DATE DUE			
DE 04 '89			
DE 22 '89	renew		

JOHN
KEATS
AND SYMBOLISM

By the same author:

Time and Mind in Wordsworth's Poetry (Wayne State University Press, Detroit, 1980)

JOHN KEATS
AND SYMBOLISM

JEFFREY BAKER

Professor of English Literature
St Francis Xavier University, Nova Scotia

THE HARVESTER PRESS · SUSSEX
ST. MARTIN'S PRESS · NEW YORK

First published in Great Britain in 1986 by
THE HARVESTER PRESS LIMITED
Publisher: John Spiers
16 Ship Street, Brighton, Sussex
First published in the United States of America by
St. Martin's Press, Inc., 175 Fifth Avenue, New York, NY 10010

© Jeffrey Baker, 1986

British Library Cataloguing in Publication Data

Baker, Jeffrey
    John Keats and symbolism.
    1. Keats, John, *1795–1821*—Criticism and
    interpretation
    I. title
    821'.7   PR4837

    ISBN 0–7108–0691–4

Library of Congress Cataloging-in-Publication Data

Baker, Jeffrey, 1925–
    John Keats and symbolism.

    Bibliography: p.
    Includes index.
    1. Keats, John, 1795–1821—symbolism. 2. Symbolism
in literature. I. Title.
PR4838.S95B35   1985   821'.7   85–26205
ISBN 0–312–44366–8

Typeset in Garamond 11 on 12 pt by Witwell Limited, Liverpool

Printed and bound in Great Britain by
Anchor Brendon Ltd, Tiptree, Essex

For Mark, Helen, Teresa and Philip

Contents

1

Introduction

I hope to do three things in this book. Firstly, and primarily, I want to examine in detail Keats' use of symbolism, by which I mean not only symbolic objects such as the nightingale, the urn, and Madeline's casement, but also symbolic personae such as Cynthia, Circe, Glaucus, Lamia, Moneta and Saturn; and symbolic action such as the awakening of the drowned lovers in *Endymion*, and the withering away of Lamia.

Secondly I want to show that a principal feature of Keats' incredibly rapid development as a poet is the swiftly increasing complexity of his symbolism. Whatever Cynthia represents, it is something simply and overwhelmingly good; whatever Circe represents it is plainly evil. But Lamia represents both the real and the unreal, as she is both victim and villain. Madeline represents both purity and eroticism, the Titans fallen divinity and fallen humankind. The full effect of Keats' symbolism in his greatest poetry, however, is much richer than mere ambiguity; the dualism is often antithetical and paradoxical to the highest and most poignant degree—one thinks, for example, of Moneta's face 'deathward progressing/To no death,' having passed 'the lily and the snow.' In fact Keats' greatest poetry, particularly in the Odes, is akin to the finest work of the metaphysicals in that his images argue with one another, there is an urgent debate not only among, but within, his most powerful symbols.

Thirdly I hope to show that this developing complexity in his symbolism parallels Keats' growing awareness of the nature and workings of the human mind and the reality with which it has to grapple. To put the matter as plainly as possible, Keats' representational images are simple while his intellectual vision is simple, they become ambiguous as he examines the difficulty of distinguishing between reality and illusion, and painfully antithetical as he discovers that reality itself, once it is known,

1

seems to be composed of irreconcilable yet inseparable opposites.

If we are to perceive fully and clearly the relationship between Keats' symbolism and his intellectual development, we must obviously, at the outset, take care to ascertain as far as possible what the general nature of that development really was. In Chapter 2, therefore, I have tried to point out the shortcomings of many current assessments, which seem to me to be oversimplistic. Keats grew, it seems to me, not from a shallow otherworldly romanticism to a grimly realistic despair, but from an aesthetically selective vision of reality to a comprehensive but bewildered one. As his sensibility expanded beyond the limitations of aestheticism, he came to realise that what we commonly call 'reality' is ambiguous at its boundaries, and paradoxical at its centre. His developing consciousness of these problems reveals itself in the manner in which his poetry deals with his principal topics—romantic love, religious mythology, and the nature and value of art.

Romantic love is the most intense manifestation of human subjectivity, and such subjectivity represents the blurred edges of reality—those ambiguous boundaries I mentioned a moment ago. In Chapter 3 then, I deal with Keats' love narratives, in which we see his delight in beauty and romantic joy gradually giving place to a concern with the increasingly painful problem of appearance and reality. In *Endymion*, although the symbolism is itself simple enough, we seem to detect from time to time an unconscious subversion of the poem's ostensible purposes. In *Lamia* and *The Eve of St Agnes* the problem has been acknowledged, and the ambiguities and ironies in the symbolic functions of the main personae, Lamia, Madeline and Porphyro, are fully controlled.

We cannot know for how long reflective mankind has concerned itself with the problems raised by the paradoxical nature of reality, but articulate mankind has obsessively done so by means of religious mythology. Keats' realisation of the great paradoxes occasioned in him not 'tragic vision,' as modern cant has it, but bewilderment, and I suggest, in Chapters Four Five and Six, that in the Glaucus episode of Endymion, and the reconstruction of the Hesiodic myth in the two *Hyperions* that he is attempting, among other things perhaps, both to express and resolve this bewilderment. The central relationship in

Endymion is one of love between the divine and the human, and the Glaucus episode suggests a fall, a redemption and a resurrection. We see here another, and perhaps unexpected, source of symbolic ambiguity—for Keats here is clearly as much aware of Biblical myth as he is of Ovidian myth. But it is in the *Hyperions* that we see the most effective symbolic dualism—the Titans are both gods and men, in both their aspirations and their fallen condition. In *The Fall of Hyperion* we see the religious concern becoming much more open and specific, and there is possibly a re-examination of Christianity taking place under the guise of the Greek machinery. Here, almost heartbreakingly, we sense the agony of the poet and man in whom the conflict of doubt and hope can find neither resolution nor relief—Moneta may be Christ or unredeemed Adam.

The final chapters of the book deal with the Odes, where all the great themes and the great paradoxes are brought together and expressed in a profoundly oxymoronic symbolism. Love, art, and immortality are discussed in terms of a funerary urn; a shortlived bird becomes a symbol of the eternal, and a grave may be a winepress. Most important, perhaps, is the fact that the function of the symbolism seems to be to express a most urgent and anguished debate—a debate of immense complexity, ending without a declared result.

I must add a note to explain what to some readers may seem an oddity in the order in which I deal with the poems. *Endymion* represents an early stage in the development both of Keats' handling of the theme of appearance and reality, and his examination of Greek myth as a source of religious understanding. For the sake of clarity, therefore, I have divided my treatment of it into two: first, part of a chapter on Keats' love narratives; second, a full chapter on the symbolic significance of the Glaucus episode, coming before the chapters on *Hyperion* and *The Fall of Hyperion*. Some readers may also think it odd that I have discussed *Lamia* before *The Eve of St Agnes*. I have done so because I wished to indicate *Lamia*'s development of the Circean theme in *Endymion*, and the relationship to Shakespeare's *Troilus and Cressida* which both poems have in common. Apart from these displacements, the treatment follows the usual order. Some readers may be irritated by the fact that I have dealt only incidentally with certain poems such as *Isabella*, and not at all with others such as the *Ode to Psyche*. My only excuse, but a sufficient one I believe, is that a full discussion of such poems, which, whatever their merits, are only indirectly relevant to my principal themes, would occupy more space than I have available for this particular project.

I must also apologise to those readers who may feel that I do not give sufficient attention to Keats' examination of the nature and value of poetry, and the role of the poet in human affairs. This is not because I do not acknowledge the importance of the topic, but because I think it inseparable from Keats' changing conception of the nature of the world which the poet serves. Since Keats undoubtedly regarded poetry as his vocation in the religious sense of that word, his understanding of the nature of art is organically connected to his understanding of larger issues.

2

The Nature of Keats' Development

For many years now, commentary on Keats' poetry has been based on the assumption that we can trace in his work a straighforward progress from otherworldly romance to realism. One scholar, introducing a collection of critical essays, provides a typical example in a general statement to which, he claims, all critics would more or less subscribe: 'The world of beauty seized or created by the imagination clashes with the tragic world of reality. Keats had too much integrity to turn away from the actual world, and nearly all his greatest poetry is an imaginative expression of this conflict ... In *Isabella* and *The Eve of St Agnes* he luxuriated in the world of romance, but his imagination had been disciplined by his experience, and he was fully aware that these poems, describing events of far away and long ago, were only a temporary escape from the pressure of reality.'[1]

That events are romantic and unreal because they happened far away and long ago is a questionable proposition, but this is not the most disturbing aspect of the statement for us. One may say that the events portrayed in *Isabella* and *The Eve of St Agnes* are unreal in so far as they are fictional, but there is, in Keats' account of them, such a remarkable grasp of the concrete that only an imagination that had looked long and carefully at real things could have achieved it. One thinks of Madeline's 'warmed jewels', for instance, and the bloodhound that 'shook his hide'. This aspect of the poem can be overlooked only if one assumes that the imagination can make bricks without straw—something Keats never assumed. Also, are we to regard as an escape from reality an account of a treacherous murder, a macabre exhumation and mutilation, and a heroine's pitiful descent into madness? This particular commentator (Kenneth Muir), seems also to have ignored Jack Stillinger's thought-provoking essay on *The Eve of St Agnes*, for the anti-romantic ironies of the poem seem to go unnoticed.[2] Again, Muir does not seem to sense the 'pressure of reality' in the decrepitude and deaths of the beadsman and palsy-twitched Angela.

The symptomatic fallacy in Muir's comments, however, is the assumption that there are two realms, the real and the unreal, and the human mind can perceive a clearly discernible boundary between them. This constitutes the besetting limitations of nearly all recent Keats criticism. One distinguished critic, introducing another collection of critical essays, actually draws a diagram with a horizontal line 'separating the actual world (below) and the ideal (above)'.[3]

Keats was not of this mind. He did not assume a clearly defined boundary between reality and unreality, nor that reality is homogeneous in nature. The world which we commonly call 'the real world' is full of living creatures, and to grasp their total reality we must know not only the creatures themselves but their relationships to one another. The most sophisticated species is mankind, and the interrelationships between its members form an inexhaustible complexity. A human being is a thing that thinks, and having thought, makes judgements. What is the status of such judgements? In a letter to Benjamin Bailey of 13 March 1818, Keats indulges in a witty castigation of the men of Devonshire:

> I think it well for the honor of Brittain that Julius Caesar did not first land in this county—a Devonshirer standing on his native hills is not a distinct object—he does not show against the light—a wolf or two would dispossess him. I like, I love England, I like its strong Men—Give me a "long brown plain" for my Morning so I may meet some of Edmund Iron sides descendants—Give me a barren mould so I may meet with some shadowing of Alfred in the shape of a Gipsey, a Huntsman or as Shepherd. Scenery is fine—but human nature is finer—the Sward is richer for the tread of a real, nervous, english foot—the eagles nest is finer for the Mountaineer has look'd into it—Are these facts or prejudices?

There is a degree of playfulness in both the criticism of the Devonshire men and the patriotic exaltation of other Englishmen, but the passage as a whole is highly serious. The question Keats approaches by way of banter is: How real is human subjectivity? He does not say 'Scenery is fine—but people are finer,' he is more specific: 'Scenery is fine—but *human nature* is finer.' The natural world is fine in itself, but finer for being the object of human perception. The real 'english foot' is a 'nervous foot', and the Sward is richer because that foot has felt it. And how real are human judgements? If Keats' criticisms of Devonshire men are justified, are his judgements in some sense 'facts'? A little further in the letter Keats makes his implication somewhat plainer, and broadens its scope:

> I am sometimes so very sceptical as to think poetry itself a mere Jack a lanthern to amuse whoever may be struck with its brilliance—As tradesmen say everything is worth what it will fetch, so probably every mental pursuit takes its reality and worth from the ardour of the pursuer—being in itself a nothing—Etheral thing may at least be thus real, divided under three heads—Things real—things semireal—and no things—Things real—such as existences of Sun Moon & Stars and passages of Shakespeare—Things semireal such as Love, the Clouds &c which require a greeting of the spirit to make them wholly exist—and Nothings which are made Great and dignified by an ardent pursuit—Which by the by stamps the burgundy mark on the bottles of our Minds, insomuch as they are able to 'conse[c]rate whate'er they look upon'.[4]

One wishes Bailey had quizzed Keats a little on this topic, so that we might have had an elucidatory sequel, for there are more than enough ambiguities and inconsistencies here—the inevitable accompaniment, perhaps, of enthusiastic but fugitive theorising. One is not quite sure why all three kinds are included under the general heading of 'Ethereal thing', since some of the things considered are 'Things real' in the most obvious sense. Also Keats can scarcely be said to define his classes—he simply gives examples of their members, and this is confusing. Why are 'Sun Moon & Stars' grouped with 'passages of Shakespeare', since they are 'Ethereal' in very different ways? Why are 'Love' and 'the Clouds' grouped together as semireal?

But in spite of this confusion one senses that Keats is saying something true and important, and that had he returned to the

topic in a more leisured 'consequitive' frame of mind we might
have had a system somewhat parallel to Karl Popper's scheme of
three worlds of reality, in which passages of Shakespeare would be
classified as 'objective knowledge'.[5] In what we have, though,
there are two vital conceptions. First, there is indeed a burgundy
mark on our minds—our subjectivity is of supreme value, and
undoubted reality. Secondly, things semireal, such as love (let us
omit clouds) become wholly real upon receiving a 'greeting of the
Spirit'. Even this is not quite clear though—Keats' enthusiastic
hurry has caused him to contract his meaning too much,
perhaps—but the most likely meaning is that love, a subjective
thing in itself, must be validated by some other subjective act.
Having been thus greeted, it becomes as real as the lover himself
and the object of his love. Love is an undoubted fact in the real
world, yet it is neither tangible nor mensurable—its reality, in any
particular case, is therefore not verifiable. Our response to
someone whom we think we love, our feelings for them, or
perhaps our mental image of them, may not be a greeting of the
spirit but mere salivation—only another greeting of the spirit can
authenticate it. The love of others for us we can only verify by
observing their behaviour, and behaviour may be simulated.

Sometimes one must not only act according to one's
judgement, but according to what one may suppose another
person's subjective state to be. If a man is wrong in his
understanding of this, he may over a period of time have given so
much spurious actuality to a false impression that when the truth
of the matter finally becomes inescapable he may be able only to
say: 'This is and is not Cressida'. In other words, there is an
irreducible element of subjectivity in human perception—as
Wordsworth says, we half create what we see. Few people will
deny that this subjective element is most intensified in the
perception of an object of sexual desire. More than half of Keats'
major poetry is concerned with sexual love, and, apart from
Isabella, is concerned at some level with this problem of knowing
the real from the subjective image.

This large preoccupation with sexual feeling is without doubt
connected closely and directly with the poet's own emotional
adventures. Various passages in his letters, as well as some of his
minor poems, reveal that his attitude to women was ambivalent.[6]
There has been a good deal of scholarly diagnosis of this common

affliction, and Keats' mother has been identified as the Jocasta in the woodpile.[7] There is no doubt that Keats became defensive in the presence of a woman who strongly attracted him—his account of Jane Cox, for example, shows him thoroughly enjoying the danger to his peace of mind while carefully setting his defences in order (1:394 – 95).

There is also another common form of ambivalence with which we may sympathise less. He flirts within social limits with Mary Frogley, Isabella Jones, and perhaps the Reynolds and Jeffrey sisters, but at Oxford he seems to have had an anonymous adventure which caused him to suspect for some time that he had caught syphilis.[8] Aileen Ward also suggests that at Teignmouth he relieved the tension of nursing his sick brother by wenching in the Devonshire meadows.[9] If these suppositions are true, then it would seem that he was circumspect with women in his own social orbit, but not with Rantipole Betty.

He may have been afraid of marriage rather than women, and there may have been several reasons for such prudence. Keats certainly looked on poetry as his vocation: 'My Imagination is a monastery, and I am its Monk,' he told Shelley in August 1820 (2:232), a statement on which Mario D'Avanzo has commented: '... the writing of poetry was for Keats a holy, priestlike task leading to divine truth.'[10] Geraldine Pederson-Krag, finding a substitute phallus in 'O Poesy for thee I hold my pen,' declares that for Keats 'Poetry ... meant a celibate masculine way of living.'[11] I am going to suggest a less high-minded reason, though one that is admirable in the honesty and self-knowledge that it implies. On 8 July 1819 Keats told Fanny Brawne 'I cannot conceive any beginning of such a love as I have for you but Beauty' (2:127). Some seven months previously he had given an account to George and Georgiana Keats of a visit to Wentworth Place made by Fanny and her friend Caroline Robinson. His description of Fanny has the usual signs of defensiveness: '... she is ignorant—monstrous in her behaviour flying out in all directions, calling people such names—that I was forced lately to make use of the term Minx'. But it is the description of Caroline that is important:

Her face is raw as if she had been standing out in a frost—her lips raw and seem always ready for a Pullet—she plays the

Music without one sensation but the feel of the ivory at her
fingers—she is a downright Miss without one set off—we
hated her and smoked her and baited her, and I think drove her
away—Miss B thinks her a Paragon of fashion, and says she is
the only woman she would change persons with—What a
Stupe—She is superio[r] as a Rose to a Dandelion—When we
went to bed Brown observed as he put out the Taper what an
ugly old woman that Miss Robinson would make—at which I
must have groan'd aloud for I'm sure ten minutes. (2:13 – 14)

One doesn't know just how cruel the baiting was—Keats may
be jocularly exaggerating in a manner that his brother and sister-
in-law would recognise—but certainly there was baiting, and it
was clearly less than kind.[12] Fanny Brawne seems to have felt some
need to come to her friend's defence. But even more unpleasant
than the baiting itself is the apparent motive for it. Some mention
is made of Caroline's social faults (and they strike the reader as
being less than Fanny's), but obviously the principal objection is
to her plainness. She is a Dandelion to Fanny's Rose. Most
interesting of all, however, is Keats' ten-minute groan at the
thought of how ugly Caroline would be as an old woman. Perhaps
the groan was prolonged by the thought that beautiful women
also may become ugly as they grow old, and this might be Fanny's
fate. Such a thought may have cast some doubt on the nature of
the greeting of the spirit which Keats had bestowed on Fanny.
Significantly the theme of the ugliness of old age smuggles itself
into *Endymion* and *The Eve of St Agnes*, and is in fact the
dramatic climax of *Lamia*, as I hope to show.

A love that could only begin with beauty might not survive
beauty, and this may be one of the considerations which made
Keats struggle so painfully against his feelings for Fanny. The
problem arises, is such love real, semireal, or a nothing? With one
exception (*Isabella*) Keats' so-called romances are struggles to get
to grips with this problem, together with the associated problem
of whether or not the object of love is in its own nature what it
appears to be to the lover. Far from escaping from the pressure of
reality, Keats is acutely aware of the problem of reality in the most
impassioned and hazardous area of human subjectivity, the
imagination sensitised by desire.

In the light of this, let us look back to the aesthetic dogma

Keats had formulated in a letter to Bailey of 22 November 1817. 'I am certain of nothing but the holiness of the Heart's affections and the truth of Imagination—What the Imagination seizes as Beauty must be truth—whether it existed before or not.' (1:184). There are two propositions here, both set forth as certainties, but we need to deal with the second one first, because, in an obvious way, the validity of the first is contingent upon it. If we turn it inside out, thus providing a corollary, we see both its weakness and its function: 'What the Imagination rejects as Ugliness must be falsehood.' This is certainly a way of sorting out the rose from the dandelion, but does it guarantee the holiness of the heart's affections? The implication is that once we have perceived the beauty of an object, our love for such an object is in some sense 'true'.

One suspects that the same greeting of the spirit is being forced into double duty; it is our perception of beauty that gives rise to love in the first place, and is then invoked a second time to authenticate love, and make the semireal thing wholly real. The unhappy dandelion receives neither greeting of the spirit, and so may be smoked, baited, and driven away. Perhaps the dandelion's consolation may be the suspicion that as the rose withers, it too will become a nothing. In its capacity to filter reality in this convenient way, one sees how readily Keats' dogma can become the basis for an aesthetic theory of art.

It would be wrong, however, to suppose that Keats' dogma was merely a pompous casuistry meant to dignify a commonplace scheme of values. It is that, certainly, but it is also a serious attempt to devise an instrument for discerning what is real and what is spurious in the semireal world of human subjectivity. Let us see what happens when Keats tries to apply it as an instrument of judgement in artistic matters: '. . . the excellence of every Art is its intensity, capable of making all disagreeables evaporate, from their being in close relationship with Beauty and Truth—Examine King Lear & you will find this exemplified throughout.' (1:192). D.G. James advises that no-one can afford to treat any judgement of Keats on Shakespeare lightly, but in this particular case I find I can take it seriously only if I read 'disagreeables' as a stunning litotes, and assume that Keats intended an ingenious and unusual meaning for 'evaporate.' James goes on to say:

But does *King Lear* exemplify this ... We can do no other than
follow our own perception and judgement, such as it is. And
when we consider *Lear*, *do* the 'disagreeables evaporate'—the
wickedness of Goneril, Regan and Edmund, the blinding of
Gloucester, the terrible deaths of Cordelia and Lear? And is
not *King Lear* much less an 'evaporation' of the terrible than a
question thrown out into the heavens by a mind speculating
and baffled, in 'aching but in fearless ignorance'?[13]

James is tactfully implying that in this instance Keats'
judgement is as shallow as his diction indicates. The context of
Keats' pronouncement makes such a conclusion almost
inescapable, for we might have rescued the dogma by a special and
weighty significance to be attached to 'intensity'. However, this
is scarcely possible. The occasion of Keats' dictum was a visit to
see Benjamin West's painting *Death on a Pale Horse*. 'There is
nothing to be intense upon,' Keats complains, 'no women one
feels mad to kiss.' No amount of tortured exegesis can cope with
the dismal implications of this. But what has brought a man of
such deep and perceptive intelligence to this kind of judgement
except the felt need to justify a dogma? Fortunately Keats himself
seems to have had qualms about his aesthetic criterion, for after
citing *Lear* as an example of it, he resumes his critique of West's
painting with an auxiliary standard of judgement: '... but in this
picture we have unpleasantness without any momentous depth of
speculation excited in which to bury its repulsiveness.' One still
regrets the urge to 'bury' unpleasantness rather than to integrate
it into a complex whole, but one is relieved to find that the means
of doing so is now 'depth of speculation' rather than the kind of
beauty one feels mad to kiss. It is a fortunate afterthought, and
points the direction of Keats' future development.

The dogma concerning beauty was, I have suggested, meant to
be a way of establishing values and authenticity in the subjective
realm, but it has very obvious uses in the world of objects. Keats is
clearly thinking of the imagination's perceptive function rather
than its esemplastic power, as his choice of verb indicates: 'What
the Imagination seizes as Beauty,' etc. The phrase 'whether it
existed before or not' hints at imagination's creative role, but
again the emphasis of the whole doctrine is on the mind's capacity
to seize the beauty in its own creation. One sees then, the manner

in which the theory can control the materials and imagery of poetry, even a poetry which is based on reality rather than dream.

Keats begins his poetic career, then, as an aesthete. But his aestheticism does not lead to a dream world; it consists in an expurgated reality so surely and firmly grasped that F.R. Leavis felt the need to distinguish Keats from his idolatrous imitators by insisting on the concrete and realistic nature of his genius.[14] If we use the term 'reality' in its narrowest sense, signifying the world of objects, then Keats' early poetry is as firmly rooted in it as his later work. The first poem, as far as we know, that he ever wrote, the *Imitation of Spenser*, has these lines:

> There saw the swan his neck of arched snow,
> And oar'd himself along with majesty.
>
> (14 – 15)

It is the second verb here that shows how deeply Keats' sensibility was stirred by the actual. It is true, of course, that in some of his early poems he proposes an escapist view of poetry: 'But there are times when those that love the bay/Fly from all sorrowing far, far away.' Yet even in his abortive tales of chivalry (*Calidore, Specimen of an Induction*), the grasp of reality is clearly meant to provide the substance of the poetry, and is not an accidental and scarcely welcome intrusion into a pleasant daydream. Let us see, by way of example, what Calidore sees as he rows across the lake:

> Scarce can his clear and nimble eyesight follow
> The freaks and dartings of the black-wing'd swallow,
> Delighting much, to see it half at rest,
> Dip so refreshingly its wings, and breast
> 'Gainst the smooth surface, and to mark anon,
> The widening circles into nothing gone.'
>
> (13 – 18)

Even in *Endymion*, as Christopher Ricks has pointed out, the 'vulgarities' which critics have traditionally found there arise from the frequency with which the poem 'touches down', so to speak, on the physical details of sexual delight—even to the point of including the slight sense of repulsion in the midst of pleasure. Ricks comments shrewdly on the suggestion of a film of saliva on Cynthia's lips in the 'embarrassing' image of 'slippery blisses'.[15]

In order to perceive clearly the real nature and direction of
Keats' poetic development, let us take one more example of his
early realism, and compare it with a passage on a somewhat similar
theme from his later poetry:

> Here are sweet peas on tip-toe for a flight;
> With wings of gentle flush o'er delicate white,
> And taper fingers catching at all things,
> To bind them all about with tiny rings.
>
> (*I Stood Tip-toe*, 57 – 60)

Butterflies are as real as sweet peas, and the first two lines enliven
our consciousness of both. The picture of 'taper fingers catching
at all things' again shows that Keats not only looks principally at
the world of objects, but he does so at leisure, closely and
lovingly. The flowers are astonishingly real, and we see them in a
rich context of other vividly real objects: a filbert hedge, wild
briar, blue bells, marigolds, a streamlet, a swarm of minnows, cool
cresses, finches with black and golden wings, the soft rustle of a
maiden's gown. There are one or two less delightful
plants—sorrel and dandelions—but no dockweed, no rank
fumiter, no stinking billy. And there are no parasites on the
flowers' tender petals, no tinge of blight, no signs of withering.
They are, like all the leafy luxuries mentioned in the poem, a
moment's ornament, and they have been chosen carefully as such.
Let us now look at one of Keats' later plants:

> ... thick, and green, and beautiful it grew,
> So that it smelt more balmy than its peers
> Of basil tufts in Florence; for it drew
> Nurture besides, and life, from human fears,
> From the fast-mouldering head there shut from view:
> So that the jewel, safely casketed,
> Came forth, and in perfumed leafits spread.
>
> (*Isabella*, 426 – 32)

The power of these lines is not their power to shock—by the
time we read them we already know about Lorenzo's head. Nor
is the effect merely one of bringing delicate beauty and
unspeakable horror into collision. The supreme power of the

lines is in the vividly expressed interrelationship between the beauty and the horror; the basil grows thick and green and beautiful, more so than its peers, precisely because it feeds on tears and rotting flesh. The effect on the reader is much too complex to be described as shock; on the one hand we are made aware of the macabre thing below the commonplace beauty, but we are also aware that the beauty flourishes because the horror is there. The relationship between life and death is more mutually active than we might suppose, and even the horror itself, 'vile with green and livid spot' (476) is, because of human love and grief, a precious thing—it was once, Keats has reminded us, 'no formless monster's head' (394). The rotting head, in one sense the most unlikely symbol of energy, is, by the paradox of life itself, the source of fresh and virile growth—The stench of the head is transmuted into the fragrance of the herb, the jewel, Keats tells us, 'Came forth, and in perfumed leafits spread.'

The most important thing to notice here is that while this passage is bringing the story of Isabella to its undoubtedly tragic ending, the lines themselves constitute a symbol of reality that cannot adequately be described as tragic. The relationships of the good and evil elements are too complex, the mutual interplay between them too energetic, the sense of revitalisation too powerful for such an easy judgement. What we have here is a symbol of the oxymoronic complexity of the real world, where 'Nurture besides, and life' are drawn from grief and death.

What brought about the change? Those critics who see Keats' development as a transition from idealism to a concern with actuality and tragic vision also usually assume that the causes or catalysts of such development were tragic events in Keats' own life. A moment's reflection makes it clear that this cannot be so. There is in such a judgement an implicit assumption that life did not begin to darken for Keats until October 1817 or thereabouts, after which all manner of appalling disasters overtook him—the Scotch reviews, the illness and death of Tom, the loss of George and Georgiana, the cold caught in the Isle of Mull, his own blood-spitting, his doomed love for Fanny Brawne, and so on. The second part of this is obviously true, the first part certainly not.

Few poets can have been more grimly reminded of death throughout their youthful lives than Keats was. When he was seven his infant brother Edward died, when he was nine his father was killed (his mother subsequently hurrying to church with Mr Rawlings, like Gertrude, within two months). At ten years old he lost his grandfather Jennings, at twelve his beloved uncle Midgley Jennings, at fourteen his mother, at nineteen his grandmother Jennings. Keats enjoyed a reasonably happy and unclouded life only between the beginning of 1815 and the autumn of 1817, but even then was not free from contact with horrors. From October 1815 to July 1816 he was a student at Guy's Hospital, and the days spent walking the wards as assistant to the ageing and reputedly incompetent William Lucas would provide powerful reminders of agony and death. Bearing all this in mind then, let us look at the literary path he charts for himself in *Sleep and Poetry*:

> First the realm I'll pass
> Of Flora and old Pan: sleep in the grass,
> Feed upon apples red, and strawberries,
> And chose each pleasure that my fancy sees;
> Catch the white-handed nymphs in shady places,
> To woo sweet kisses from averted faces,—
> Play with their fingers, touch their shoulders white
> Into a pretty shrinking with a bite
> As hard as lips can make it: till agreed,
> A lovely tale of human life we'll read.
> And one will teach a tame dove how it best
> May fan the cool air gently o'er my rest;
> Another, bending o'er her nimble tread,
> Will set a green robe floating round her head,
> And still will dance with ever varied ease,
> Smiling upon the flowers and the trees
> Another will entice me on, and on
> Through almond blossoms and rich cinnamon.
>
> (101 – 118)

The only items here that are strictly unreal are Flora and old Pan; the rest undoubtedly have objective correlatives. This is the realism of the epicure, though we might more kindly say it is the therapeutically selected realism of a sensibility that has been too regularly assailed by grief and the ugliness of suffering. Whatever it is, Keats knew it to be a starting point only: 'Can I ever bid these joys farewell?/ Yes, I must pass them for a nobler life,/Where I may find the agonies, the strife/Of human hearts' (122 – 25). But I suggest that when Keats did bid these joys farewell, it was not in accordance with this prearranged plan. Epicurean pleasure of this kind is only possible while one's sensibility is limited, while one cannot see the death beneath the basil. One may choose one's experience only while the elements of experience seem to be separable, while good and evil seem to form a mixture rather than a compound. Keats abandoned his bower of bliss when he realised that life's opposites are fused and indivisible.

He was brought to this perception not by a calamitous event in his own life, but by a moment of insight on the shore at Teignmouth in the spring of 1818:

> Dear Reynolds, I have a mysterious tale
> And cannot speak it. The first page I read
> Upon a Lampit Rock of green sea weed
> Among the breakers—'Twas a quiet Eve;
> The rocks were silent—The wide sea did weave
> An untumultuous fringe of silver foam
> Along the flat brown sand. I was at home,
> And should have been most happy—but I saw
> Too far into the sea; where every maw
> The greater on the less feeds evermore:—
> But I saw too distinct into the core
> Of an eternal fierce destruction,
> And so from happiness I far was gone.
> Still am I sick of it: and though today
> Ive gathered young spring leaves, and flowers gay
> Of Periwinkle and wild strawberry,
> Still do I that most fierce destruction see,
> The Shark at savage prey—the hawk at pounce,
> The gentle Robin, like a pard or ounce,
> Ravening a worm.
>   (*Epistle to John Hamilton Reynolds*, 86 – 105)

There has long been a consensus that this passage represents a turning point in Keats' development, but what has perhaps not

been noted sufficiently is that he probably did not actually see
'that most fierce destruction'. One cannot see very far into the
sea when the waves are breaking on the shore, and there is little
reason to suppose that Keats actually saw a shark. He had
known for some time, obviously, that sharks did eat smaller sea-
creatures, hawks ate smaller birds, and robins devoured worms.
Now he realised that such activity is eternally going on
throughout nature, that it is not a mere snag or an evaporable
disagreeable, but a system, and a necessary one. Writing to
George and Georgiana some twelve months later, he comments
on altruism (which he calls 'disinterestedness'), and speculates
that if it were carried to its highest pitch it would destroy
human society, since man is necessarily as predatory as the
animals: 'For in wild nature the Hawk would lose his Breakfast
of Robins and the Robin his of Worms. The Lion must starve as
well as the swallow.' (2:79). The death of the prey is the life of
the predator, and the ugliness of 'that most fierce destruction'
takes place within 'An untumultuous fringe of silver foam'.
About a month after this distressing perception he wrote the
stanza about Lorenzo's head concealed in the pot of basil, and
another week later, in a prose letter to Reynolds, he wrote the
Chamber of Maiden thought passage:

> I compare human life to a large Mansion of Many
> Apartments, two of which I can only describe, the doors of
> the rest being as yet shut upon me—the first we step into we
> call the infant or thoughtless Chamber, in which we remain as
> long as we do not think—We remain there a long while, and
> notwithstanding the doors of the second Chamber remain
> wide open, showing a bright appearance, we care not to
> hasten into it; but are at length imperceptibly impelled by the
> awakening of the thinking principle—within us—we no
> sooner get into the second Chamber, which I shall call the
> Chamber of Maiden-thought, than we become intoxicated
> with the light and the atmosphere, we see nothing but
> pleasant wonders, and think of delaying there for ever in
> delight: However among the effects this breathing is father of
> is that tremendous one of sharpening one's vision into the
> <head>heart and nature of Man—of convincing ones nerves
> that the World is full of misery and Heartbreak, Pain,

Sickness and oppresion—whereby This Chamber of Maiden Thought becomes gradually darken'd and at the same time on all sides of it many doors are set open—but all dark—all leading to dark passages—We see not the ballance of good and evil. We are in a Mist. (1:280 - 81)

There are three points implicit in this passage which I believe are important. First, Keats' wish for a life of sensations rather than thoughts (see the letter to Bailey, 22 November 1817, 1:185) is now seen to be immature, belonging to the infant Chamber. If one accepts, as I do, W.W. Beyer's interpretation of 'sensations' as 'intuitive perceptions through the senses', then the doctrine about beauty and truth has become rather vulnerable.[16] Secondly, 'the awakening of the thinking principle' does not pitch us immediately into darkness, but into a Chamber which is bright and full of pleasant wonders. This however becomes darkened as we *convince* our nerves (the verb is significant) that the world is full of hearbreak and pain. Teignmouth was such a Chamber, with the beauty of the seashore,. and the fields sprinkled with periwinkles and wild strawberry. It was the nascent thinking principle that enabled Keats to conceive of 'The Shark at savage prey'. His imagination had, as always, seized the beauty of the scene; it required a more sober, cautionary, and ultimately more perceptive power to reveal the fuller truth within it.

In other words, the greeting of the spirit whereby one endowed a semireal thing with full reality—that is by perceiving its beauty—has been abandoned. It is by the application of intelligence and knowledge that full reality can now be known. The principle of beauty has been replaced by the thinking principle—and this is the real nature of Keats' development—from aestheticism to a fully integrated sensibility. This is a very different matter from abandoning the unreal in favour of the real, for it recognises the effort involved in knowing the real. For when intelligence and knowledge are brought to bear on our perception of the world, a simple judgement becomes impossible—one cannot comfortably slip from a romantic posture to a stoic one.

This brings us to the third of the implications which I suggested were important in this pasage. What we achieve in the second Chamber is not tragic vision—we do not now realise that the world is ugly and not beautiful, evil and not good, we realise that it is good, evil, beautiful, ugly, comic, tragic, noble, ignoble, intelligible and absurd, and that all these opposites exist incorrigibly together. Our state is neither despair nor resignation, but bewilderment. 'We see not the ballance of good and evil. We are in a Mist.' One might compare the penultimate phrase with the longing Keats expressed in the *Epistle to Reynolds* for 'the lore of good and ill' (75). The implication both of the *Epistle* and the Chamber of Maiden Thought is that such an understanding may yet be possible, the bewilderment may not be permanent. The second Chamber has dark passages leading from it which we feel impelled to explore—the thinking principle having been awakened we must go on thinking—for we are in a 'large Mansion of Many Apartments'. Keats' phrase has a curiously stimulating echo of *St John* 14:2, 'In my Father's house are many mansions.' This then, is the state of mind in which Keats wrote his greatest poetry—bewildered, frightened, disillusioned, but still vigorously explorative.

It is necessary now to see this state of bewilderment in its relationship to the doctrine of negative capability. The first thing to note is that Keats promulgated the doctrine in a letter to George and Tom Keats at the end of December 1817, three months before his distressing experience at Teignmouth:

> I had not a dispute but a disquisition with Dilke, on various subjects; several things dovetailed in my mind, & at once it struck me, what quality went to form a Man of Achievement especially in Literature & which Shakespeare possessed so enormously—I mean *Negative Capability*, that is when a man is capable of being in uncertainties, Mysteries, doubts, without any irritable reaching after fact & reason—Coleridge, for instance, would let go by a fine isolated verisimilitude caught from the Penetralium of mystery, from being incapable of remaining content with half knowledge. This pursued through Volumes would perhaps take us no further than this, that with a great poet the sense of Beauty overcomes every other consideration, or rather obliterates all consideration. (1:193-94)

The are two valuable insights that one may safely infer from this passage. First, a state of uncertainty may be fruitful for a poet. Second, a poet should not try to alleviate his own philosophic discomfort by imposing on his experience a meaning which he has achieved by 'an irritable reaching after fact & reason'. 'We hate poetry that has a palpable design upon us' (1:224), and such a kind of poetry probably comes from a poet who has first had a palpable design upon himself.

But it is equally important, I believe, to understand what Keats does not mean by the passage. The use of the words 'irritable reaching' suggests that the kind of philosophical reason that the poet objects to is the superficial and dogmatic kind that has been adopted to meet a need, consequently everything must be seen in relation to it, and nothing must be allowed to threaten it. But Keats can scarcely be objecting to a philosophical position that has been long and deeply held, and that informs but does not distort the sensibility. He does not include *Paradise Lost* and *The Divine Comedy* among the poetry that has a palpable design upon us—though in one sense both poems plainly have. In other words, one must not equate negative capability with a state of philosophic uncertainty—it is the capacity to endure such uncertainty without grasping for ready-made solutions that Keats values so highly.

It would be fallacious to suppose then, that Keats would not have hoped for some alleviation of his state of bewilderment, or that he feared he would be any less a poet had he achieved 'the prize/High reason and the lore of good and ill'. Indeed five months after the *Epistle to Reynolds* he not only expresses his fear and anguish with great poignancy, he also explicitly asks for enlightenment:

> Read me a lesson, Muse, and speak it loud
>   Upon the top of Nevis, blind in mist!
> I look into the caverns, and a shroud
>   Vaporous doth hide them,—just so much I wist
> Mankind do know of hell; I look o'erhead,
>   And there is sullen mist,—even so much
> Mankind can tell of heaven; mist is spread
>   Before the earth, beneath me,—even such,
> Even so vague is man's sight of himself!
>   Here are the craggy stones beneath my feet,—

Thus much I know, that, a poor witless elf,
    I tread on them,—that all my eye doth meet
Is mist and crag, not only on this height,
But in the world of thought and mental might.

Most striking here is the way in which the imagery of mist has developed since the Chamber of Maiden Thought passage. 'We know not the ballance of good and evil. We are in a Mist.' Being in a mist in a large mansion of many apartments is much less frightening than being in a mist on a dangerous mountain. In the former one may grope about, and explore dark passages with comparatively little fear—on the latter one had much better sit still and hope for a clearance. In this sense the need for negative capability has clearly increased since the Teignmouth experience. But even so it is only the panic-stricken blundering about that is to be inhibited. One cannot sit on a mountainside for ever. The whole point of the geographical image is that one must ultimately try to find one's way.

The image of mental bewilderment as a kind of physical disorientation occurs several times in the letters:

I have no meridian to date Interests from, or measure circumstances—Tonight *I am all in a mist* [My italics] (2:167).

You see how puzzled I am—I have no meridian to fix you to—being the slave of what is to happen (2:211).

I have been so very lax, unemployed, unmeridian'd and objectless these two months (2:227).

The implication is, once again, that negative capability is not an entirely passive state—there must come a point at which one must try to fix one's position—as the mist clears, perhaps, look for landmarks and try to establish one's latitude.

A little less than three years after writing the *Epistle to Reynolds* Keats died in horror, with 'no kind hope smoothing down his suffering—no philosophy—no religion to support him' (2:368). But in the last few years of his life, those years of bewilderment, 'unmeridian'd', 'all in a mist', his mind had remained 'a thoroughfare for all thoughts' (2:213). One sees in the great poetry a progressive openness to all experience, a growing freedom from the stifling principle of beauty (though it makes an ambiguous final bow in the *Ode on a Grecian Urn*), an increasing willingness to explore the dark passages leading from the Chamber of Maiden Thought.

It is not unlikely that one of the things he was searching for in his explorations was some religious principle to which both his mind and heart could give assent. Severn's letters from Rome, if one discounts, as one probably should, their author's frankly wishful thinking, indicate that he did not find such a principle. But perhaps it would be more accurate to say that he was trying to recover, rather than find, a religious principle. In spite of his hatred of the Church of England, and his violently expressed anticlericalism, there is good reason to suppose that, at least until the Teignmouth episode, Keats held some form of non-Christian belief. There are several references to God in his letters, made soberly and without mockery; and there are two occasions when Keats attempts a sort of spontaneous theology. The most famous of these is a scheme of non-Messianic salvation:

Call the world if you Please "The Vale of Soul-making" Then you will find out the use of the world (I am speaking now in the highest terms for human nature admitting it to be immortal which I will here take for granted for the purpose of showing a thought which has struck me concerning it.) I say 'Soul making' Soul as distinguished from an Intelligence—There may be intelligences or sparks of the divinity in millions—but they are not Souls <the>till they acquire identities, till each one is personally itself. I[n]telligences arc atoms of perception—they know and they see and they are pure, in short they are God—how then are Souls to be made? How then are these sparks which are God to have identity given them—so as ever to possess a bliss peculiar to each ones individual existence? How but by the medium of a world like this? This point I sincerely wish to consider because I think it a grander system of salvation than the chryst <e> ain religion — or rather it is a system of Spirit-creation—This is effected by three grand materials acting the one upon the other for a series of years—These three Materials are the *Intelligence*—the *human heart* (as distinguished from intelligence or Mind) and the *World* or

Elemental space suited for the proper action of *Mind and Heart* on each other for the purpose of forming the *Soul* or *Intelligence destined to possess the sense of Identity*. I can scarcely express what I but dimly perceive—and yet I think I perceive it—that you may judge the more clearly I will put it in the most homely form possible—I will call the *world* a School instituted for the purpose of teaching little children to read—and I will call the *human heart* the *horn Book* used in that School—and I will call the *Child able to read, the Soul* made from that school and its hornbook. Do you not see how necessary a World of Pains and troubles is to school an Intelligence and make it a soul? A Place where the heart must feel and suffer in a thousand diverse ways! Not merely is the Heart a Hornbook, it is the Minds Bible, it is the Minds experience, it is the teat from which the Mind or intelligence sucks its identity—As various as the Lives of Men are—so various become their souls, and thus does God make individual beings, Souls, Identical Souls of the sparks of his own essence—this appears to me a faint sketch of a system of Salvation which does not affront our reason and humanity—I am convnced that many difficulties which christians labour under would vanish before it—There is one wh[i]ch even now Strikes me—the Salvation of Children—in them the Spark or intelligence returns to God without any identity—it having had no time to learn of, and be altered by, the heart—or seat of the human Passions. (2:102 - 103)

Undoubtedly this scheme raises more problems than it solves, and one isn't sure that it really solves the one it sets out to tackle. Keats sees his scheme as being superior to the Christian one because it does away with the need for an 'arbitrary interposition of God', and thus seems to make human beings achieve salvation entirely by their own efforts. However, the '*World* or *Elemental space*, has to be properly suited for the 'action of Mind and Heart on each other'—in other words the vicissitudes of life must be set at the correct level for the Soul-making business to work. The pains and troubles of the world are just enough, and no more. Salvation has thus been pre-ordained by God—'and thus does God make individual beings, Souls, Identical Souls of the sparks of his own essence'. To many readers this will also seem to be an arbitrary act of God—not an interposition in that it involves no historical act—but none the less it is an act without which mankind could not be saved. The major point though is that Keats seems to have intended his scheme to be more humanistic than the Christian one, and it turns out to be in fact less so, as John Jones has rather sternly pointed out:

> The automatic nature of the process is what strikes an observer first. The world is a "place where the heart must feel and suffer in a thousand diverse ways"; and in the inevitable course of feeling and suffering, it becomes a soul and at the same time furnishes us with a working model of Keats' private (as he supposes) "system of salvation". Provided one stays alive one cannot help growing into a soul and a saved soul. The scene therefore appears theologically as well as morally empty.[17]

In attempting to remove the divine saviour, Keats has in fact removed human will.

Keats' other theological attempt concerns the nature of life after death:

> ... we shall enjoy ourselves here after by having what we called happiness on Earth repeated in finer tone and so repeated ... have you never by being surprised with an old Melody—in a delicious place—by a delicious voice, fe[l]t over again your very speculations and surmises at the first time it operated on your soul—do you not remember forming to yourself the singer's face more beautiful that it was possible and yet with the elevation of the Moment you did not think so—even then you were mounted on the Wings of Imagination so high—that the Prototype must be here after—that delicious face you will see—what a time! I am continually running away from the subject. (1:185)

Earl Wasserman and like-minded critics are almost certainly right in finding neo-Platonic antecedents for this—Keats' use of the word 'Prototype' is strongly suggestive. But there may also be Athanasian suggestions. For the truth which dreaming Adam waked to find was Eve in her unfallen splendour, and the Christian doctrine of the resurrection of the body implies that at the last day the saved will reassume their glorified bodies—real flesh and blood, but 'in finer tone'.

Whatever the shortcomings of Keats' theological endeavours, the most important thing is that he made them, and thought sufficiently seriously on these matters to communicate his theorisings to such correspondents as Bailey and the George Keatses. And one should remember that the Vale of Soul-making passage was written a long time after the Teignmouth experience. That his mind was so vigorously exercised by religious matters has lately become increasingly recognised by commentators, most notably, perhaps, by Robert Ryan, and, from a radically different point of view, Stuart Sperry.[18] Both these critics, unfortunately, are inclined to look for final decisions, Ryan rather tentatively, Sperry somewhat more dogmatically.

My own view is that one finds no decision in the poetry, but one certainly finds debate—and it is perhaps time now for commentators to recognise how much of Keats' major poetry is concerned with these matters—one sees the preoccupation beginning in *Endymion*, and intensifying in the two *Hyperions*. As it intensifies, it becomes more and more a conflict between symbols, or within antithetically ambiguous symbols. But one does not find in any of these poems anything which one might sensibly call a philosophical 'position'—only an anguished puzzlement. Consequently, although I have found it necessary in these introductory chapters to indicate briefly what I take to be the true nature of the development of Keats' thought and sensibility, it is not my purpose in this book to use the poems as documents for an inner biography. My concern is with the poetry itself, and largely with the great poetry. I begin my close analysis of his symbolism, then, at the point where his aestheticism is beginning to be challenged by his awakening thinking principle, in *Endymion*, *Lamia*, and *The Eve of St Agnes*.

3

The Love Narratives

Discussion of *Endymion* has for a long time been dominated by the question whether it is a Platonic allegory of the human soul in search of ideal beauty, or an entirely naturalistic celebration of sexual love. I do not propose to reproduce the opposing arguments here, any reader who is interested in the debate should consult Jacob D. Wigod's essay 'The Meaning of *Endymion*', where the main points are adequately summarised.[1] I do not propose, either, to make yet another exegesis of the overworked 'pleasure thermometer' passage (1:777 – 807), in spite of the importance Keats himself attached to it. I wish rather to draw attention to a passage in Book 2 which I believe really states the twin themes of the poem:

> The woes of Troy, towers smothering o'er their blaze,
> Stiff-holden shields, far-piercing spears, keen blades,
> Struggling, and blood, and shrieks—all dimly fades
> Into some backward corner of the brain;
> Yet, in our very soul, we feel amain
> The close of Troilus and Cressid sweet.
> Hence, pageant history ...
> ... the silver flow
> Of Hero's tears, the swoon of Imogen,
> Fair Pastorella in the bandit's den,
> Are things to brood on with more ardency
> Than the death-day of empires. Fearfully
> Must such conviction come upon his head,
> Who, thus far, discontent, has dared to tread,
> Without one muse's smile, or kind behest,
> The path of love and poesy. But rest,
> In chafing restlessness, is yet more drear

Than to be crush'd in striving to uprear
Love's standard on the battlements of song.
(2:8 – 13; 30 – 41)

Now this passage, particularly the last two lines, might well be
used as the starting point of the naturalistic critics' case for
reading the poem as an erotic fantasia, and if it were a clear and
unmistakable statement of the supreme goodness of simple
sexual feeling one might rightly base such an argument upon it.
But an erotic fantasia needs no heroism, no struggle, no tension,
no heartbreak, no hope of ultimate triumph, no defiance of the
rest of the world. Eroticism needs only itself. Something quite
different is suggested by love's standard fluttering on the
battlements of song. It is *romantic* love that Keats is celebrating, a
more fully human sentiment than simple eroticism, capable of
enduring all vicissitudes.

So great a value is attributed to such love that Keats seems to
make an epic claim for his poem. As Milton had asserted that his
divine cosmogony was as truly an epic theme as the wrath of
Achilles, and as Wordsworth had made a similar claim on behalf
of his celebration of the human mind, so Keats seems to claim
heroic status for his tale of love—and, going further than Milton
and Wordsworth, waves aside the battles of the *Iliad* as he does
so—'hence pageant history.' So brisk a dismissal of the Greek
epic sits oddly with the delight in Homer celebrated in his most
famous sonnet. But the preposterousness of Keats' implication is
not the greatest oddity of these lines. One might point to 'sweet'
as a very questionable adjective for Cressida, for example. But
more inexplicable is the unchronological silhouetting of Troilus
and Cressida's embrace against the flames of Troy, an image
which unerringly reminds us of the lovers who caused the
destruction, the 'far-piercing spears, keen blades,/ Struggling, and
blood, and shrieks'. We have immediately before our eyes
Troilus, the most foolishly besotted of all betrayed lovers, and
Cressida, whose name is a by-word for infidelity, but beyond
them we perceive Paris, whose blood was so madly hot that no
discourse of reason could secure his consent to an end of the
slaughter, and Helen, whose freshness so ambiguously made stale
the morning, and of whom it was said that for every false drop in
her bawdy veins a Grecian's life had sunk (*Troilus and Cressida*,

2:2:78 – 9; and 4:1: 69 – 70).

These Shakespearean associations, so inescapably evoked by Keats' picture, might well make us think that it was time for Aphrodite's colours to be lowered, yet the poet most strangely adduces them, along with the sufferings of Hero, Imogen and Pastorella, as preludes to the raising of Love's standard on the battlements of song. Most odd, however, is Keats' description of himself as working 'without one muse's smile or kind behest'. This may be simple modesty, but it may also be an acknowledgement that the muse is unlikely to ratify a project that links 'love and poesy' in the manner Keats is proposing to do here. For when Keats describes himself as 'treading the path of love and poesy' he is not, I think, merely saying that he is extolling love through the medium of poetry. 'Poesy' for him was probably not a rather precious synonym for 'poetry'; it signified the happy, picture-making imagination without which poetry could not be written at all.

It would require too long a digression to establish an indisputable definition of the term as Keats understood it, but most readers will probably agree with the general import of it which I infer from certain passages in *Sleep and Poetry*. That poesy is a visualising power seems clear from lines 62 – 79 and 101 – 21, and that the pictures it makes are, or ought to be, beautiful and happy ones is explicitly stated in lines 241 – 7. Perhaps at this point we should remember that Keats seems to use the terms 'poesy,' 'imagination,' and 'fancy' interchangeably (in the *Ode to a Nightingale* he certainly equates 'poesy' and 'fancy'), and though on one occasion in his letters he seems to differentiate them (see *Letters* 1:170), he never attempts the careful distinction that Coleridge makes in *Biographia Literaria*. For him all these terms refer to the mental power that seizes upon and delights in things of beauty, and subsequently recalls and recreates them. It is not the business of poesy to perceive and recreate horror and ugliness; on the contrary, its most important function is to evaporate such disagreeables. To this selective, delightful, and reassuring power, Keats also attributes authenticity. When Keats speaks of 'treading the path of love and poesy' then, he is identifying two themes. But these are not separable, parallel themes (Keats refers to one 'path'), they interpenetrate each other, for though the imagination can be sensitive and vigorous without sexual desire, love must necessarily intensify and energise it almost alarmingly. Nonetheless, Keats seems to be saying, the imagination is to be trusted even when it is spellbound by love. It is all the more astonishing then, that he proclaims his themes against a background drawn from *Troilus and Cressida*, and this background is perhaps the most dramatic example of Keats' unconscious subversion of his own purpose.

Here then is one of the principal difficulties of Endymion. We know from his letters that in fact Keats' response to beautiful women was ambivalent and defensive. It seems though, at this stage in his career, he was determined to refute in literature what he conceded in life. We rightly judge that the faults of *Endymion* are those of immaturity, but that immaturity consists to a large extent in Keats' reluctance to acknowledge and to assimilate into his artistic consciousness the treacherous doubt that accompanied his most wishful beliefs. Hence perhaps, the strain, the obsessional heaping of pleasure on pleasure—everything about the poem which a disgusted Lord Byron described as 'outstretched poesy'.[2] But in spite of this attempt to smother his scepticism with beauty, Keats' doubts do insinuate themselves into the poem. For whatever Cynthia represents—ideal beauty, truth, and happiness in love, the soul's ultimate desire—Circe represents its perfect imitation. There is a major conflict in the poem between these symbolic personae, and in a vital respect it remains undecided. But there are also minor conflicts between the main theme and its subsidiaries—the subsidiaries infiltrating the poem with treasonous symbolism.

The sense we have that in spite of the narrative line *Endymion* is not a poem but merely a heap of verses derives, I believe, from the uneasy relationship between the whole and its parts. The great romantic theme is carried by the main story of the ultimately triumphant love of Endymion and Cynthia, but to this tale two sub-stories are loosely tacked, and a third is much more strongly connected. It is hard to decide whether or not these minor love tales are meant to ratify the main plot in the manner of a Shakespearean sub-plot; what one does feel is that they modify it in variously disconcerting ways.

The first tale is the legend of Venus and Adonis—peculiarly apt in one sense, for it is another goddess-mortal relationship. In another sense it is most inappropriate, for in spite of the manner in which Keats glosses over Adonis' wounds, we are reminded of the horror of his death. The second love tale is that of Alphaeus and Arethusa, and Keats again overwhelms the ugliness and pain of the original myth as he found it in his Ovidian source, with a surfeit of poesy. Gone is the brutality of Alpheus' pursuit and siege, gone is Arethusa's terror:

> Then what a heart had I! the Lamb so fears
> When howling Wolves about the Fold she heares:
> So Heartlesse Hare, when trayling Hounds drawe nye
> Her sented Forme; nor dares to move an eye.
> Nor went he on, in that he could not trace
> My further steps; but guards the clowd and place.
> Cold sweats my then beseiged limbs possest:
> In thin thick-falling drops my strength descreast.[3]

In Keats' prettified version Arethusa has become a coquette: 'Ah, have I really got/ Such power to madden thee?' (2:955 - 56). Nevertheless, the kind of reader Keats could reasonably expect would be likely to know and recall the Ovidian ugliness and suffering.

The Glaucus myth in Book 3 is not only, at first sight, much more appropriate as a reinforcement of the main narrative theme, it is also organically connected with it. Glaucus, like the main hero, has endured an ordeal (a much more dreadful one than Endymion's), and the end of his sufferings heralds both the triumph of his own love for Scylla and that of innumerable other loves too, in a kind of amorous apocalypse. Not only is Love's standard upreared on the battlements of song, but Neptune's palace rings with universal joy, occasioned by the achieved immortal happiness of thousands of lovers (3:924 - 34). Glaucus' thousand years of suffering having been adequately indicated, this triumph surely justifies the imagination putting its trust in what it has seized as beauty. Unfortunately there is something in the heart of the Glaucus story that is deeply subversive of this hope. Let us compare certain descriptive passages from Book 1 with others from Book 3:

> ... she had
> Indeed, locks bright enough to make me mad;

And they were simply gordian'd up and braided,
Leaving, in naked comeliness, unshaded,
Her pearl round ears, white neck, and orbed brow;
The which were blended in, I know not how,
With such a paradise of lips and eyes,
Blush-tinted cheeks ...'
  'Ah! see her hovering feet,
More bluely vein'd, more soft, more whitely sweet
Than those of sea-born Venus, when she rose
From out of her cradle shell ...'
    'She took an airy range,
And then towards me, like a very maid,
Came blushing, waning, willing, and afraid,
And press'd me by the hand ...'
'I was distracted, madly did I kiss
The wooing arms which held me.'
    (1:612 - 19; 624 - 7; 633 - 6; 653 - 4)

'When I awoke, 'twas in a twilight bower;
Just when the light of morn, with hum of bees,
Stole through its verdurous matting of fresh trees.
How sweet, and sweeter! for I heard a lyre,
And over it a sighing voice expire.
It ceased—I caught light footsteps; and anon
The fairest face that morn e'er look'd upon
Push'd through a screen of roses. Starry Jove!
With tears, and smiles, and honey-words she wove
A net whose thralldom was more bliss than all
The range of flower'd Elysium ...'
'She took me like a child of suckling time
And cradled me in roses.'
    (3:418 - 28; 456 - 7)

The lines from Book 1 describing Cynthia are more detailed in their treatment of the beauties of her form and features; the lines on Circe more concerned with the beauties surrounding her—the nearest direct description is that she has 'the fairest face that morn e'er look'd upon.' The most significant difference, of course, in the two descriptions, is that the Circe lines contain certain indications of the treacherous nature of her beauty and wiles, but these are surely the products of the narrator's hindsight. At the time the thralldom was at work his deception was complete. And if the reader did not already know the happy ending of the myth, he would have no means of knowing that Endymion is not similarly deceived—is he not still 'a tranced vassal' (3:460) of Cynthia's beauty as Glaucus was of both Scylla's and Circe's? How is the infatuated imagination to distinguish between a loving goddess and a divine witch?

Perhaps we may clinch the point with one more comparison, this time of the lovers' perception of reality once their imaginations have been deprived of sexual glamour. For Endymion, bereft of his vision,

> '... all the pleasant hues
> Of heaven and earth had faded: deepest shades
> Were deepest dungeons; heaths and sunny glades
> Were full of pestilent light; our taintless rills
> Seem'd sooty, and o'er-spread with upturn'd gills
> Of dying fish; the vermeil rose had blown
> In frightful scarlet, and its thorns out-grown
> Like spiked aloe.'
>
> (1:691 - 8)

After Circe has stolen from his side while he was sleeping, Glaucus awakes to find

> '... the barbed shafts
> Of disappointment stuck in me so sore,
> That out I ran and search'd the forest o'er.
> Wandering about in pine and cedar gloom
> Damp awe assail'd me; for there 'gan to boom
> A sound of moan, an agony of sound,
> Sepulchral from the distance all round.
> Then came a conquering earth-thunder, and rumbled
> That fierce complaint to silence; while I stumbled
> Down a precipitous path, as if impell'd,
> I came to a dark valley.'
>
> (3:480 - 89)

Endymion's disappointment is temporary, part of his purifying ordeal; Glaucus' disenchantment is permanent, part of a thousand years of punishment. But there is nothing in the way the lovers' experiences, either of bliss or deprivation, are rendered, to which one could point and say, 'This is how to tell the difference between a goddess and an enchantress, between love and thralldom.' In this, of course, Keats is being entirely true to life, but not to either of his themes, or his pet maxim.

More ominously, love and witchcraft deprive their subjects not only of discernment, but of will. Endymion, justifying himself to Peona, says 'she had/ Indeed, locks bright enough to make me mad;' Glaucus, justifying himself to Endymion, says 'Who could resist? Who in this universe?' (3:453). To use the terms Shakespeare attributes to Troilus, 'will' has overwhelmed 'judgement' in the minds of both lovers. Endymion, we may conclude, merely turns out to be lucky, Glaucus, like Troilus, not so. *Endymion*, in fact, is a 'problem' poem, and has a particular affinity with *Troilus and Cressida*, sharing the play's main problem, the difficulty of distinguishing between appearance and reality. Also, an awareness of this affinity with the play may be another of the buried doubts indicated by the context in which Keats proclaimed his theme—Troilus and Cressida embracing amid the flames of Ilium.

In *Lamia* the affinity with Shakespeare's play is subtler and more comprehensive. In *Endymion* appearance and reality were symbolised by separate personae, Circe and Cynthia; the unhappy Glaucus was merely the victim of witchcraft, Endymion merely the fortunate object of true love. The problem of how to distinguish between a goddess and a sorceress is suggested implicitly, and being merely an implicit suggestion can be forgotten in the happiness of a triumphant ending for all concerned. In *Lamia* this problem is no longer a suppressed minor theme, it is the principal concern, and it is presented as a dilemma of human subjectivity which is always potentially tragic. The problem is now fully acknowledged, the various forms of ambivalence by which it is expressed are all controlled, and there is no sense of unwitting sabotage from unconscious sources.

The new mastery of his subject is reflected in Keats' development of a highly sophisticated symbolism. True and false beauty are no longer represented by separate personae; Lamia, as we shall see, represents both. On the other hand, the mind of the

lover has been divided into two, Lycius representing the hungry
and affective part of his sensibility, Apollonius the cognitive
aspect. One sees how fundamental the Shakespearean affinity is:
Cressida is throughout the play an undividable incorporate; it is
Troilus' consciousness that is, finally, divided. The fatal error of
the Trojan prince was his inability to distinguish between reality
and an illusion which he had himself created on the basis of that
reality. Hence when his Apollonius shows him the reality clasped
in Diomed's arms, he sees two Cressids, the woman his cognitive
self compels him to see, and the image whose beauty his
imagination has seized as truth, and cannot yet relinquish.

There is a clear sense, then, in which Lycius and Apollonius
represent what Troilus and Ulysses represent. There is an equally
clear sense in which Lamia represents what Cressida represents,
but we cannot make a simple transfer of either their characters or
their dramatic rôles. In Shakespeare's play only Troilus is
unaware of Cressida's nature, which is flawed in a way that
Lamia's is not; in Keats' narrative the reader is, at the outset, only
marginally better off than Lycius, but knows much more than
Lycius at the end.

Jackson Bate points out that Lamia is deliberately conceived as
an enigma: 'To begin with we are never sure whether she is
essentially a woman or a serpent ... Nor do we know whether she
is a mortal or an immortal, or something that falls between, or,
more probably something essentially different from either
category, though capable of participating in both.'[4] I suggest she
is capable of participating in both because she is both—she is and
is not a real woman because she represents reality invested with
illusion. Both in *Troilus and Cressida* and in *Lamia* the problem
of appearance and reality is made painfully ironic by the fact that
the appearance is largely of the beholder's making.

In reading Part 1 of *Lamia* let us first consider the mixture of
beauties and disagreeables, and then watch the manner in which
the latter are 'evaporated'. In lines 35 - 46 compare the Lamia
Hermes hears with the one he sees. '... he heard a mournful
voice,/ Such as once heard, in gentle heart, destroys/ All pain but
pity.' But he found 'a palpitating snake'. The participle evokes
that chill of repulsion that Emily Dickinson called 'zero at the
bone'. Perhaps we might gain a better idea of what Lamia
represents in the poem if we paid more attention to the symbolic

function of her serpent form. A 'cirque-couchant' snake scarcely makes an acceptable phallic image in itself, but 'palpitating' in this context suggests a predatory animal force that we may well take as representative of the male appetite. As a symbol then, Lamia represents three things: sexual desire; the object of that desire; and the glamorous phantasm created by that desire. We should note too that in her serpent form Keats finds her both repulsive and sickeningly beautiful. To understand the serpent symbol fully, one must remember Keats' own ambivalent attitude to desire, particularly that unexpected instinctive puritanism revealed in his marginal comment in Burton's *Anatomy of Melancholy*:

> Here is the old plague spot; the pestilence, the raw scrofula. I mean that there is nothing disgraces me in my own eyes so much as being one of a race of eyes, nose and mouth beings in a planet called the earth, who all from Plato to Wesley have always mingled goatish, winnyish, lustful love with the abstract adoration of the deity.[5]

Thus the horror of the word 'palpitating' in the description of Lamia's serpent form springs from that sliding pulsation that suggests a menacing, brutish energy. But the word develops its full force here because all its suggestions contrast so sharply with the helpless and piteous suggestions of Lamia's plaint. Here, one feels, must be the reality; both the 'lady bright' and the 'mournful voice' must be illusions. Lamia, in one of her symbolic aspects, is truly venomous, though her poison is delicious, paralysing not the nervous system but the development of emotional life. The point can be made by comparing the life she seeks for herself, and will offer Lycius, with the life proposed by Keats for the true poet:

> And can I ever bid these joys farewell?
> Yes, I must pass them for a nobler life,
> Where I may find the agonies, the strife
> Of human hearts.
>
> (*Sleep and Poetry*, 122 - 5)

'When from this wreathed tomb shall I awake!
When move in a sweet body fit for life,
And love, and pleasure, and the ruddy strife
Of hearts and lips!'

(1:38 - 41)

The echoes are astonishing, but it is plain that Lamia means very different things by 'life', 'strife', and 'hearts' from the meanings intended in the earlier poem. The strife she seeks risks no agony, the joy she will offer is not found in the core of pain.

The mixture of loveliness and repulsion in Lamia is not as simple as I have suggested here. She does not merely sound human and look monstrous, in her serpent form she has a loathsome beauty that bewilders and dazzles by its excess and multifariousness:

She was a gordian shape of dazzling hue,
Vermilion-spotted, golden, green, and blue;
Striped like a zebra, freckled like a pard,
Eyed like a peacock, and all crimson barr'd;
And full of silver moons, that as she breathed,
Dissolv'd, or brighter shone, or interwreathed
Their lustres with the gloomier tapestries—
So rainbow-sided, touch'd with miseries,
She seem'd at once, some penanced lady elf,
Some demon's mistress, or the demon's self.
Upon her crest she wore a wannish fire
Sprinkled with stars, like Ariadne's tiar:
Her head was serpent, but ah, bitter-sweet!
She had a woman's mouth with all its pearls complete:
And for her eyes: what could such eyes do there
But weep, and weep, that they were born so fair?
As Proserpine still weeps for her Sicilian air.

(1:47 - 63)

There are certain specific contrasts that Keats makes plain: the prevailing brilliance is 'interwreathed ... with the gloomier tapestries', the lustrous 'rainbow-sided' body is 'touch'd with miseries', and the eyes weep because they are so beautiful. But the ambiguity embedded in the description is more than is implied by 'bitter-sweet'. When one penetrates the migraine dazzle and the mazy pattern one perceives a gaudiness that is sickening in its abundance, and reaches a height, not · of pathos, but of grotesquerie in the vision of a reptilian head with human lips, teeth, and weeping eyes. Also when Lamia speaks, her voice either comes 'as through bubbling honey' (65), or it is a hiss, 'swift lisping' (116). Her metamorphosis too, has a similar nauseating brilliance:

> Left to herself, the serpent now began
> To change; her elfin blood in madness ran,
> Her mouth foam'd, and the grass, therewith besprent,
> Wither'd at dew so sweet and virulent;
> Her eyes in torture fix'd and anguish drear,
> Hot, glaz'd, and wide, with lid-lashes all sear,
> Flash'd phosphor and sharp sparks, without one
> cooling tear.
> The colours all inflam'd throughout her train,
> She writh'd about, convuls'd with scarlet pain:
> A deep volcanian yellow took the place
> Of all her milder-mooned body's grace;
> And, as the lava ravishes the mead,
> Spoilt all her silver mail, and golden brede,
> Made gloom of all her frecklings, streaks and bars,
> Eclips'd her crescents, and lick'd up her stars:
> So that, in moments few, she was undrest
> Of all her sapphires, greens and amethyst,
> And rubious argent: of all these bereft,
> Nothing but pain and ugliness were left.
>
> (1:146 - 64)

There is even an ambiguity in the last two words—they can mean simply 'remained', or 'left behind, discarded'. It immediately becomes clear that the latter is the important suggestion. Lamia is now 'a lady bright,/ A new born beauty new and exquisite'.

What evil, if any, does this curiously immaculate conception represent? From what does Apollonius wish to save Lycius, and Keats, perhaps, to save himself? Apart from a certain amount of preliminary teasing and sexual witchcraft meant to entrammel Lycius more securely, we can point to nothing that Lamia does that seems, at first sight, even mildly harmful. On the contrary she brings Lycius great happiness, and is sufficiently devoted to him to enjoy his tyranny, and, in order to appease his social pride, to risk the disaster which in fact overtakes her. Nevertheless I am going to suggest that the implication of the whole poem is that Apollonius is right, that Lycius' death is not his old tutor's fault, and that Lamia, in one of her aspects, is indeed a destructive being.

Lamia is both the symbol and agent of the power that created her, sexual fantasy. As Douglas Bush says, she 'is not ideal at all, except as a symbolic object of sensuous dreams'.[6] I suggest she is also a real object of sensuous dreams, as I hope to show later. Meanwhile let us look more closely at what she does for Lycius, and see whether it is as harmless as it appears. She creates an expurgated world for her lover, and she does so effortlessly. All delights come at will, free from disagreeables. This, indeed, is her distinctive power:

> Ah, happy Lycius! for she was a maid
> More beautiful than ever twisted braid,
> Or sigh'd, or blush'd, or on a spring-flowered lea
> Spread a green kirtle to the minstrelsy:
> A virgin purest lipp'd, yet in the lore
> Of love deep learned to the red heart's core:
> Not one hour old, yet of sciential brain
> To unperplex bliss from its neighbour pain;
> Define their pettish limits, and estrange
> Their points of contact, and swift counterchange;
> Intrigue with specious chaos, and dispart
> Its most ambiguous atoms with sure art;
> As though in Cupid's college she had spent
> Sweet days a lovely graduate, still unshent,
> And kept his rosy terms in idle languishment.
>
> (1:185 - 99)

Cupid's college is an ivory tower set among shadowy waters. 'To unperplex bliss from its neighbour pain' is not a means of achieving fulness of living, nor of fitting oneself to be a great poet. The principle of trying to select one's experience has affinities with the Pre-Rephaelite manifesto proclaimed by John L. Tupper:

... the subjects of Fine Art should be drawn from objects which address and excite the activities of man's rational and benevolent powers, such as: acts of justice,—of mercy—good government—order ... but not of gluttony, anger, hatred or malevolence.[7]

Tupper's principle seems quite priggishly moral, but let us see where it leads. Oscar Wilde says, in 'The Critic as Artist':

Art does not hurt us. The tears that we shed at a play are a type of the exquisite sterile emotion that it is the function of art to waken. It is through Art ... and through Art only, that we can shield ourselves from the sordid perils of actual existence ... All art is immoral.[8]

If the honeymoon consciousness is to be indefinitely prolonged, it too must avoid the sordid perils. Arrested sexual feeling partakes of the same nature as aesthetic consciousness, and may be the unacknowledged origin of such consciousness.

Let us now examine Lycius, and the nature of his love. He is first introduced as an object of Lamia's projected vision, and he is perceived, romantically of course, as a 'young Jove with calm uneager face' (1:218), but when he is brought directly before the reader, his presence is announced with a noise of abrasive realism: 'his galley now/ Grated the quaystones.' He has been to offer vows, sacrifices, and petitionary prayers, apparently for successful love, for 'Jove heard his vows, and better'd his desire' (1:229). The implication is that Lycius has asked, not for a particular woman, but for a woman. Jove's response, by leading him aside 'over the solitary hills' (1:233) provides him with an object of desire better than he could conceive hitherto. If Keats is serious, and not being ironic or figurative about Jove's irresponsible part in this affair, then Lamia does have a real existence, and is not merely a phantasm created by young libido. Lamia, in fact, is a composite figure, and the objective element in Keats' conception of her will become fully apparent in Part 2. Meanwhile we must note that Lycius, immediately before encountering Lamia, is eager to fall in love. He has encountered the 'palpitating snake' before the 'lady bright.'

At the first sight of her he plunges into fevered infatuation. He drinks from a 'bewildering cup' (1:253), he yearns to kiss her in 'due adoration' (1:255), he swoons 'murmuring of love, and pale with pain' (1:289), his life is 'entangled in her mesh' (1:295), 'And every word she spake entic'd him on/ To unperplex'd delight and pleasure known' (1:326 - 7). He is in the same plight as Troilus:

> 'O, be thou my Charon,
> And give me swift transportation to those fields
> Where I may wallow in the lily-beds
> Propos'd for the deserver!'
>
>   'I am giddy; expectation whirls me round;
> The imaginary relish is so sweet
> That it enchants my sense; what will it be,
> When that the wat'ry palates taste indeed
> Love's thrice repured nectar? Death, I fear me,
> Sounding destruction, or some joy too fine,
> Too subtle potent, tun'd too sharp in sweetness
> For the capacity of my ruder powers.'
>
>   (*Troilus and Cressida*, 3:2:10 - 13,17 - 24)

'Imaginary relish' is the palpitating snake in the grass for both Troilus and Lycius; the original cause of their 'sounding destruction', though the immediate cause in each case is the resolute insistence on reality urged by Ulysses and Apollonius respectively.

There is a difference, though, in the work done by the infatuated visions of Troilus and Lycius. The perfections with which the Trojan's mind invests Cressida remain tangibly biological:

> ... her hand,
> In whose comparison all whites are ink
> Writing their own reproach; to whose soft seizure
> The cygnet's down is harsh, and spirit of sense
> Hard as the palm of ploughman.
>
>   (1:1: 55 - 9)

The disaster Troilus fears is also biological. He can hardly be supposing that he might expire from excessive pleasure; it is the

failure of his 'ruder powers' he dreads. This, it may be is a form of
impotence, brought on by 'some joy ... Too subtile potent'.
Troilus may be using the word 'Death' as a derivative from the
common Elizabethan slang sense of the verb 'to die', in which case
'sounding destruction' would certainly follow a premature
'death'. But even if Shakespeare intended a less specific meaning
than this, Troilus is plainly fretting about the possibility of sexual
failure, and he acknowledges the part that would have been played
in this by indulgent fantasy.

Lycius too faces failure, also due to overheated imagination,
but the form is different. He is, Lamia tells us, a scholar; when he
encounters her he is returning from a religious observance, his
mind is shut up in 'mysteries' and 'wrapp'd like his mantle' (1:241
– 2), his train of thought lost 'In the calm'd twilight of Platonic
shades'. (1:236). (It may be worth remembering that Keats at this
time claimed to find in 'abstractions' his 'only life'—*Letters*
1:370.) Although Lamia's appearance jolts him from this musing,
the cast of his mind no doubt influences how his imagination
works on the apparition before him. Troilus glamourises
Cressida: Lycius, like Porphro in *The Eve of St Agnes* gazing on
the kneeling Madeline, spiritualises his lady:

> 'Stay! though a Naiad of the rivers, stay!
> To thy far wishes will thy streams obey:
> Stay! though the greenest woods be thy domain,
> Alone they can drink up the morning rain.'
>   (1:261 – 4)

Lamia quickly picks up the cue:

> 'If I should stay ...'
> 'What canst thou say or do of charm enough
> To dull the nice remembrance of my home?'
>
> 'Thou art a scholar, Lycius, and must know
> That finer spirits cannot breathe below
> In human climes, and live.'
>   (1:271; 274 – 5; 279 – 81)

This is teasing, of course, but the substance of it is worth brief scrutiny. Lamia claims, being a goddess, to find earthly flowers too rough. The decadent aesthetes, we remember, ultimately found that nature was uncomfortable. When Lamia's 'finer spirit' is eventually persuaded to dwell in Corinth, she can scarcely be said to live there, she has servants to do that for her. Meanwhile, she is too shrewd to overplay her teasing, and hastens to assure Lycius (who, she realises, 'could not love in half a fright') that she is a real woman, with nothing more than throbbing blood in her veins. Indeed she is a real woman, but one who has been transformed by her lover's imagination, (that 'palpitating snake') into an image from which all mundane flaws have been removed. Being fantasy, her beauty is unearthly; being real, she is fully endowed with 'women's lore'. With the advantage her double nature gives her, she can play wooing games to perfection—'every word she spake entic'd him on' (1:326).

She imitates superbly a kind of human behaviour that Keats found both attractive and alarming, the flirtatious tormenting whose purpose may or may not be invitation.[9] It is perhaps a real women's very human if rather foolish response to the advantage her lover's imagination has given her. We need to bear this in mind if we are to grasp all that is going on in lines 1:328 - 39, which have been more commonly misunderstood even than the lines about philosophy clipping an angel's wings:

> Let the mad poets say whate'er they please
> Of the sweets of Fairies, Peris, Goddesses,
> There is not such a treat among them all,
> Haunters of cavern, lake, and waterfall,
> As a real woman, lineal indeed
> From Pyrrah's pebbles or old Adam's seed.
> Thus gentle Lamia judg'd and judg'd aright,
> That Lycius could not love in half a fright,
> So threw the goddess off, and won his heart
> More pleasantly by playing woman's part,
> With no more awe than what her beauty gave,
> That, while it smote, still guaranteed to save.

By far the most perceptive comment on these lines has been made by Georgina S. Dunbar:

The joking use of 'treat' will jar on the ears of those who want a dignified grand passion, but Keats has not made his lovers dignified. He poked fun at the ever-smitten and red-eared Hermes, the withering Tritons, the coquettish Lamia, and the swooning Lycius. She is a perfect example of scheming, clever, but enchanting femininity, and he is the perfect example of the gullible lover who is bewitched into believing he is playing the dominant male at the very moment when he is helplessly entrapped by the lady's coy wiles.[10]

Lamia's symbolic function is complex—one aspect of it is the representation of an image created by the male libido, but another aspect is the representation of a real woman taking advantage of the glamorous creation for her own purposes. She is woman being what man thinks he wants her to be. Hence the sardonic notes struck by 'treat', 'old Adam', 'playing woman's part', and 'guaranteed to save'. Keats made a careful study of Dryden before writing *Lamia*, and he obviously learnt more than a superior skill in versification.

From this point on, Lamia begins a change in nature, less spectacular than her metamorphosis from serpent form, but dramatically far more interesting. Her womanhood gradually becomes exclusively real. When Lycius muffles his face and shrinks closer into his mantle upon encountering Apollonius in the streets of Corinth, Lamia's trepidation, dissembling, and suspicion are familiarly human:

> "Why do you shudder, love, so ruefully?
> Why does your tender palm dissolve in dew?"—
> "I'm wearied," said fair Lamia: "tell me who
> Is that old man? I cannot bring to mind
> His features:— Lycius! wherefore did you blind
> Yourself from his quick eyes?"
>
> (1:369 – 74)

The child of Ouranos is becoming a daughter of Eve. The change gathers speed in Part 2. When she detects a weakening of her hold on her lover, her response is characteristic of flesh and blood: 'she began to moan and sigh/ Because he mus'd beyond her' (2:37 – 38). When the threat to her love is grave, she becomes a distraught, cast-off mistress:

> "You have deserted me;—where am I now?
> Not in your heart while care weighs on your brow:
> No, no, you have dismiss'd me, and I go
> From your breast houseless: ay, it must be so."
>
> (2:42 – 5)

Or a desperate wife:

> The lady's cheek
> Trembled; she nothing said, but pale and meek,
> Arose and knelt before him, wept a rain
> Of sorrows at his words; at last with pain
> Beseeching him, the while his hand she wrung,
> To change his purpose.
>
> (2:64 – 9)

She is in fact begging him not to proceed with a wedding, yet she looks and sounds like a heartbroken woman struggling to save a marriage. When Lycius becomes domineering, her response may or may not be true to a certain kind of feminine psychology—'She burn't, she lov'd the tyranny,' (2:81), but when Lycius asks her questions she prefers not to answer, she is fully human: 'Lycius, perplex'd at words so blind and blank,/ Made close inquiry; from whose touch she shrank,/ Feigning a sleep' (2:102 6 104).

This complication of Lamia's nature was, I believe, a part of Keats' intention in his original conception of the poem, and in the changes she undergoes he is representing what he suspects is the usual progress of love in real life. Infatuated eyes create much of what they see, and superimpose a radiant vision on an unsuspecting human being. The dazzle obscures, perhaps totally for a time, the person whom it invests, and she may be Cressida. That such a possibility was in Keats' mind is indicated in a letter to Fanny Brawne written in February 1820: 'My greatest torment since I have known you has been the fear of you being a little inclined to the Cressid' (*Letters*, 2:256).

But even if the person whom the radiance invests is not Cressid, a tragic outcome remains possible. The vision survives satisfaction for a period, but ultimately an ordinary woman must emerge from the erotic haze. Traditional wisdom used to say that as the process continues, the 'faery power/ Of unreflecting love' will develop into a sober affection capable of flourishing by the light of common day. But if it doesn't, there will almost certainly be a suffering female victim—not Lamia, who will have vanished as she does in the poem, but the unhappy woman whom Lamia once invested. To this extent Claude Finney is certainly right when he says: 'Keats' sympathy throughout the romance is with Lamia.'[11] We are all familiar with the misgivings Keats had about Fanny Brawne, but a study of Lamia should alert us to the more important misgivings he had about himself. London was Keats' Corinth, with all 'her populous streets and temples lewd' (1:352), 'Men, women, rich and poor' (1:355), 'many a light' flaring from 'wealthy festivals' (1:357 – 8), throwing 'their moving shadows on the walls' (1:359).

Keats needed his friends too, with their 'Corinth talk' (1:231), and their philosophical and literary speculations. Charles Brown may well have been his bald-headed, sharp-eyed mentor whose cruel speculation about Caroline Robinson's old age may have roused fears for an elderly Fanny Brawne. A little later, desperately ill and jealous, he felt sickened by the 'brute world' which Fanny was 'smiling with' (*Letters*, 2:312), but when in good health he was a man of that world, and it did not seem so brutal. What safety can there be for a dream love in a daylight world? Certainly Apollonius' intervention saves the lovers from a drawn-out, embittered anti-climax: 'Too short was their bliss/ To breed distrust and hate, that makes the soft voice hiss.' (2:9 – 10).

Let us now pay some attention to Apollonius and the effect of his intervention. Early Wasserman has rightly identified his symbolic function: 'Apollonius is not an independent value, but an inherent faculty of the mortal Lycius ... He is, in other words, Lycius' own conceptual brain.'[12] In fact he is to Lycius what Ulysses was to Troilus, the intelligence that can distinguish between appearance and reality. Therefore he does not turn Lamia back into a serpent, as we might have expected, he merely speeds up the humanising process that has already begun. Under his gaze she withers swiftly into reality, and disappears. Once he has turned his scrutiny upon her, her eyes grow dull and fixed, with the vacuity of death. 'There was no recognition in those orbs' is clearly meant to remind us of Banquo's glare (*Macbeth*,

3:4:95 – 96). Her skin coarsens, 'no azure vein/ Wander'd on fair-
spaced temples' (2:272 – 73). She grows old, tired, and ill, as all
women must:

> ... no soft bloom
> Misted the cheek; no passion to illume
> The deep-recessed vision:—all was blight;
> Lamia, no longer fair, there sat a deadly white.
>
> (2:273 – 6)

The tragedy for Lycius, perhaps, was not Lamia's vanishing, but
the wreckage of her beauty.

If Lycius is in some sense Keats, why does he die? I suggest two
reasons. First, he has had no time to adjust to the accelerated
decay of his love. Having lived so intensely in an expurgated
world, he cannot survive being bundled so swiftly back to the real
one, though we should note that he had already begun to drift
back to it. His love had begun to ebb, but at a normal human
pace. Lamia's complaints were justified; she had become, for
Lycius, a possession to be displayed:

> 'What mortal hath a prize, that other men
> May be confounded and abash'd withal,
> But lets it sometimes pace abroad majestical,
> And triumph, as in thee I should rejoice
> Amid the hoarse alarm of Corinth's voice.
> Let my foes choke, and my friends shout afar,
> While through the thronged streets your bridal car
> Wheels round its dazzling spokes.'
>
> (2:57 – 64)

This is already something less than love. The selfishness at the
heart of such feeling is beautifully emphasised by Keats in the use
he makes of the old Elizabethan conceit of lovers 'looking babies'
at each other. In John Donne's *Good Morrow* the image suggests
mutual self-offering and honest dealing: 'My face in thine eye,
thine in mine appears,/ And true plain hearts do in the faces rest.'
Compare this with 'He answer'd, bending to her open eyes/
Where he was mirror'd small in paradise.' Lycius' glamorous
mistress reflects a glamorous image of himself and his sense of self

grows rapidly; she is *his* silver planet—he, presumably, the sun. The marriage on which he now insists is a means to secure ('trammel up and snare'—2:52) the prize that other men may be 'confounded and abash'd withal'. So much for the holiness of the heart's affections.

The second reason why Lycius dies is that he represents a Keats whom Keats rejected, and the nineteenth century beatified. Already sick of being a pet lamb in Hunt's sentimental farce, Keats was trying to save himself from the Keatsians. But the poet loved the outworn self who died in the poem, and perhaps still loved too the perilous principle of beauty in all things that died with him. Apollonius' achievement is therefore felt as a destructive thing:

> Do not all charms fly
> At the mere touch of cold philosophy?
> There was an awful rainbow once in heaven:
> We know her woof, her texture; she is given
> In the dull catalogue of common things.
> Philosophy will clip an Angel's wings,
> Conquer all mysteries by rule and line,
> Empty the haunted air and, gnomed mine—
> Unweave a rainbow.
>
> (2:229 – 37)

But what does philosophy destroy? Charms merely, the ornaments which Fancy imposes on things—pretty cherubs, Oberon's crown and jewelled cloak. True, not everyone would be willing to categorise Noah's rainbow thus, but Keats probably would. The mystery which sober objectivity conquers is the spurious mystery with which romantic fantasy has overlaid reality, not the philosophic mystery which many people find at the heart of the commonplace. Also, the list of things destroyed contains no genuinely humane values. If any things other than mere charms have been destroyed, they are Keats' desperately formulated propositions concerning beauty, imagination, and the heart's affections.

The problem of appearance and reality was discussed in *Lamia* by means of a highly sophisticated ambivalence of tone, diction and symbolism. In *The Eve of St Agnes* the theme is expressed by contrasts, most of which are strong and obvious. Youthful energy is set against moribund age, snarling trumpets against muttered prayers, moonlight against darkness, social delight against loneliness, erotic warmth against sterilising cold; and in the dramatic climax of the poem, love is enjoyed in the midst of murderous hate. These oppositions engage the reader's attention so forcefully that it takes a little time to become aware of certain less obvious contrasts and ambiguities. I suggest that these subtler oppositions are in fact the most important ones, and that once we have identified them we shall find in them both the origin and purpose of the poem.

Perhaps the most important of these is the contrast between religious and superstitious behaviour. It is easy to miss this, as Jack Stillinger has done in his otherwise admirable essay on the poem:

> If we recall Keats' agnosticism, his sonnet *Written in Disgust of Vulgar Superstition* (Christianity), and his abuse in a spring 1819 journal letter of 'the pious frauds of Religion' (*Letters*, II, 80), we may be prepared to see a hoodwinked dreamer in the poem even before we meet Madeline. He is the old Beadsman, so engrossed in ascetic ritual that he is sealed off from the joys of life ... By brooding 'all that wintry day,/ on love and wing'd St Agnes saintly care' (43 – 4), Madeline presents an obvious parallel with the Beadsman. Both are concerned with prayer and ascetic ritual; both are isolated from the crowd and from actuality. A second point is that the superstition is clearly an old wives' tale: Madeline follows the prescription that 'she had heard old dames full many times declare' (45). It is called by the narrator a 'whim'.[13]

If we recall Keats' agnosticism we must also recall his negative capability, and his insistence that the needs of art overcome all other considerations. For dramatic purposes he was evidently prepared to acknowledge that Christianity, pious fraud though it might be, had a more substantial ethical content than a whim or an old wives' tale; and that the self-seeking petitionary ritual practised by Madeline and the many pious oaths ejaculated by Porphyro constitute no more than a frivolous parody of the prayers offered by both the Beadsman and Angela. In fact we cannot grasp the full scope of what Stillinger himself has so valuably pointed out—the anti-romantic ironies of *The Eve of St Agnes*—unless we are prepared to see the distinction made throughout the poem between religious and superstitious behaviour (or, as Douglas Bush puts it, between 'religious and quasi-religious piety'),[14] and the part it plays in expressing the whole problem of appearance and reality. In particular we shall miss the irony in the complex symbolic status of Madeline in the poetic, rather than the dramatic, climax of the poem.

In regard to this distinction we should first note a barely concealed paradox in the legend that triggers the plot. That a saint martyred for virginity should become the particular friend of young maidens in love may seem paradoxical in itself, but more clearly so is the fact that Agnes appears to have instituted a fairly rigorous physical and mental discipline (going 'supperless to bed', maintaining the guard of the eyes, and performing 'ceremonies due') in order to procure a high degree of physiological stimulation while innocently asleep. One might add that while the legend itself is merely superstitious, the paradox within it is fundamentally religious, since it reflects the notion that certain things can be secured only by renunciation.

The superstition is the mainspring of such plot as the poem has:

> They told her how, upon St Agnes' Eve,
> Young virgins might have visions of delight,
> And soft adorings from their loves receive
> Upon the honey'd middle of the night,
> If ceremonies due they did aright;
> As, supperless to bed they must retire,
> And couch supine their beauties, lily white;
> Nor look behind nor sideways, but require
> Of Heaven with upward eyes for all that they desire
>
> (46 – 54)

The favour Madeline asks of St Agnes is akin to that which Browning's bishop proposed to ask on behalf of his bastard sons: 'And have I not St Praxed's ear to pray/ Horses for ye, and brown Greek manuscripts,/ And mistresses with great smooth marbly limbs?'[15] The bishop's case is not complicated by any felt need to offer his patron any kind of self-denial; Madeline must go hungry and ignore the lively festivities of the evening in order to be rewarded with an erotic dream. Yet Madeline's behaviour, like the bishop's is fundamentally irreligious; she offers St Agnes propitiatory rites, not prayers, and her state of mind is enchantment, not devotion. She herself, as I think Keats suggests, may be unaware that such distinctions might be made, since she is 'Hoodwink'd with faery fancy' (70). Thus in spite of the reference to Madeline's reliance on 'wing'd St Agnes' saintly care' (44), the reader is more impressed by old Angela's perception that 'my lady fair the conjuror plays' (124). Porphyro too at first assesses Madeline's doings realistically; he is moved to tears not by thoughts of her piety, but by 'those enchantments cold/ And Madeline asleep in lap of legends old' (134 – 35), and he hopes by means of his strategem to 'see her beauty unespied ... / While legion'd fairies pac'd the coverlet/ And pale enchantment held her sleepy-eyed' (166 – 69). Later, when he actually sees Madeline on her knees, his judgement falters.

It is in the sensibility of Porphro that we find the most significant ambivalence, and I suggest it is an authorial one. Keats seems to have been unsure of, or not fully conscious of, his basic purpose. The poem was first written between 18 January and 2 February 1819, but in September of that year Keats proposed certain revisions. After line 54 he added the following stanza:

> 'Twas said her future lord would there appear
> Offering as sacrifice—all in the dream—
> Delicious food even to her lips brought near:
> Viands and wine and fruit and sugar'd cream,
> To touch her palate with the fine extreme
> Of relish: then soft music heard; and then
> More pleasure followed in a dizzy stream
> Palpable almost; then to wake again
> Warm in the virgin morn, no weeping Magdalen.

He also altered lined 314 – 22 to read as follows:

> See while she speaks his arms encroaching slow
> Have zon'd her, heart to heart—loud, loud the dark
> > winds blow.

For on the midnight came a tempest fell,
More sooth for that his close rejoinder flows
Into her burning ear;—and still the spell
Unbroken guards her in serene repose,
With her wild dream he mingled as a rose
Marryeth its odour to a violet.
Still, still she dreams—louder the frost wind blows.[16]

In spite of that 'pleasure ... palpable almost', and the implication of 'no weeping Magdalen', the ladies for whom Keats was at this time pretending scorn might well have read the first revision with little shock; its purpose seems merely to explain the Agnes legend more fully. Put both revisions together, however, and it becomes clear that Keats is insisting that, in the very act of awakening Madeline Porphyro has intercourse with her. The row which followed these proposed changes has become famous, and I need not go into its details here. The climax was a warning from the publisher, John Taylor, that if Keats would not 'so far concede to my Wishes as to leave the passage [314–22] as it originally stood, I must be content to admire his Poems with some other Imprint.' (*Letters*, 2:183). In the end Keats did concede, though on proof-reading the poem he insisted on a few minor, less controversial changes. As a result, the received text of the poem has, as John Barnard says, 'a somewhat ambiguous authorial approval.'[17]

Taylor's editorial prudence has not cost us dearly, there is little to choose between the text as we now have it, and as it would have been with the September revisions incorporated. What we should note in this whole incident are the reasons Keats seems to have given for the proposed changes. Their purpose was to make the poem less 'smokeable', that is, less vulnerable to charges of sentimentality and romantic simplicity. Keats in fact is flinching before the critics. Porphyro therefore must be made more manly; the reader must not be allowed to suppose him, at Madeline's bedside, 'such an eunuch in sentiment as to leave a [Girl] maid with that Character about her, in such a situation' (*Letters*, 2:163).

Greater sexual explicitness, however, was not to be the only remedy for sentimentality. The last lines of the poem were now to read:

> Angela went off
> 'Twitch'd with the Palsy; and with face deform
> The beadsman stiffen'd, 'twixt a sigh and laugh,
> Ta'en sudden from his beads by one weak little cough.[18]

These lines illustrate well the danger of revising out of fear, with the artistic consciousness not fully engaged. Keats wished, according to Woodhouse, 'to leave on the reader a sense of pettish disgust, by bringing Old Angela in (only) dead stiff & ugly.—He says he likes that the poem should leave off with this Change of Sentiment' (*Letters*, 2:162 – 63). Keats largely fails in his purpose. It is not clear why we should feel disgust rather than pity for the old beldame, but whatever we feel for Angela quickly gives place to bewilderment about what precisely the Beadsman was doing at the moment of his death. If 'stiffen'd' means 'died,' then 'twixt' indicates that he had just sighed and was about to laugh—raising the question whether an author can reasonably claim to know this. If we construe the words as meaning that the Beadsman's final breath made a sound something between a sigh and a laugh (and Keats must have heard many death-rattles), then this does not square well with 'one weak little cough'. The reader is too busy trying to rationalise a meaning out of these lines to feel pettish disgust.

A point to bear in mind now is that none of the proposed changes would have actually introduced anything new into the poem; they would simply have reinforced and made more explicit what is already there. (In doing so, I believe they would have constituted an overemphasis.) The dispute about the September revisions simply brought into the open the reasons for a certain ambivalence of tone and characterisation. Keats, it seems, had from the beginning suspicions about the poem's simple chivalric tone. But I suspect that his real fear was something more important than being flyblown on the review shambles. I suggest that this fear may have been of sexuality itself, and that it may have been strengthened by increasing doubts about the validity of his dogma about beauty, truth, and imagination. Certainly the ambiguity of the poem turns out to be immensely fruitful, because although the ostensible subject matter is a simple mediaeval tale with a simple romantic hero, its real substance is a delicate exploration of a complex erotic sensibility, and the conflicting idealisations created by that sensibility. Bearing this in mind then, let us now examine the behaviour and consciousness of Keats' hero.

Although the account of Porphyro given in 'The Hoodwinking of Madeline' is an invaluable corrective to traditional and neo-Platonic views of the poem, he is none the less a more complex figure than Jack Stillinger supposes. True, we cannot be comfortable with his character as a romantic hero, though he displays all the usual attributes. He rides across the moonlit heath 'with heart on fire' (75), he implores all saints 'to give him sight of Madeline' (78),—the St Praxed's tradition of prayer again—he longs to gaze, kneel and worship at the shrine of his love, and he ventures in, most hero-like, to the castle of his hyena foemen, to pluck, in the manner of Hotspur, the flower of romance and fulfilment out of the nettle danger. Yet he may also be seen, by almost any standards, as a blackguard; not because he seduces Madeline, but because he does so after he has promised so fervently that he will not:

> 'I will not harm her, by all saints I swear,'
> Quoth Porphyro: 'O may I ne'er find grace
> When my weak voice shall whisper its last prayer,
> If one of her soft ringlets I displace,
> Or look with ruffian passion in her face:
> Good Angela, believe me by these tears;
> Or I will, even in a moment's space,
> Awake, with horrid shout, my foemen's ears,
> And beard them, though they be more fang'd than wolves
>   and bears
>   (145 – 53)

The worst aspect of this is Porphyro's emotional blackmail of a frail and terrified old woman who apparently loves him. It is not his treatment of Madeline that is so out of key with the ostensibly prevailing tone of the narrative, (though one is not impressed by Keats' 'rhodomontade' about the inevitability of the seduction), it is his cruelty to a 'palsy-stricken, churchyard thing' (155). But perhaps we should hesitate to accuse him of hypocrisy or calculation. One may defend his broken promises on the usually shaky ground that he meant them at the time, and in fact in his case such a defence is not so feeble as it first seems. I suggest that Porphyro is more than a rather shabby character; he is, like Lycius, a symbolic persona representing again a male sensibility in love, incapable of distinguishing between object and phantasm. But he may be unlike Lycius in one vital respect—he is as much ignorant of his own nature and motives as he is about the object of his love. Certainly he deceives Angela, certainly he takes an advantage which he had sworn not to take, but Keats gives us no reason to suppose that these wrongdoings were part of a premeditated design, nor that they are in keeping with his normal behaviour. For we know nothing of his normal behaviour, he exists for us only as a lover, and therefore symbolises the doting man whose practical deceit springs first from self-deceit. For as the poem proceeds there is such persuasive evidence of a fundamental emotional volatility and duality of vision that one must suppose his behaviour springs from these, not scheming duplicity.

To consider this more fully, let us examine his two visions of Madeline. From his closet he sees her hurry into her bedroom and kneel down to pray, whereupon he grows faint. He does so, it is too frequently assumed, because he is a Keatsian hero, and therefore given to swooning. If Keats had wanted to make his hero more manly, he might have excised his tears and giddy spells. But there is an excellent reason for Porphyro's reaction: 'Porphyro grew faint,/ She knelt, so pure a thing, so free from mortal taint' (224 – 25). In spite of his failure to see the distinction Keats makes between religion and superstition, Jack Stillinger makes an excellent point on this matter:

> Though many reasons will suggest themselves why Porphyro grows faint, a novel one may be offered here. In his copy of *The Anatomy of Melancholy*, after a passage in which Burton tells how 'The Barbarians stand in awe of a fair woman, and at a beautiful aspect a fierce spirit is pacified', Keats wrote: 'abash'd the devil stood.' He quotes from Book IV of *Paradise Lost*, where Satan is confronted by the beautiful angel Zephon: 'Abasht the Devil stood,/ And felt how awful goodness is, and saw/ Virtue in her shape how lovely, saw, and pin'd/ His loss' (846 – 849). But since Burton speaks of standing 'in awe of a fair woman', Keats must also have recalled Book IX, in which

Satan's malice is momentarily overawed by Eve's graceful innocence: 'That space the Evil one abstracted stood/ From his own evil, and for the time remain'd/ Stupidly good' (463 – 5). Porphyro's faintness may in some way parallel Satan's moment of stupid goodness.[19]

But there is an irony in Keats' lines which we ought not to miss, similar to the irony of Shakespeare's scene where Hamlet spares the defenceless Claudio at his prayers. After Hamlet has left the stage, the king reveals that his prayers have been invalid. But in Keats' scene we know all the time what the nature of Madeline's exercise really is. She only appears to have what Stillinger attributes to her, 'the status of one of St Agnes' lambs unshorn' (*loc. cit.*). As she kneels down to do what she thinks of as praying, she is merely fulfilling the requirements of an old wives' tale, and is soliciting a love dream.

I believe this irony to be important. Keats is not mocking Madeline's behaviour, yet throughout this stanza the reader is always aware that what is being described is not piety but a posture of piety. Like Porphyro, Madeline is a symbolic persona (we know nothing of her except as a young girl in love), and she represents a sensibility that does not fully know itself. Although her piety is spurious, it is not hypocritical—there is nothing to indicate that she recognises her behaviour as anything other than true petitionary prayer. But her symbolic function is, as I indicated earlier, highly complex, for she unwittingly imposes her own deception on Porphyro. She represents sexual desire that does not recognise the nature of the behaviour it prompts (in this her function precisely parallels Porphyro's); and she also represents contrasting aspects of an object of such desire, and in the great bedroom scene we see her dissolve from one image to another. Let us look carefully, yet once more, at the poem's most famous stanzas:

> A casement high and triple-arch'd there was,
> All garlanded with carven imag'ries
> Of fruits, and flowers, and bunches of knot-grass,
> And diamonded with panes of quaint device,
> Innumerable of stains and splendid dyes,
> As the tiger-moths deep-damask'd wings;

And in the midst, 'mong thousand heraldries,
And twilight saints, and dim emblazonings,
A shielded scutcheon blush'd with blood of queens and kings.

Full on this casement shone the wintry moon,
And threw warm gules on Madeline's fair breast,
As down she knelt for heaven's grace and boon;
Rose-bloom fell on her hands together prest,
And on her silver cross soft amethyst,
And on her hair a glory, like a saint:
She seem'd a splendid angel, newly drest,
Save wings, for heaven:—Porphyro grew faint
She knelt, so pure a thing, so free from mortal taint.

(208 – 25)

It is not only Madeline's genuflection and praying hands that transmute her supernatural soliciting into an appearance of devotion; the major work is done by the moonlight and the stained glass. The 'rose-bloom' from the magic casement emphasises and spiritualises her her hands and breasts, and for a significant moment focuses attention on her pectoral cross. Her hair is not yet freed from its 'wreathed pearls', but the rose-bloom catches a few intractable and otherwise scarcely visible strands, and creates upon them a halo. We know that the business she is about is incorrigibly earthy, but to the unfortunate Porphyro 'she *seem'd* a splendid angel' (my italics). In the mind of the besotted spy in the closet, her appearance is that of a nun at her devotions, Agnes herself perhaps, or even the one woman reputedly 'free from mortal taint'. The fruition of love seems impossible. But Porphyro is deluded by that spiritualising moonlight, which is not merely working its magic on the figure of Madeline, but working also in co-operation with the watcher's intoxicated fancy. The fact that the whole tableau is spurious is emphasised ironically by the superbly detailed realism and intensity of the imagery, and by our memory of another praying figure, stripped of glamorous warmth and colour:

Numb were the Beadsman's fingers, while he told
His rosary, and while his frosted breath,
Like pious incense from a censer old,

Seem'd taking flight for heaven, without a death,
Past the sweet Virgin's picture, while his prayer
                                        he saith. (5 – 9)

There is one thing more to note about the moonlight which so
enhances Madeline. One should not, I think, see it merely as a
theatrical lighting effect; it is possible that the light gains more
than colour from the glass through which it passes. The 'panes of
quaint device', the royal scutcheon, the blazonings and heraldries
symbolise a chivalric social order, though one that includes hyena
foemen and barbarian hordes, and the 'twilight saints' represent a
moral scheme which pervades that social order, and on which
indeed it is ostensibly based. The light that falls on Madeline
transforms her as it does because it is saturated not merely with
colour, but with the values whose capacity to idealise
womanhood is most commonly manifested in images of Mary.
The 'gules' from the royal scutcheon is also the 'bloom' from a
rose window. But the physical light can hold these values only
because it finds a corresponding light in Porphyro's mind, a
consciousness inevitably coloured by the values of his age.
Porphyro's erotic fancy has stultified itself by transforming
Madeline from a woman into an image.

'Anon his hart revives,' and now he half perceives and half
creates another Madeline:

                ... her vespers done,
        Of all its wreathed pearls her hair she frees;
        Unclasps her warmed jewels one by one;
        Loosens her fragrant boddice; by degrees
        Her rich attire creeps rustling to her knees:
        Half-hidden like a mermaid in sea-weed,
        Pensive awhile she dreams awake ...
                                        (226 – 32)

Note first the sense of relieved tension as Madeline loosens her
hair, freeing it from its 'wreathed pearls', and no doubt shattering
its halo at the same time. Porphyro's imagination is thereby
released from religiose enchantment. Now we see Keats' mastery
of the erotic power of reticence. What must we imagine to know
that Madeline's jewels are warmed, and how near to her flesh

must we be to sense the fragrance of her loosened bodice? What picture is gradually revealed by the sound of 'by degrees/ Her rich attire creeps rustling to her knees'? But again the most arresting description is of a posture: 'Half-hidden, like a mermaid in sea-weed.' Again, the source of power is reticence, for Keats trusts the reader to perceive the figure behind the specified image. Madeline among her discarded clothes suggests an image more archetypal than a mermaid in sea-weed; she is Aphrodite, new born, rising amid the sea-foam:

> But the hidden boy
> Stretched forth his left hand; in his right he took
> The great long jagged sickle; eagerly
> He harvested his father's genitals ...
>
> The genitals, cut off with adamant
> And thrown from land into the stormy sea,
> Were carried for a long time on the waves.
> White foam surrounded the immortal flesh,
> And in it grew a girl.[20]

We should now remember that Porphyro never existed, and that all that I have attributed to his erotic sensibility must be attributed to the poet's. It is true that Keats, a non-Christian living in an intolerantly Protestant milieu, would not be himself so readily conscious of Mary as his imagined Porphyro would be, but even in nineteenth-century England the Virgin was probably still the remote and unacknowledged image behind man's idealisation of woman. As a chastening influence she had not yet been superseded by Jocasta. Also if Porphyro's conflicting visions of Madeline are, as we may reasonably suppose, really Keats' visions of his own fiancée, then Aphrodite's victory was clearly a necessity.

But Keats was not able to accept with composure all the consequences of the goddess' triumph. It seems possible that he took more from his classical sources than the image of beauty rising from the sea. Certainly the contrasts in *The Eve of St Agnes* become more understandable once we have grasped the nature of Aphrodite as she is presented in Hesiod's fifth *Homeric Hymn*. The laughter-loving goddess found her amusement in match-

making between deities and mortals. Zeus, however, perhaps
sensing the horror latent in such mischief, devised condign
retribution, and soon the daughter of Earth and Heaven found
herself in love with a mortal herdsman. On the morning after she
has enjoyed her lover Anchises, she stands by his bed and explains
the necessary anguish of mortal love. She tells him of the fate of
Tithonous, whose divine mistress Eos secured for him the
privilege of immortality, but forgot to stipulate that this should
be accompanied by everlasting youth. Consequently Tithonous
lives for ever, locked away in a secret room, babbling endlessly,
and increasingly oppressed by more and more loathsome
consequences of age. Aphrodite continues:

> I would not have you be deathless among the deathless gods
> and live continually after such a sort. Yet if you could live on
> such as you are now in look and form, and be called my
> husband, sorrow would not then enfold my careful heart. But
> as it is, harsh old age will soon enshroud you—ruthless age
> which stands some day at the side of every man, deadly,
> wearying, dreaded even by the gods.[21]

We are reminded of the punishment of Glaucus, the withering of
Lamia, and the cause of Keats' ten-minute groan. Presumably the
pain of the immortals was worse than the human experience, for
they had to watch their lovers grow old while remaining
themselves young and vigorous. But the human experience is bad
enough. This perhaps is why *The Eve of St Agnes* abstains from all
but the slightest hint of lasting happiness for the lovers. We do
not see them arrive at the promised home beyond the southern
moors; our last glimpse is of their sneaking out into the stormy
night and, in order to grasp Keats' ironic purpose we do not need
to fantasise, as Herbert G. Wright has done, that they met their
deaths in the storm.[22] Let us suppose the best for them. At the
end of it all they will be like the Beadsman and Angela. Porphyro,
who spurred across the moors with heart on fire will shuffle,
meagre, barefoot, wan; Madeline, who danced along with vague
regardless eyes will hobble off, beset with busy fears, and agues in
her brain.

The poem gives poignant forewarnings. When Porphyro has
been told that his beloved is playing the conjuror, he sits and

gazes at old Angela, 'like puzzl'd urchin on an aged crone/ Who keepeth clos'd a wond'rous riddle-book,/ As spectacled she sits in chimney nook' (129 - 31). It is a decrepit Madeline he sees, still conjuring. While he is protesting 'may I ne'er find grace/ When my weak voice shall whisper its last prayer' (146 - 7) the Beadsman's frosted breath is taking flight for heaven. When Keats tells the story, these forewarnings, and worse, have already come to pass, for 'they are gone—ay, ages long ago/ These lovers ...' (370 -71).

Perhaps the greatest anti-romantic irony in *The Eve of St Agnes* is the one detected by Claude Finney: '[Keats] drew the device of setting youthful love in a background of family feud from *Romeo and Juliet*, but he invented and added from his own grim experience of life the second and enveloping background of natural decay and death.'[23] Perhaps the greatest clash of appearance and reality springs from love's spurious sense of invulnerability—kind nature's gentlest boon. Youthful imagination may spiritualise or glamourise the object of its passion, but the human truth, the truth Keats feared, is that men can take neither Agnes nor Aphrodite to bed with them, they must be content with a 'real woman, lineal ... From Pyrrah's pebbles'. The wonderfully fertile contrasts and ambiguities of the poem spring, perhaps, from Keats' suspicion that he could never be so content.

The central symbol of the poem consists in Porphyro's dual vision of Madeline, and is dramatically manifested in her swift change, in his eyes, from untouchable virginity to sensual womanhood. But this ambiguous vision is set in the midst of an undoubtedly real world, one full of antithetical extremes. Perhaps the most painful and ominous of these is the contrast between the young, rich and healthy lovers and the old, poor and sick servants. (One might note in passing that this is precisely the paradoxical context in which the traditional marriage service insists on setting the love between man and woman.) The contrast between the lovers and the servants expresses the most inescapable of experiential paradoxes, the simultaneously creative and destructive power of time.

It was, I believe, the awakening of the thinking principle that made Keats fully aware of the world's conflicting blessings and horrors. From this point on Keats' work is increasingly concerned with the problem of grasping and assimilating such a world, of finding, if possible, some principle of unity and intelligibility in human experience. In so far as the most basic and general meaning of the word 'religion' is 'a binding together again' the major part of Keats' greatest poetry is, among other things, concerned with religion. In the next three chapters I propose to examine how he adapts for his purpose the symbolism of the Greek mythology of the relationship of gods and goddesses to men and women.

4

Endymion and Glaucus

We do not need to solve the problem of appearance and reality in order to know that the identifiably objective world has within itself a much greater problem. The world into which we find we have been born both delights and torments us, nourishes us and kills us, and between the certainties of birth and death no individual has any assurance that the experiential opposites will balance each other. Even on the largest scale we cannot be sure of the equity of fertility and death—the regenerative cycle may be deceptive and things may indeed be running down. But a puzzlement about the final destiny of all things is not the most immediate and painful problem; what most challenges us is the eternal co-presence of opposites. During Keats' year in Guy's Hospital as a student and dresser, these opposites must have presented themselves most vividly to him—his days spent among the sick and dying, his evenings devoted to the joy of poetry. The poems he wrote at this time, notably *Specimen of an Induction* and *Calidore*, seem to reflect a determination not only to keep the opposites apart, but to ignore the horrors altogether. Clearly this could not last. Even if Keats could have forgotten the frequent hearses that had beseiged his gates since childhood, his medical experience made it inevitable that he must soon acknowledge that good and evil incurably infect each other.

In view of this we ought not to be surprised to find the beginnings of Keats' concern with religious matters in *Endymion*. I propose now to return to an examination of that poem, and in particular to an analysis of the symbolic nature of the Glaucus episode. John Middleton Murry has said of *Endymion*: 'Essentially the poem is the effort to create a thing of beauty before the spirit is darkened; to make the creation of the poem itself a defence against the onset of doubts and miseries and feverous speculations, of which he had only too clear a presentiment. It is the poem of maiden experience and maiden thought, indeed, but they are conscious of their doom.'[1] That being so, the supposedly allegorical elements may be an attempt to stiffen a defence which Keats knows to be shaky, and particular passages may be attempts to cope with the disturbances of maiden thoughts as they arise. We also know that in his letters Keats was sometimes given to speculation about man and his destiny of a kind that we might call (a little unkindly perhaps) extempore theology. The 'Chamber of Maiden Thought' passage, for example, is a sensitive account of the soul's development from innocence to knowledge; and the 'Vale of Soul-making' is an essay in primitive soteriology. Morris Dickstein seems to find a quasi-theological thread running through *Endymion*. Speaking of the catalogue of 'things of beauty' with which the poem begins, he comments:

> Keats ... endows the beauteous forms with metaphysical permanence and timelessness. He describes them as 'An endless fountain of immortal drink,/ Pouring unto us from the heaven's brink.' They are transcendental objects which make a joyful appearance in a world of time and change, as God in divine revelation, makes a transfiguring incursion into history. And Keats' last line—'They always must be with us or we die'—has the urgency of a desire for salvation itself ... There is perhaps no better way we can penetrate to the centre of *Endymion* than by taking up this transcendental motif.[2]

In regard to the poem as a whole Dickstein may be overstating his case, but in regard to the Glaucus episode in particular his point is very germane. We must remember also that Book 3 was written at Oxford, while Keats was staying with Bailey, future Archdeacon of Colombo. It is not surprising then, if we find in the Glaucus episode a kind of poetical theology, but we must be cautious about classifying that theology and putting a name to it. It is not, I feel sure, a neo-Platonist scheme, and it is not, *pace* Ronald A. Sharp, the dogmatic basis of a religion of beauty.[3] The safest name I can coin for it has, unfortunately, a currently fashionable ring—alternative theology. One remembers that the Vale of Soul-making theory is quite explicitly this—a 'grander scheme of salvation than the chryst[e]ain religion'. However, when Keats launches himself on such a venture, there is about both his thought and expression an inescapable gravitational pull from the scheme he is trying to replace. I believe we have, in the Glaucus episode, an example of this system-making urge, bravely independent in purpose, but succumbing finally to that gravitational pull. Unfortunately Keats' alternative myth is no match for the Biblical one: in the absence of a clearly realised unifying principle, the distracting force distorts and vitiates the poet's virtually impromptu scheme.

Keats presents the events of the Glaucus story in what he conceives to be the most dramatically effective order; I now propose to reorganise the narrative into a simple chronological order, so that the parallels with and divergences from the Biblical narrative may be more immediately apparent. Keats' myth, although it does not deal with creation, begins very near the beginning. Endymion, wandering about the ocean bed, finds, among shipwrecks and sea-encrusted relics of human affairs (breast-plates, shields, golden vases and so forth), a uniquely interesting literary source: 'mouldering scrolls,/ Writ in the tongue of heaven, by those souls/ Who first were on the earth' (3:129 – 31). A letter to Jane and Marianne Reynolds written about this time speaks of a particular letter from Brown to Mrs Dilke as something Keats 'would rather see than the original copy of the Book of Genesis' (*Letters*, 1:159). Endymion too passes by the opportunity, but the suggestion has been made that we are going to be concerned with origins—not of man and the universe perhaps—but the origins of man's folly and pain.

The story begins then, with man's innocence. Glaucus had been, according to his own account, 'a lonely youth on desert shores' (3:339), enjoying a full life of natural happiness, so much in harmony with nature that even the sea-beasts protected him from danger. His occupation was fishing, and he gave fish to 'the poor folk of the sea-country' (3:368), never revealing himself as the provider of this bounty. With this life he ought to have been contented, but:

> 'Fool! I began
> To feel distemper'd longings: to desire
> The utmost privilege that ocean's sire

> Could grant in benediction: to be free
> Of all his kingdom.'
>
>   (3:374 – 8)

In wishing for the freedom of Neptune's kingdom, Glaucus is in a sense wishing to be equal with Neptune, an equality to which he ought not to aspire. His fault, then, is hubris. He does in fact 'eat the apple', and lives in the depths with all the ease and freedom of the sea-god himself. But the consequence of his fall from innocence is that his emotions become ungovernable; he becomes distracted by passion for the beautiful Scylla, and in the torment of his desire invokes the aid of a goddess-witch: 'And in that agony, across my grief/ It flashed, that Circe might find some relief' (3:411 – 12). Circe herself appears to him, and he now becomes even more enthralled by her beauty than he had been by Scylla's, though he is unaware of her identity: 'With tears, and smiles, and honey-words she wove/ A net whose thralldom was more bliss than all/ The range of flower'd Elysium' (3:426 – 28). After a period of rapturous love the enchantress abandons him, and he, wandering in agony, finds her again and recognises her for what she truly is:

> 'In thicket hid I curs'd the haggard scene—
> The banquet of my arms, my arbour queen,
> Seated upon an uptorn forest root;
> And all around her shapes, wizard and brute,
> Laughing, and wailing, grovelling, serpenting,
> Showing tooth, tusk, and venom-bag, and sting!
> O such deformities!'
>
>   (3:497 – 503)

Circe now pronounces Glaucus' fate:

>   'Thou has thews
> Immortal, for thou art of heavenly race:
> But such a love is mine, that here I chase
> Eternally away from thee all bloom
> Of youth, and destine thee towards a tomb.'
>
>   (3:588 – 92)

In Ovid's version of the myth, Glaucus claims to be a god: '"*non ego prodigium nec sum fera belua, virgo, sed deus" inquit "aquae".*' (*Metamorphoses* 13:917 - 18). In Keats' version we should note that Circe's description of him stops short of attributing divinity, though he is 'of heavenly race', and meant to be immortal. In this he is much more like Adam than the classical figure. For he now loses his privilege of immortality, and will suffer the decrepitude of age, a thousand years of living death. After the enchantress has pronounced his punishment, Glaucus is, again like Adam, driven out of his 'garden': 'A hand was at my shoulder to compel/ My sullen steps; another 'fore my eyes/ Moved on with pointed finger' (3:604 - 606). On returning to the sea he finds that he has, by his fault, brought death into his world: 'Upon a dead thing's face my hand I laid/ I look'd—'Twas Scylla!' (3:618 - 19).

Before long Glaucus is given a promise that the curse will ultimately be lifted, and that he will avoid the death his transgression had incurred. After witnessing a shipwreck, Glaucus finds an old man's hand emerging from the waves, offering him a scroll. He takes it, and reads:

> 'In the wide sea there lives a forlorn wretch,
> Doom'd with enfeebled carcase to outstretch
> His loath'd existence through ten centuries,
> And then to die alone. Who can devise
> A total opposition? No one. So
> One million times ocean must ebb and flow,
> And he oppressed. Yet he shall not die,
> These things accomplish'd:-If he utterly
> Scans all the depths of magic, and expounds
> The meanings of all motions, shapes, and sounds;
> If he explores all forms and substances
> Straight homeward to their symbol-essences;
> He shall not die. Moreover, and in chief,
> He must pursue this task of joy and grief
> Most piously;-all lovers tempest-tost,
> And in the savage overwhelming lost,
> He shall deposit side by side, until
> Time's creeping shall the dreary space fulfill:
> Which done, and all these labours ripened,
> A youth, by heavenly power lov'd and led,

> *Shall stand before him; whom he shall direct*
> *How to consummate all.'*
>
> (3:689 – 710)

Endymion did not pause to study *Genesis*, but Glaucus has joyfully read *Isaiah*: 'And your covenant with death shall be disannulled, and your agreement with hell shall not stand' (28:18). At the end of his millenium of redemptive suffering Glaucus recognises Endymion as the prophesied saviour. He greets him with joy, tells him his story, shows him Scylla's tomb and the cemetery of drowned lovers, tears up the prophetic scroll and hands him the fragments. Endymion strews these fragments first on Glaucus, then on the dead lovers. Glaucus is rejuvenated, and the lovers rise from the dead. The redemptive act completed, Endymion and all the redeemed proceed to the sea-god's palace for an apocalyptic climax of joy and reconciliation.

One sees immediately the basic elements which Keats' scheme has in common with the Judaeo-Christian one (perhaps these elements are inescapable in any mythopoeic theodicy). First, as we have noted, Keats has 'Adamised' Ovid's Glaucus. He is an immortal man, not a god, and he incurs a fall from innocence, due to hubristic sin, a punishment and an expulsion from a kind of paradise, a long period of suffering and labour, lightened by the promise of deliverance, and finally ended by the ultimate arrival of the saviour, who performs a redemptive act, followed by the resurrection of the dead and a final restoration of divine friendship.

The differences from the Christian scheme are considerable, and while some may be inadvertent and perhaps purposeless, others, one feels, reflects Keats' temperament and preoccupying ideas. Glaucus, though like Adam in so many ways, is not the human prototype—he has neighbours for whom he performs charitable acts. Like Adam, his sin is presumption, but it is entirely self-engendered; he has not fallen in love with Scylla when his fall occurs; and there is no supernatural agent of temptation involved. Keats' Adam cannot shuffle off his guilt on to 'the woman thou gavest to be with me', nor to any beguiling serpent (*Genesis* 3:12 – 13).

Keats' most important divergence from the Biblical scheme concerns the saviour and his redemptive act. Mario D'Avanzo has said that in Book 3 Endymion 'chooses to become the redeemer of all suffering mankind and saves not only Glaucus and Scylla but countless others entombed by Circe'.[4] D'Avanzo is right, though he chooses to assume tacitly a point which I think needs to be stated formally as an assumption. For Endymion's liberating act is a circumscribed one—it sets free only lovers, and at that only lovers who have been shipwrecked. There is, however, an apocalyptic tone about the whole passage that makes it not unreasonable to suppose that the raising of the lovers is a synecdoche for a general resurrection of the dead; and, as a corollary to this, that love in the sexual sense is a synecdoche for a wider, all-encompassing kind of love.

The importance of such synecdoches is now clear; Endymion is a universal saviour, as D'Avanzo suggests, and his redemptive act is an expression of divine caritas. He is, however, unlike the Biblical saviour in certain very important respects. Christ was double-natured; Endymion is exclusively human, though 'by heavenly power lov'd and led'. Christ in the garden sweated blood in his agony for mankind; Endymion's sufferings are largely self-pitying until he prays for Alpheus and Arethusa—compassion, innate in Christ, had to be learned by Endymion. Compared to the forty days in the wilderness and the agony in the garden, Endymion's sufferings are trivial. Indeed, without such a comparison they still seem trivial, as John Jones has pointed out: 'I stress the flimsiness of the rigours endured by Endymion because the belief (which almost everybody shares) that the poem is too sweet stems as much from the boring insubstantiality of its pains as from the exorbitance of its luxuries.'[5] Christ's redemptive act involved horrifying physical suffering; Endymion merely scatters scraps of paper over the dead lovers.

These differences from the Christian scheme are the vital ones, I think, and reveal the nature of Keats' need for an alternative theology. Christ's divine nature and his 'arbitrary interposition' in human affairs seem to deny man's ability to save himself by his own efforts. The appalling pain that seems inseparable from Christianity not merely in Christ's passion but in martydroms through all centuries since his death is more than Keats can bear to contemplate—one remembers his comments to Leigh Hunt on 'the dreadful Petzelians and their expiation by blood' (*Letters*, 1:137). Both the arbitrariness of divine intervention and the notion that salvation is available only through pain would be, one must think, not only repellent to his sensibilities, but an affront to his humanism. Yet, ironically, traces of both these elements are there in the poem as a whole. The initiatives of Cynthia and Venus towards their human lovers constitute a species of grace, and both Endymion's unsatisfactory griefs and Adonis' glossed-over wounds are in some sense means of redemption.

This last reflection brings us back to that planetary tug exercised by orthodox religious tradition. So far, in discussing the Glaucus myth, I have been identifying the similarities and differences in the theological concepts involved in *Endymion* and the Biblical account. I now wish to consider something which is, for a student of literature, far more interesting. The conflict that most concerns us is not between rival mythologies but between the cultural and symbolic treasuries associated with the myths.

There emerges from an elucidation of Keats' Glaucus myth a certain doubleness both in the personae and the action. Glaucus, the primal man whose fault brought death into the world, becomes Glaucus/Adam, and the long-promised deliverer becomes Endymion/Christ. But there is another dimension to this doubleness and, in order to see it more clearly, we must examine again the symbolic status of Glaucus. There is something familiar about Keats' description of Endymion's first encounter with him:

> He saw far in the concave green of the sea
> An old man sitting calm and peacefully.
> Upon a weeded rock this old man sat,
> And his white hair was awful, and a mat
> Of weeds were cold beneath his cold thin feet.
>   (3:191 – 5)

The memory is quickly identified in Wordsworth's *Resolution and Independence*:

> Now, whether it were by peculiar grace,
> A leading from above, a something given,
> Yet it befel, that, in this lonely place,
> When I with these untoward thoughts had striven,
> Beside a pool bare to the eye of heaven

I saw a man before me unawares:
The oldest man he seemed that ever wore grey hairs.

(50 – 56)

When we remember the old man stirring the pools with his feet in search of leeches, the resemblance grows very close, and we can hardly suppose the borrowing to have been unwitting or purposeless. One function of the Wordsworthian echo is doubtless to strengthen the sense of the numinous in Keats' passage—we remember the leech-gatherer's ghostly endurance: 'In my mind's eye I seemed to see him pace/ About the weary moors continually' (129 – 30). But more important, I think, is the memory of the sense of providence in *Resolution and Independence*, the suggestion Wordsworth makes, with a kind of pre-emptive tentativeness, that the encounter was supernaturally ordained. The poet sees the man as possibly being 'from some far region sent/ To give me human strength' (111 – 12), and the encounter as possibly resulting from 'peculiar grace/ A leading from above, a something given'. Keats has no need of such tentativeness; he is constructing a myth, not commenting on an incident from ordinary life.

But the memories alert us not only to the nature of Glaucus, but to the nature of the meeting and of the recognition which now takes place. The meeting was divinely pre-ordained, and man recognises his saviour. The sense of doubleness in the symbolic action, of one mythology 'ghosting' another as it were, thus becomes unusually strong in Glaucus' words 'Thou art the man!' (3:234)—the Keatsian humanist version of Peter's 'Thou art the Christ' (*Matthew* 16:16).'

Glaucus is not merely the Biblically 'historical' Adam of *Genesis*; he represents by his millenial endurance and decrepitude the inherited Adam in all mankind—though not a biological prototype he is the 'first man' who has now been joined by the 'second man'. When he is rejuvenated by Endymion he symbolically casts off the ruined body of the 'first man', and this symbolic function of Glaucus becomes important in the resurrection of the lovers which immediately follows it. Keats' description of this yields the most powerful sense of mythological ghosting—the sense of doubleness affects not only the symbols and symbolic action, but the tone, phraseology, visionary intensity and sense of climax. Let us look at Keats' passage first, and then at the source which glimmers through it:

'A power overshadows thee! Oh brave!
The spite of hell is tumbling to its grave.
Here is a shell; 'tis pearly blank to me,
Nor mark'd with any sign or charactery—
Canst thou read aught? O read for pity's sake!
Olympus! we are safe! Now, Carian, break
This wand against yon lyre on the pedestal.'

'Twas done: and straight with sudden swell and fall
Sweet music breath'd her soul away, and sigh'd
A lullaby to silence.—'Youth! now strew
These minced leaves on me, and passing through
Those files of dead, scatter the same around,
And thou wilt see the issue!—'Mid the sound
Of flutes and viols, ravishing his heart,
Endymion from Glaucus stood apart,
And scatter'd in his face some fragments light.
How lightning-swift the change! a youthful wight
Smiling beneath a coral diadem,
Out-sparkling sudden like an upturn'd gem,
Appear'd, and, stepping to a beauteous corse,
Kneel'd down beside it, and with tenderest force
Press'd its cold hand and wept,—and Scylla sigh'd!
Endymion with quick hand the charm applied—
The nymph arose: he left them to their joy,
And onward went upon his high employ,
Showering those powerful fragments on the dead.
And, as he pass'd, each lifted up its head,
As doth a flower at Apollo's touch.
Death felt it to his inwards; 'twas too much:
Death fell a weeping in his charnel-house.

(3:759 – 88)

Keats may have had several sources for this passage, but there is one, unacknowledged certainly, and unwitting perhaps, that reveals itself all too powerfully—the poetry wilts at the comparison:

The first man is of the earth, earthy: the second man is the Lord from heaven.

As is the earthy, such are they also that are earthy; and as is the heavenly, such are they also that are heavenly.

And as we have borne the image of the earthy, we shall also bear the image of the heavenly.

Now this I say brethren, that flesh and blood cannot inherit the kingdom of God; neither doth corruption inherit incorruption.

Behold, I show you a mystery; we shall not all sleep, but *we shall all be changed.*

In a moment, in the twinkling of an eye, at the last trump: for the trumpet shall sound, and the dead shall be raised incorruptible, and we shall be changed.

For this corruptible must put on incorruption, and this mortal must put on immortality.

So when this corruptible shall have put on incorruption, and this mortal shall have put on immortality, then shall be brought to pass the saying that is written, *Death is swallowed up in Victory.*

O Death, where is thy sting? O grave, where is thy victory?

(1 *Corinthians* 15:47 - 55)

The most dramatic parallels here are the ones I have italicised, but we must note some less explicit ones. Keats has made concrete St Paul's powerful abstractions. Glaucus decrepitude is the realisation in time of his corruptibility and mortality; his sudden 'outsparkling' youth is the realisation, the 'putting on', of his incorruption and immortality. His lightning-swift change is the pattern for the universal regeneration—the lovers do not all sleep, they participate in Glaucus' renewal. (For a moment Glaucus, not Endymion, is the Christ-figure; his weeping over the corpse of Scylla is reminiscent of Christ weeping for Lazarus before raising him from the dead.) The last trump has been softened and sweetened to the ravishing tones of flutes and viols. Finally, and pervasively, there is the sense throughout Keats' passage that in Glaucus and Endymion we have an actualisation of St Paul's 'first man' and 'second man'. The parallel is by no means exact, Endymion is 'of the earth earthy' too, he is not 'the Lord from heaven'—but it is dramatically functional, for as, in Keats' first man, all died, even so, in his second man, all were made alive.

Let us now look at the way in which Keats' eschatology differs from Christian orthodoxy. Although Glaucus seems to have been subjected to a particular judgement and punishment, there is in Neptune's palace no general and final judgement, no eternal separation of the sheep from the goats. If we add this to the list of Keatsian divergences we already have—no scourging at the pillar, no crowning with thorns, no crucifixion, no martyrdoms, we may be inclined to think that Keats was trying to construct a surrogate religion which was to be a far more comfortable affair than the orthodox one. In so doing, it may be that he was not merely turning his back on what seemed to him a corrupt church and a brutal theology, but also on the real world where, whether within God's providence or not, men and women are, in various ways, crucified every hour of every day. It is significant in this connection that his divergences from his classical sources are equally anaesthetising. We have already noted that Adonis' agonising wounds were beautified away, and Arethusa's terror quite overlooked. Glaucus, in Ovid's version, was a Caliban-like monster, with his lower limbs distorted grotesquely into the form of a fish, and his pursuit of Scylla, like Alpheus' pursuit of Arethusa, brutally predatory. Far from achieving immortal bliss with Glaucus, Scylla suffers dreadful pain and bestial deformity inflicted by Circe:

> Now Scylla came; and wading to the wast,
> Beheld her hips with barking dogs embrac't.
> Startes back: at first not thinking that they were
> Part of her selfe; but rates them, and doth feare
> Their threatening jawes: but those, from whom she flies,
> She with her hales. Then looking for her thighes,
> Her legs and feet; in stead of them she found
> The mouthes of *Cerberus*, inviron'd round
> With ravening Curres.[6]

Once fixed in her place in the sea by Circe's spite, she becomes cruel in her turn, robbing Ulysses of his companions. Only when he came to write *Hyperion* was Keats able to accept the horrors of the mythology he thought he loved. The religion which we might call Keatsianity avoids the beastliness in Jew and Greek alike, and the Vale of Soul-making is its belated gospel. If there were just enough evil in the world to bring out the best in humankind, Keats' patchwork theology would do admirably. If there is to be no arbitrary interposition of God in human affairs—a little circumscribed notion—then we must hope that the world will not be worse than we can cope with.

However, it is plainly much worse, as Keats himself perceived in the *Epistle to John Hamilton Reynolds*: 'But I saw too distinct into the core/ Of an eternal fierce destruction' (96 – 97). The Vale of Soul-making passage, written more than a year later than this, seems to be a regression (temporary perhaps) to an *Endymion* world view, wherein 'disagreeables' are mild enough to be 'evaporated' away like Adonis' wounds, once they have fulfilled their soul-making function. Perhaps in this clash between the *Epistle to Reynolds* and the Vale of Soul-making we see the dilemma of optimistic, theistic humanism. Non-theistic humanism naturally and logically adopts a posture of stoic resignation. However, the doctrine of incarnation is for those who can believe it, Christianity's trump card. In Christ, God suffers all that man suffers, and also in Christ a man's suffering achieves mankind's salvation. In the Glaucus episode, in spite of Endymion's role as mankind's saviour, there is no hint of incarnation.

I have discussed this matter of the mingling of Greek and Christian elements rather lengthily, but I believe with justification. The mere fact that Keats feels a need for on-the-spot mythmaking is another indication of a fundamental lack of confidence in the aesthetic dogma *Endymion* was designed to promulgate, and the mythopoeic pastiche which results is as great a cause of the failure of Book 3 as the unharnessed poesy is of the rest of the work. For the effect of the mingling of the two fields of imagery really is pastiche—there is no fusion, no acclimatisation of the borrowed material into its new environment. The dual vision adds no sense of depth or solidity to the figures, nor of deep significance to the symbolic action. What we have is rather a sense of blurred edges and ritualistic parody. We sense this principally in Endymion himself, who performs a Christ-like function without in any other way becoming a Christ-like being. His redemptive act is in itself so trivial that it scarcely modifies his characteristic self-pity and self-absorption. But what makes the matter worth examining at this length is the fact that a similar mingling of Jewish and Greek elements occurs in *Hyperion*, but with much greater success. There the blurred images focus into rounded figures, the discordant echoes become harmonic resonances. By what alchemy the transmutation is achieved it is impossible to say, but the coarse alloy of *Endymion* becomes something rare in *Hyperion*.

5

Hyperion

I have divided this chapter into four sections, because I find its argument (no doubt due to the limitations of my own per-spicuity) irreducibly complex. In the first section I try to establish that although Keats' ostensible purpose was to use Apollo's triumph as a symbol of the superiority of the kind of poetry he now wished to write, his interest was almost immediately seduced by the larger myth of the Olympian rebellion, and his sympathy was captured by the fallen Titans. I believe that Keats did not intend to use the theogonic myth as a political or psycho-anthropological allegory, but as a means of expressing his own philosophic bewilderment (which he assumes, I think, to be representative of a widespread human condition), and with this end in view he purposefully renders his gods ungodlike.

In the second section I suggest that Keats' bewilderment was caused by the loss or weakening of his own non-Christian and perhaps rather idiosyncratic religious faith, and that this loss of faith in its turn was caused not by personal catastrophe but by a perception that good and evil are permanently and inseparably present together in the world.

Section three suggests that for these reasons Keats' dethroned gods have a complex symbolic function. First, they each in turn (those who speak, that is) represent Keats in the process of losing faith—as they discover their contingent nature they discover also the limitations of a particular form of theism. Secondly, they represent mankind, suffering from the conflict between divine aspiration and mortal limitation; and in their painful ignorance they ask the philosophical questions articulate man has always asked.

In the fourth section I try to show that their symbolic complexity is made yet more complex by the manner in which their appearance, actions and speeches remind us of certain of the historical figures of the Christianity Keats had rejected. In this respect, perhaps, they symbolise rather poignantly something which now seems not discarded, but lost.

1

In Book 4 of *Endymion* Keats apostrophises his hero in his status as Cynthia's husband: 'felicity/ Has been thy meed for many thousand years' (4:776 – 7), and promises him 'Thy lute-voic'd brother will I sing ere long' (4:774). This reminds us first that Apollo and Cynthia were brother and sister (a fact we remember the more easily if we think of them as Phoebus and Phoebe), and second that *Hyperion*, in spite of its title, was meant to be about Apollo. The epithet 'lute-voic'd' is an indication that Keats' principal interest was in Apollo as the mythological prototype of the poet—'The Father of all verse'. That being so, one might ask why the particular story about Apollo that Keats proposed to use constitutes, in the terminology of art criticism, a 'detail' of a much larger myth—the creation myth of Hesiod's *Theogony*. The explanation that most readily offers itself is that Hesiod's evolutionary principle enables Keats to suggest in the triumph of Apollo the progress of poesy from the fanciful plaything that his own early verse exemplifies to the great humanist achievements of Shakespeare and Dante.

There is a great deal of truth in this, and we may well see the proposed downfall of Hyperion as the 'death' of the early Keats, and the apotheosis of Apollo as Keats' regeneration as a 'mighty Poet of the human Heart' (*Letters* 2:115). None the less, there is a danger in thus selecting a detail. The Apollo story must be put into Hesiod's larger context, and thus put at risk of being subsumed into that context. I believe when we read *Hyperion* we do not see this happening, we see that it has already happened. Keats' interest, and therefore ours, is too firmly rooted in the defeated Titans and the questions they ask for an apotheosed Apollo ever to displace or greatly reduce it. Before he put pen to paper, Keats' original theme, which may have been within his capabilities, had been devoured by an enormously greater conception, well beyond his powers at that time.

Many critics have argued that Keats intended to reduce the

cosmic theme to manageable dimensions by using it for the purposes of social allegory, or psycho-anthropological myth. I am going to suggest, however, that Keats became preoccupied with the larger myth not as a framework for an allegorical purpose, but as a thing in itself dealing with a matter of permanent and absorbing interest to mankind. The substance of *Hyperion* is, I believe, a poetic critique of the central religious conceptions embodied in Hesiod's work. Furthermore this critique constitutes an acknowledgement of the failure of Keats' own beliefs.

One of the greatest oddities of the poem is a problem which Keats seems, perversely enough, to have made for himself. In a society that had been conditioned for fourteen or fifteen centuries in a monotheistic tradition, he could scarcely hope to establish 'true' divinity for the gods of classical tradition. But for his purpose it was scarcely necessary to do so. Presumably he looked for an educated audience, and such an audience would be familiar with classical mythology, and therefore quite ready to enter into a tacit agreement with an author who wanted to write about Saturn, Apollo, and Jove and call them 'gods'. But Keats chose not to make use of a convention which was readily available; on the contrary he took pains to draw attention to the ungodlike nature of his chief personae. The first suggestion comes from Thea, who reminds Saturn that 'heaven is parted from thee, and the earth/ Knows thee not, thus afflicted, for a God' (1:55 – 56), and Coelus, father of the Titans, laments to Hyperion:

'For I have seen my sons most unlike Gods.
Divine ye were created, and divine
In sad demeanour, solemn, undisturb'd,
Unruffled, like high Gods, ye liv'd and ruled:
Now I behold in you fear, hope, and wrath;
Actions of rage and passion; even as
I see them on the mortal world beneath,
In men who die.'

(1:328 – 35)

The fact that the gods cannot be recognised as such is not in itself a major difficulty—classical mythology abounds in divine disguises, and the Bible describes the moment of Christ's recognition by Peter as a uniquely dramatic event. But what Keats is doing here is to make the convention on which it seems he ought to rely less easy to accept. Having reminded us of how gods ought to be—'solemn, undisturb'd,/ Unruffled'—he thrusts their flawed humanity on our attention. But this is not the worst. In Book 2 he makes it quite clear that not only do his gods not look like gods, in certain important respects they are not gods. The key passage occurs in Oceanus' speech:

> 'We fall by course of Nature's law, not force
> Of thunder, or of Jove. Great Saturn, thou
> Hast sifted well the atom-universe;
> But for this reason, that thou art the King,
> And only blind from sheer supremacy,
> One avenue was shaded from thine eyes,
> Through which I wandered to eternal truth.
> And first, as thou wast not the first of powers,
> So art thou not the last; it cannot be:
> Thou art not the beginning nor the end.'
>
> (2:181 – 190)

Our willing suspension of disbelief can hardly survive this. In order to accept, for the sake of the literary experience we value, the divinity of Saturn, Apollo and Jove, we have to shelve the principal tenet of the monotheistic tradition which is an inescapable part of our culture. This remains true even for those who have no religious belief, for it is rooted in our thinking that if there is a God, he must be an uncreated creator. The very word 'theogony' has no place in monotheistic thought—there can be no genealogy of God. Almost equally rooted is the idea that if the universe is not absurd, we shall find its meaning in the nature of its uncreated sustainer. If there is a God, he is the beginning and the end. It is worth repeating here that in regard to *Hyperion* there would be no such stuff in our thoughts if Keats had not put it there.

The matter becomes particularly important when we remember that Oceanus' comment applies also to the Olympians. He is quite specific about their vulnerability: 'another race may drive/ Our conquerors to mourn as we do now' (2:230 – 231). He offers this not as a hope for an eventual spiteful comfort, but as a plain observation that both groups of gods are subject to an eternal law; so, of course, is Apollo. Keats has thus rendered his hero's divinity circumscribed, if not actually spurious, even before his apotheosis. Why has he done so?

2

The only defensible answer, I think, to the question why Keats so insistently dethrones his gods is that at this stage of his career he cannot do otherwise. The reason for this is more complicated than is often implied; it is not a matter of moving from complacency to pessimism. As Middleton Murry has said: 'There is no sadder poem in English than *Hyperion*, but its sadness is not the icy chill of intellectual despair.'[1] Nevertheless one certainly detects something akin to a loss or weakening of religious faith. In recent years it has become increasingly recognised that Keats' anti-clericalism did not imply atheism or even agnosticism. Robert Ryan has made a good case for Keats having an ill-defined but genuine belief in God, and there are certain allusions in the letters which are too unambiguous to be ignored. One might note in particular that the argument of the Vale of Soul-making theory takes for granted the existence of God, and states the immortality of the human soul as a basic assumption.[2]

But it does seem that during the months before he began *Hyperion* Keats became aware of the inadequacy of his religious conception. As the universe grew larger and more complex in his eyes, his God seemed smaller and simpler. This problem, I suggest, came to dominate his more specific examination of the role of the poet in human affairs. If the poet was to be 'A humanist, Physician to all men' (*The Fall of Hyperion* 1:190), then he must have something to add to the general human conception of the nature of things. Thus the general religious preoccupation swallowed up the specific preoccupation with poets and poetry; consequently the theogony of Hesiod's myth swallowed up the 'detail' of the overthrow of Hyperion by Apollo. Let us examine briefly what we may reasonably suppose to have been the nature of the religion which Keats now found to be inadequate.

Some time in the spring of 1817, Keats and Leigh Hunt in a mood of pretentious enthusiasm, crowned each other with laurel wreaths in the manner of the ancient bards. While this was going on they were visited by a group of ladies, whereupon Hunt doffed his bays, but Keats decided to outface his embarrassment, and kept his crown on till the visitors departed. Three poems resulted from this gauche episode—the sonnets *On Receiving a Laurel Crown from Leigh Hunt* and *To the Ladies Who Saw Me Crowned*, and the later of the two odes to Apollo. Walter Evert has pointed out the astonishing implications of the latter poem, in which Keats makes an act of sorrow and reparation for his blasphemous presumption:

> ... where slept thine ire,
> When like a blank idiot I put on thy wreath,
>   Thy laurel, they glory,
>   The light of thy story,
> Or was I a worm—too low crawling for death?
>
> (7 – 10)

> ... who did dare
> To tie for a moment thy plant round his brow,
>   And grin and look proudly,
>   And blaspheme so loudly,
> And live for that honour, to stoop to thee now?
>   O Delphic Apollo!
>
> (31 – 6)

No doubt Keats is merely scolding himself for his silliness and conceit, but the self-accusation seems inappropriately harsh, and the address to the god too self-abasing for figurative purposes merely. There emerges from this poem a sense not merely of humiliated self-esteem, but of quasi-religious penitence. Evert reminds us that for Keats Apollo was the most important of all the Greek gods. He presided over four realms, astronomy, medicine, the sun, and poetry. In all these realms his function was to preserve a system of harmony both within the realms themselves and in their relationship to one another. In view of this function, Evert maintains, Apollo is the indispensable central symbol of Keats' 'metaphysical hypothesis', which he summarises thus:

The complete spiritual cycle of individual human life and growth is comparable to the annual cycle of physical life and growth in external nature. These cycles are not only comparable by developmental analogy but are harmonious with each other because identically subject to the influence of a single beneficent power, or law, which manifests itself in and through them. This power is the law of universal harmony, by which all existing things are held in balanced interrelationship with each other.

If Evert is right, then Apollo symbolised for Keats the power that sustains the universe. He was also a particularly appropriate god for a poet to worship, for as god of poetry he presided over the ripening of the human intellect:

The process of intellectual ripening, however, is confined in its direct operation to those who acknowledge the god and are peculiarly able to perceive his power and influence, i.e. the poets. It is the poet's function to receive, interpret, and transmit knowledge of the god to men who ordinarily feel his influence less directly and who, without the poet's aid, do not properly understand it.[3]

Robert Ryan maintains that although Keats' cast of mind was empirical, and distrustful of abstract reasoning, (a tendency which would have been strengthened by his medical studies under Astley Cooper) he 'never abandoned the belief that a Supreme Intelligence governed the universe'. Ryan goes on to say:

Keats' imagination [could] operate within two completely different mythic systems—which I will call arbitrarily Theist and Apollonian. He appears to experience no intellectual difficulty, no hesitation or embarrassment, in passing from one to the other. It is clear that for Keats the two systems are distinct and separate, one presided over by the 'great Maker' and 'Framer of all things', the other by 'the great Apollo'.[4]

I believe that Ryan is largely right, but his last sentence relates rather oddly to the one before it. The ease with which Keats could move from the Theist to the Apollonian system would itself seem to indicate that there was a good deal of common ground, and it is reasonable to suppose that his conception of the 'Framer of all things' would be powerfully modified by his image of the central figure in his 'metaphysical hypothesis'. In short, it would be entirely natural if the nebulous and unformulated religious belief that Keats had was a form of Apollonian theism.

Nevertheless, by the time he came to write Apollo's epic, he could no longer 'acknowledge the god'. This may have been due to certain calamities of life, (the loss of George and Georgiana Keats, and the threatening illness of Tom), but more probably to that distressing philosophical insight which he represents as having been achieved on the sands of Teignmouth (*Epistle to J.H. Reynolds*). This had almost certainly destroyed the metaphysical and aesthetic hypothesis that Apollo symbolised. Even if it were still possible to perceive a grand principle of harmony in the universe, that harmony was often preserved at great cost. The balance of nature was achieved not by the ministrations of a kindly god, but by an unfeeling system:

> ... I saw too distinct into the core
> Of an eternal fierce destruction.
> And so from happiness I far was gone.
> Still am I sick of it; and though today
> I've gathered young spring leaves, and flowers gay,
> Of periwinkle and wild strawberry,
> Still do I that most fierce destruction see—
> The shark at savage prey, the hawk at pounce,
> The gentle robin like a pard or ounce,
> Ravening a worm.
>
> (*Epistle to Reynolds*, 96 – 105)

Neither Apollo nor the soothing law he represents can cope with this vision. Yet within six months of experiencing this sickening enlightenment, Keats begins *Hyperion*. He knows that his metaphysical hypothesis has failed, but he still cherishes the visionary world in which it had been embodied. Thus, I think, we can now define the two conflicts which generate the poetic energy of *Hyperion*: first, that between the surviving, undiminished love for the symbolism of his former religious conception and his acknowledgement of that conception's inadequacy; second, that between the specific Apollonian myth concerning the nature of poetry and the theogonic myth which overwhelms it.

We can now perceive a rather complex form of that symbolic dualism which I maintain is a principal feature of Keats' greatest poetry. The personae of *Hyperion* represent two figurative schemes which operate simultaneously. In the first, and supposedly principal scheme, the gods symbolise evolutionary progress, particularly in regard to the nature of poetry, and within this scheme it is possible to distinguish between the old gods and the new, and make judgements about them. In the second, and supposedly minor scheme, they symbolise a failed anthropomorphic religion, and in this scheme Titans and Olympians are indistinguishable. The power of the poetry is in the simultaneous effect of the two schemes, the sustained parallelism of the specific and the universal. We shall find this dualism of the personae operating in five principal ways: in their discovery of limitation and mortality; in the questions they ask; in their appearance and postures; in their newly discovered sense of paradoxical experience; and in their attempt, notably in Oceanus' speech, to find a new understanding of themselves and their status in the universal scheme of things. This dualism between specific and universal is, in all the operative modes I have specified, complicated by a mythological dualism (as in *Endymion* Book 3) in the form of memories from another religious culture.

3

Keats dethrones his gods then, including the ones whose triumph the poem was intended to celebrate, because Apollonian theism cannot solve the problems revealed by the horror perceived on the sands of Teignmouth. The Greek gods now find that they are not responsible for the universe, and they have only circumscribed powers within it. Take, for example, the tormented Hyperion, trying to escape from the repulsive visions that have invaded his palace:

> ... he fled
> To the eastern gates, and full six dewy hours
> Before the dawn in season due should blush,

> He breath'd fierce breath against the sleepy portals,
> Clear'd them of heavy vapours, burst them wide
> Suddenly on the ocean's chilly streams.
>
> (1:263 – 8)

He has flung open the gates for a very human reason—night being unendurable he wishes day to come, though it is six hours to dawn. But it is not this nervous frailty that reduces his divinity, it is the fact that he cannot do what he so painfully longs to do:

> Fain would he have commanded, fain took throne
> And bid the day begin, if but for change.
> He might not;—No, though a primeval God:
> The sacred seasons might not be disturb'd.
> Therefore the operations of the dawn
> Stay'd in their birth.
>
> (290 – 95)

Keats evidently thought the adverbial clause in the third sentence had become necessary. We are to continue to think of Hyperion as a sort of god, just as we would have done according to convention if Keats had not made it difficult to do so. He continues to make it difficult in these lines, for Hyperion merely presides over certain regularities—he cannot suspend or alter astronomical laws because they are not his laws, any more than they are Kepler's—and his successor will be in precisely the same position. It is ironic that the father of the Titans, after confessing himself in an equally secondary role ('My life is but the life of winds and tides/ No more than winds and tides can I avail'—1:341 – 42) should exclaim 'But thou canst' (1:343). The whole point of the poem is that Hyperion can't. A more intense irony follows: 'Meantime I will keep watch on thy bright sun,/ And of thy seasons be a careful nurse' (1:347 – 48). At first it may seem that he is offering to take over a tautological function, for it has already been indicated that the sacred seasons may not be disturbed, whether a god is keeping watch or not. It may be, however, that Keats' implication is that a god is necessary as a source of energy—he must turn the handle of a machine he did not make and may not modify. He is not a prime mover, merely an operative with a limited function.

Saturn presents a similar case. When we first meet him, in his impassioned grief, examining the possibilities of retaliation, we are so impressed by the grandeur of his questions and the pity of their cause that we do not notice their implications:

'But cannot I create?
Cannot I form? Cannot I fashion forth
Another world, another universe,
To overbear and crumble this to naught?
Where is another Chaos? Where?'
(1:141–5)

Keats tells us that this utterance alarmed the Olympians, but it is not clear why. Saturn's last two questions supply a negative to his first. He can form and fashion a universe—he has already done so. Oceanus alludes to this: 'Great Saturn, thou/ Hast sifted well the atom-universe.' Clearly he could sift another mass of maximum entropy if he could find one. But the implication is irresistible that he cannot create one.

One finds no difficulty in the notion that one of the most important symbolic functions of the Greek deities was to represent second causes not yet understood by human science—they are 'gods of the gaps' in fact. But it is very strange to have our attention painstakingly and repeatedly drawn to this fact by a poet with a highly serious mythopoeic intention. We make sense of it, I think, if we perceive that intention as a critique of the old myth of the genealogy of the gods. Keats is showing us, in these passages, the gods discovering that they are not gods. He is also, I suspect, recognising not only the inadequacy of his own religious beliefs, but also that a certain kind of romantic humanism had come to the end of its tether. For the gods discovering their limits look very like men abandoning their aspirations—'Cannot I create? Cannot I fashion forth . . .' and so on. Man cannot, by the power of either his imagination or his science recreate the 'heaven he lost erewhile' (1:124). The poet is not a saviour-hero, he is simply a man speaking to men.

Let us now look at how this sense of loss is rendered in the poetry. The symbolic doubleness here is very different in its effect from that in *Endymion*. There is no blurring of outline in *Hyperion*; the figures have depth, contour, and a weight of reality that they could not have if they were merely effulgent gods. Saturn is pitiably real precisely because we are made aware of his loss of aura. Consider the work done in the following lines by the placing of the last epithet:

> Upon the sodden ground
> His old right hand lay nerveless, listless, dead,
> Unsceptred.
>
> (1:17 – 19)

Consider too the place where Saturn sits—the 'shady sadness of a vale'. 'Sadness' no doubt surprised Keats when its propriety declared itself to him, for in his annotation of *Paradise Lost* he says: 'There is cool pleasure in the very sound of vale. The English word is of the happiest chance.'[5] It was perhaps the vision at Teignmouth that made 'sadness' possible in this context; beauty is interpenetrated by pain. This is the nature of things, as Keats now knows; good and evil are universally and inseparably compounded. The change in sensibility shows itself when we compare these lines from 'I stood tip-toe'

> How silent comes the water round that bend;
> Not the minutest whisper does it send
> To the o'erhanging sallows.
>
> (65 – 7)

with these from *Hyperion*:

> A stream went voiceless by, still deadened more
> By reason of his fallen divinity
> Spreading a shade: the Naiad 'mid her reeds
> Press'd her cold finger closer to her lips.
>
> (1:11 – 14)

In 'I stood tip-toe' the quietness and motionlessness constitute another form of beauty and pleasure in an environment rich in gentle loveliness. In *Hyperion* too the locale is one which, to a younger Keats, would have seemed wonderfully beautiful—a forested vale, feathered grass, a stream with reeds and an institutional Naiad. But now the silence is voicelessness, the stillness is deadness. In a shrewd ambiguity Keats suggests that the whole scene has been invaded by Saturn's weight of sorrow, for if we observe even the slightest line-end pause after 'divinity', the silent deadness of the stream, and perhaps the whole 'shady sadness' seems to be a consequence of divinity having fallen; the completion of the syntax by 'spreading a shade' does little to mitigate the impression. The river-nymph, too, has been humanised to a puzzled and timorous girl.

The ambiguity of lines 11, 12, and 13 is a key to the whole opening scene of the poem. There is, in the vale, 'Not so much life as on a summer's day/ Robs not one light seed from the place it fell' (1:8 – 9), the falling leaf is dead, Saturn's 'old right hand' is dead, the stream is 'deadened more'. Yet it is a misjudgement to say, as one critic has done, that 'All is negative here ... we are in a world of death'.[6] Apart from the falling leaf everything is actually alive; the deadened stream does move, though voicelessly; Saturn is in fact fully alive, and the anguish of his grief implies no moribund sensibility. The naiad, though motionless with apprehension, strikes a notably living posture. The whole scene and the figures in it are real and living as the scenery and figures in *Endymion* are not, because we see them with both eyes, so to speak, focussing both life and mortality into a single picture that has the depth and presentness of the actual.

To take the optical metaphor a little further, what Keats achieved at Teignmouth was not tragic vision but binocular vision. The lines in the *Epistle to Reynolds* describing the 'eternal fierce destruction' are intermingled with these passages:

> 'Twas a quiet eve;
> The rocks were silent, the wide sea did weave
> An untumultuous fringe of silver foam ...

> ... today
> I've gathered young spring leaves, and flowers gay
> Of periwinkle and wild strawberry.
> (89 – 91; 99 – 101)

The artistic consequence of the Teignmouth experience was, as we have seen, a startling increment in poetic power, a new sense of dimension and oxymoronic dualism in diction and imagery.

The human consequence was profoundly distressing, but it was
not a state of despair. Keats was too perceptive and too mentally
energetic merely to exchange one Cyclops eye for another. One
of the advantages of humanising his gods was that he could use
them to externalise his own tumultuous emotions and thoughts.
To put Lord Byrons's patronising phraseology to better use, the
gods in *Hyperion* contrive to speak much as John Keats might
have been supposed to speak.[7] Hyperion, seeing repulsive visions
for the first time in his palace, where he 'should have been most
happy', responds thus:

> 'O dreams of day and night!
> O monstrous forms! O effigies of pain!
> O spectres busy in a cold, cold gloom!
> O lank-eared Phantoms of black-weeded pools!
> Why do I know ye? Why have I seen ye?'
> (1:227–31)

The ugliness briefly dominates Hyperion's vision: 'The blaze, the
splendour, and the symmetry,/ I cannot see—but darkness, death
and darkness' (1:241 – 2). Keats at Teignmouth experienced a
similarly dreadful persistence of vision: 'Still am I sick of it ...'
(99), 'Still do I that most fierce destruction see' (102). Hyperion is
resilient: 'Saturn is fallen, am I too to fall?' (1:234); 'Fall! No, by
Tellus and her briny robes,/ Over the fiery frontier of my realms/
I will advance a terrible right arm' (1:246 – 48). Keats too recoils
with healthy energy: 'Away ye horrid moods! Moods of one's
mind!' (105 – 106); 'I'll dance,/ And from detested thoughts in
new romance/ Take refuge' (110 – 112). Although this is self-
delusory—the thing Keats has seen is not a mood of one's mind,
and no amount of taking refuge will restore the lost simplicity of
vision—it is none the less healthy because it is energetic. It is
interesting to remember that Keats told Sarah Jeffrey in May
1819: 'I must choose between despair & Energy—I choose the
latter' (*Letters* 2:113). Keats will not sink into the apathy of
negativism; the vitality of his intellectual being must ultimately
seek for a more comprehensive and sophisticated metaphysical
hypothesis, or else contrive somehow to remain fully alive
without one. Meanwhile negative capability restrains any longing
for a permanent bolt-hole either in romance or resignation.

The next phase of his response to his Teignmouth experience, after the revulsion and rejection had passed, was bewilderment. Shortly before beginning *Hyperion* Keats sat on Ben Nevis, 'a few feet from the edge of that fearful precipice', and meditated on his situation as 'a poor witless elf', seeing only a shroud of vapour in the chasms below him, and 'sullen mist' in the heavens above him—'Even so vague is man's sight of himself'.[8] The mood is one of ignorance, uncertainty and disorientation so complete and fundamental that 'bewilderment' scarcely describes it—perhaps we need to borrow the Greek word $'\alpha\pi o\rho\iota\alpha$, for increasingly from now on in his poetry Keats asks what philosophers might call aporetic questions, to which no answers seem possible.

It is worth spending some time looking at the many questions asked in *Hyperion*, for as I have indicated earlier they form one of the ways in which the symbolic dualism of the divine figures manifests itself. Keats having humanised his gods, they too can experience $'\alpha\pi o\rho\iota\alpha$; consequently, apart from the long speeches of the formal Titan debate, a very large proportion of what the gods say takes the interrogative form. In fact the very first divine utterance is a question, Thea's 'Saturn, look up!—though wherefore poor old King?' (1:52). This is not an aporetic question but a rhetorical one—Thea knows full well that Saturn's exhausted oblivion is a relief from suffering. But she cannot even supply this answer without framing a question: 'I cannot say "O wherefore sleepest thou?"/For heaven is parted from thee...' (1:54-5). There seems to be no point in waking Saturn: 'O thoughtless, why did I/ Thus violate thy slumbrous solitude?/Why should I ope they melancholy eyes?' (1:68 - 71). When Saturn wakes, his first sentences are not grammatically interrogative, but they are questions: '... tell me if this feeble shape/ Is Saturn's?' (1:98 - 9) But his most poignant words are both effectively and formally questions:

> 'Who had power
> To make me desolate? Whence came the strength?
> How was it nurtur'd to such bursting forth,
> While Fate seem'd strangled in my nervous grasp?'
> (1:102–5)

To the first of these questions there is a simple answer, 'Jove', but to the second and third only a spurious answer is offered, in Book 2, by Oceanus: 'We fall by course of Nature's law' (2:181) means that the Titans have been overthrown because things are as they are, and not otherwise. Oceanus answers the form of Saturn's question, but not its import. Within the universe of the Greek gods perhaps no other answer is available, except unsatisfactory words such as Μοιρα or 'αναγκη .

Saturn's second series of questions we have already seen; his third occurs in his speech to the Titan assembly:

> 'O Titans, shall I say "Arise!"—Ye groan:
> Shall I say "Crouch!"—Ye groan. What can I then?
> O Heaven wide! O unseen parent dear!
> What can I?'
>
> (2:157 – 60)

The first two questions are merely expressing conditions, and together with their answers they constitute a statement of Saturn's dilemma. But they lead directly to the reiterated third question, the poetic power of which lies in its ambiguous nature. In view of the fact that the Titan debate follows, it appears to be a simple interrogative to which various answers are expected. Following the statement of the dilemma, however, it sounds rhetorical—one answer only being possible and obvious: 'Nothing.' This, though not aporetic in itself, nonetheless expresses 'απορια . As such it is a highly dramatic expression of the bewilderment directly stated in the preceding lines:

> 'Not in my own sad breast,
> Which is its own great judge and searcher out,
> Can I find reason why ye should be thus:
> Not in the legends of the first of days
> . . .'
> 'Not there, nor in sign, symbol, or portent
> Of element, earth, water, air, and fire
> . . .'
> 'Can I find reason why ye should be thus.'
> (2:129–32; 139–40; 149)

The next six lines relate the bewilderment directly to the Titans' immediate situation—the import is 'How did we come to lose the war?' But in the lines I have quoted a much more general question is implied in 'why ye should be thus'. Saturn, one suspects, is speaking for Keats, asking why humanity is the kind of species it is, and why it is in the situation that so baffles and daunts it.

It may be objected that the series of questions asked by Hyperion, Thea and Saturn cannot really bear the double load I have suggested because they are 'plot-required'—it is inevitable that the defeated Titans should ask why 'palpable Gods,/ Should cower beneath what, in comparison,/ Is untremendous might' (2:153–5). The objection loses much of its force when we find Apollo voicing a series of questions, different in their particular application, but also expressing bewilderment. When he asks Mnemosyne 'How cam'st thou over the unfooted sea?/ Or hath that antique mien and robed form/ Mov'd in these vales invisible till now?' (3:50 – 52), he is reasonably sure that the second possibility is the true fact—Mnemosyne has been invisibly present long before she appears. This implies some foreordained destiny for Apollo—he sees 'purport in her looks for him'—but what is that destiny, and who ordained it? Again, why, living in so beautiful a place as Delos, conscious of his marvellous gifts and destined greatness, is he weeping? Mnemosyne poses the reader's question: 'Tell me youth,/ What sorrow canst thou feel ... Explain thy griefs ... show they heart's secrets' (3:68; 70; 76). Most significantly, Apollo cannot do so:

> 'O why should I
> Feel curs'd and thwarted, when the liegeless air
> Yields to my step aspirant? Why should I
> Spurn the green turf as hateful to my feet?'
> (3:91 – 4)

The second question partly answers the first—Apollo feels that he is greater than he knows—but in doing so raises a much greater question: why does he feel this sense of destiny and special purpose? Now these questions are, like those of the Titans, dramatically appropriate to the situation in the poem; the sense of their double import is also clear. In view of what Apollo symbolises (after dreaming of Mnemosyne he woke to find a golden lyre at his side) he is, when he asks the questions, speaking for Keats. Most commentators agree that for Keats poetry was akin to a religious vocation—raising the question where the gifts and the sense of duty and destiny come from. As for the question why Apollo weeps, conscious of such gifts, the answer is implicit in the image of his tears trickling down his golden bow—the god of poetry must himself be a mighty poet of the human heart, and feel the giant agony of the world. His tears foreshadow the sufferings of his apotheosis, his 'dying into life' which, as Stuart Sperry says: 'represents that *martyrdom* to the human heart and its knowledge that Keats could already foresee as the necessary culmination of his poem.'[9] But notice how the sense of personal election leads directly, as it must, to the most fundamental religious questions:

> 'Are there not other regions than this isle?
> What are the stars? ...'
>   Where is power?
> Whose hand, whose essence, what divinity
> Makes this alarum in the elements?'
>   (3:96-7; 103-5)

The isle is Delos, and the 'alarum' is 'cloudy thunder', but these specifics do nothing to restrict the universal application of the questions. Apollo, not yet a god, is speaking for mankind, as are the fallen Titans in their bewilderment. We see then, a suggestive affinity between Saturn and Apollo—they share an ambiguous status, the one a fallen god, the other a god not yet apotheosed. Together, I suggest, and with the dynasties they represent, they symbolise mankind, at the same time fallen and aspiring, and suffering both in consequence of the fall and the aspiration. Most significantly, Saturn and Apollo ask the same question: 'Who had power?' and 'Where is power?'

    The abandonment of the poem is now in sight, because in its progress a theme has evolved which overpowers the theme which Keats envisaged at the outset. To return for a moment to Evert's account of Keats' metaphysical hypothesis: 'It is the poet's function to receive, interpret, and transmit knowledge of the god to men who ordinarily feel his influence less directly and who, without the poet's aid, do not properly understand it.' But in *Hyperion* it seems that the god, the poet, and the mass of humankind share a common bewilderment, in the face of which Oceanus' thesis that 'tis the eternal law/ That first in beauty should be first in might' (2:228 - 9) becomes an absurd bathos.

The need to render Oceanus' thesis adequate to its intended function in the poem has called forth a good deal of critical casuistry. The popular apologia maintains that the beauty of the greatest poetry will be one that knows, shares, and expresses the worst of human suffering. But Keats has, wittingly or unwittingly, undermined this sophisticated understanding of the idea. The representatives of this compassionate beauty ought not themselves to be the cause of suffering. But they are, as Enceladus makes plain:

> 'Speak! roar! shout! yell! ye sleepy Titans all.
> Do ye forget the blows, the buffets vile?
> Are ye not smitten by a youngling arm?
> Dost thou forget, sham Monarch of the Waves,
> Thy scalding in the seas? ...'

> 'The days of peace and slumbrous calm are fled;
> Those days, all innocent of scathing war,
> When all the fair Existences of heaven
> Came open-eyed to guess what we would speak:—
> That was before our brows were taught to frown.'
>   (2:316–20; 335–9)

Keats offers nothing which would allow us to suppose that Enceladus is lying or distorting. Reasonably, we may take the Olympians for aggressive villains, and Jove for the arch-tyrant and future torturer of Prometheus: 'O let him feel the evil he hath done' (2:332). But, as John Jones has said: 'The "first in beauty should be first in might" thesis could never be adequate to human suffering,' even without this subversion from within.[10] Not surprisingly then, we find the poem faltering towards its breakdown immediately after Apollo's great question 'Where is power?' The 'knowledge enormous' that we are asked to suppose will make a god of him reads more like a syllabus than an enlightenment: 'Names, deeds, gray legends, dire events, rebellions,/ Majesties, sovran voices, agonies,/ Creations and destroyings ...' (3:114 - 16). Most importantly, it does not answer the questions that Apollo, and before him Saturn and Hyperion have been asking.

Keats can describe, distantly and vaguely, the physical pains of Apollo becoming a god, but not the transfigured Apollo who has become a god. We do not know whether or not at this time Keats could still conceive of such a being, but the evidence is strong that he couldn't represent one. An attempt then, to construct an ending to the poem, to build out of second-hand parts a conception adequate to the questions the poem had been asking, would have constituted an 'irritable reaching after fact and reason', and a spurious answer thus achieved might well block an authentic one. This is perhaps what D.G. James had in mind when he described Keats' abandonment of the poem as: 'the greatest achievement of romanticism; in it the Romantic mind beheld its own perplexity and condemned itself.'

4

In spite of the pain and fear occasioned by his state of bewilderment, Keats had sufficient moral resolution to rest content without answers if adequate answers did not present themselves. Nevertheless, in his brave but distressing state of mind, the cultural power of a rejected tradition once more presented itself. To quote James again:

> It was all very well for Shelley to say of Keats that 'he *was* a Greek'; he could play the Greek to perfection, but for Keats or anyone else living at thousands of years remove from Greek civilisation and after thousands of years of Christian culture to *be* Greek is simply impossible. And indeed, what Keats wished to convey in *Hyperion* must inevitably have shattered, indeed did shatter, the loyalty he conscientiously felt to the imagination of Greece which gave him his material.[11]

This brings us to the third way in which, I suggested, the symbolic dualism of the gods is rendered—in their appearance and postures. Keats' gods not only have human lineaments, but these are sometimes specifically recognisable. We notice this first in the way that the figures of Thea and Saturn stimulate our memories—our sense of their humanity depends in part on a sense of faltering recognition. We hear a surprisingly familiar tone in the following:

> 'Look up, and tell me if this feeble shape
> Is Saturn's; tell me, if thou hear'st the voice
> Of Saturn; tell me, if this wrinkling brow,
> Naked and bare of its great diadem,
> Peers like the front of Saturn.'
>
> (1:98 – 102)

Our first memory, of course, is Shakespearean. The voice and phraseology is Lear's, as is the situation, a king 'Naked and bare of his great diadem':

> 'Does any here know me? This is not Lear.
> Does Lear walk thus? Speak thus? Where are his eyes?
> Either his notion weakens, or his discernings
> Are lethargied.—Ha! waking? 'Tis not so.—
> Who is it that can tell me who I am?'
>
> (4:4:225–9)

Thea has the voice of Cordelia in another scene when she refrains from waking 'the poor old King' (1:52), lamenting that 'ocean too ... has from thy sceptre passed, and all the air/ Is emptied of thy hoary majesty' (1:57 – 9). But both Saturn and Lear are asking questions rhetorically in order to draw attention to their obscured authority—divine or divinely ordained—and both are thus elaborating on the most dramatic of such questions: 'Whom do men say that I am ... Whom say ye that I am?' (*Matthew* 16:13,15). But Saturn is in worse case than Lear; Lear lost a kingdom; Saturn a heaven. There is a general sense then, established by the memories of Lear, of humanity fallen from divine privilege rather than fallen deity. Keats' figures look and sound more like the desolated Lear and Cordelia than like vanquished Titans. But they also look like exiled Adam and Eve in their first stunned wretchedness—an impression strengthened by the ambiguity I have noted earlier in the lines: 'A stream went voiceless by, still deaden'd more/ By reason of his fall'n divinity/ Spreading a shade.' There has been a fall, and the world seems infected by it. But by far the most intriguing memories are evoked by Thea weeping at Saturn's feet:

> ... the while in tears
> She touch'd her fair large forehead to the ground,
> Just where her fallen hair might be outspread
> A soft and silken mat for Saturn's feet.
>
> (1:79–82)

Keats, sensing though perhaps not identifying something almost archetypal here, fixes the image and bathes it in light:

> One moon, with alteration slow, had shed
> Her silver seasons four upon the night,
> And still these two were postured motionless,
> Like natural sculpture in Cathedral cavern
>
> (1:83–6)

Keats has indeed turned living beings into statues here, and yet the sculpture remains poignantly human. Ian Jack has commented:

> It seems likely that a number of passages of literature and a number of visual images all contributed to Keats' description. One of them may even have been a tombstone, for the posture of Saturn and Thea is reminiscent more than anything else of a sculptural group on a funeral monument—a fact which makes it interesting to note that Keats refers to a cathedral both in the passage itself and in the description of Fingal's Cave in the letter which lies behind this part of the poem. Some forgotten portrayal of a mourning father and daughter may well have helped to inspire the passage—a father with head bowed and eyes closed in sorrow, a daughter whose hair lies unregarded by her father's feet.[12]

Such a mutually grieving father and daughter again bring to mind Cordelia, kneeling, as she proposed to do, for her father's blessing. But there is yet another memory to identify. Ian Jack is curiously wrong in in describing the woman's hair as 'unregarded'—it is the last thing we can disregard in Keats' picture, forming as it does a 'soft and silken mat for Saturn's feet'. May not one of the 'forgotten portrayals' have been of the following:

> And behold, a woman in the city, which was a sinner, when she knew that Jesus sat at meat in the Pharisee's house, brought an alabaster box of ointment,
>
> And stood at his feet behind him weeping, and began to wash his feet with her tears, and did wipe them with the hair of her head, and kissed his feet, and anointed them with the ointment.
>
> (*Luke* 4:37–8)

The comparison has limitations of course—Thea may look like Mary Magdalen, but Saturn looks like Christ only insofar as Thea's posture makes him appear to do so. But in his speech to the kneeling goddess at his feet he says two things which are rather unexpected in a Greek god, and have resonances which are not Greek:

> 'I am smother'd up,
> And buried from all godlike exercise
> Of influence benign on planets pale,
> Of admonitions to the winds and seas,
> Of peaceful sway above man's harvesting,
> And all those acts which Deity supreme
> Doth ease its heart of love in.'
>
> (1:106–12)

That the gods were administrators of natural laws is familiar enough, that they performed their functions out of love is much less characteristically Greek. But there is also, in Saturn's speech, a more readily identifiable element. When he is considering his response to the Olympian triumph, he foresees an ultimate restoration:

> 'Yes, there must be a golden victory;
> There must be Gods thrown down, and trumpets blown
> Of triumph calm, and hymns of festival
> Upon the gold clouds metropolitan,

> Voices of soft proclaim, and silver stir
> Of strings in hollow shells; and there shall be
> Beautiful things made new for the surprise
> Of the sky-children ...
>
> ... Cannot I create?
> Cannot I form? Cannot I fashion forth
> Another world, another universe,
> To overbear and crumble this to naught?'
>   (1:126–33; 141–4)

Saturn is envisaging more than the joy of victory—it is a Titan apocalypse that he looks forward to, and one detects Biblical trace elements:

> And I saw a new heaven and a new earth: for the first heaven and the first earth were passed away ...
> And God shall wipe away all tears from their eyes; and there shall be no more death, neither sorrowing nor crying, neither shall their be any more pain; for the former things are passed away.
> And he that sat upon the throne said, Behold, I make all things new.
>   (*Revelation* 21:1,4,5)

The fourth way in which the gods perform their double function is in their own discovery of the doubleness of experience itself. We find implicitly and explicitly expressed throughout the poem what we might call the Christian paradoxes. These are now perhaps most familiar to the modern reader through T.S. Eliot's adaptation of the insights of St John of the Cross: 'the way up is the way down, the way forward is the way back.'[13] In *Hyperion* the first explicit statement of the theme is made by Oceanus. Beyond their despair the Titans may find comfort:

> 'I bring proof
> How ye, perforce, must be content to stoop
> And in the proof much comfort will I give,
> If ye will take that comfort in its truth.'
>   (2:177–80)

The truth that the Titan's must acknowledge is their place in the scheme of things. Their previous happiness in their unconquered state was spurious; in their apparent security they were all, like their king, 'blind from sheer supremacy'. Now they must recognise themselves as contingent beings, subject to the divine teleology of 'eternal law':

> 'As Heaven and Earth are fairer, fairer far
> Than Chaos and blank Darkness ...
> So on our heels a fresh perfection treads,
> A power more strong in beauty, born of us
> And fated to excel us, as we pass
> In glory that old Darkness; nor are we
> Thereby more conquer'd than by us the rule
> Of shapeless Chaos.'
>
> (2:206–7; 212–17)

The Titans can gain an invulnerable peace, and thus achieve a kind of victory out of their defeat in war. But Oceanus' comfort is indeed cold comfort, and perhaps has a stoic element at least equal to the Christian element. Clymene, however, goes much further. She has accepted the truth Oceanus proposes, and has found a matchless joy interpenetrating her grief:

> 'There came enchantment with the shifting wind,
> That did both drown and keep alive my ears.
> I threw my shell away upon the sand,
> And a wave fill'd it, as my sense was fill'd
> With that new blissful golden melody.
> A living death was in each gush of sounds,
> Each family of rapturous hurried notes,
> That fell, one after one, yet all at once,
> Like pearl beads dropping sudden from their string:
> And then another, then another strain,
> Each like a dove leaving its olive perch,
> With music wing'd instead of silent plumes,
> To hover round my head, and make me sick
> Of joy and grief at once.'
>
> (2:276–89)

Clymene's mention of 'living death' foreshadows the most intense form of the paradox, experienced, curiously enough, not by any of the Titans, but by Apollo:

> Soon wild commotions shook him, and made flush
> All the immortal fairness of his limbs;
> Most like the struggle at the gate of death;
> Or liker still to one who should take leave
> Of pale immortal death, and with a pang
> As hot as death's is chill, with fierce convulse
> Die into life: so young Apollo anguish'd.
>
>   (3:124–30)

Apollo's apotheosis is very far from Christ's crucifixion; even in his new-found maturity it is hard to imagine Keats dealing effectively with such ugly suffering. Nevertheless we should note that Keats expresses his hero's 'death' in terms of an analogue—Apollo in his anguish is '*like* one who should take leave/ Of pale immortal death and ... Die into life'.

In this last passage again we sense the poem faltering; there is a suggestion of unsuccessful straining for something beyond Keats' power to do. But perhaps it would be fairer to say beyond his power to do again, because the image of divine suffering he is struggling for here he has already achieved once, superbly. Apollo as a god in pain can never win our attention from Saturn. Apollo was meant to be, in his 'dying into life', the pattern for theTitans' acceptance of the 'eternal law'—he was, in a sense, to be both conqueror and saviour. But those wild commotions, flushes and pangs do not achieve the moving power of the following, where Saturn is approaching the place where the fallen Titans have gathered to mourn their loss:

> Then Thea spread abroad her trembling arms
> Upon the precincts of this nest of pain,
> And sidelong fix'd her eye on Saturn's face:
> There saw she direst strife; the supreme God
> At war with all the frailty of grief.
>
>   (2:89–93)

The power of this is not entirely explained as the statement of an enormous paradox. The notion of a God at war with frailty and succumbing to it, of the divine stricken with human grief, as he approaches the place where his fellows are in anguish has a parallel:

> Then when Mary was come where Jesus was, and saw him, she fell down at his feet, saying unto him, Lord, if thou hadst been here, my brother had not died.
> When Jesus therefore saw her weeping, and the Jews also weeping which came with her, he groaned in the spirit and was troubled.
> And said Where have you laid him? They said unto him, Lord, come and see.
> Jesus wept.
>
> *(John* 2:32 – 5)

Perhaps the most powerful way in which the symbolic doubleness of the gods is expressed is the one I mentioned last—their attempt to come to terms with a new perception of themselves and their destiny. It is also in this respect that we find the most significant Biblical influences. John Jones has observed: 'Oceanus it is who now asks them [the fallen gods] to see their Titanic woes as part of a process called Beauty's triumph ... the poem never got written, and what we have bends inwards upon Oceanus' speech with all possible emphasis.'[14] Clearly the speech is meant to express the thesis of the poem, but it more powerfully expresses the theme which overwhelmed that thesis, for Oceanus is the Titans' Hesiod:

> 'Great Saturn, thou
> Hast sifted well the atom-universe;
> But for this reason, that thou art the King,
> And only blind from sheer supremacy,
> One avenue was shaded from thine eyes,
> Through which I wandered to eternal truth.
> And first, as thou wast not the first of powers
> So art thou not the last; it cannot be:
> Thou art not the beginning nor the end.
> From Chaos and parental Darkness came
> Light, the first fruits of that intestine broil,

That sullen ferment, which, for wondrous ends
Was ripening in itself. The ripe hour came,
And with it Light, and Light, engendering
Upon its own producer, forthwith touch'd
The whole enormous matter into Life.
Upon that very hour, our parentage,
The Heavens and the Earth, were manifest.'
                                        (2:182 – 99)

This theogony is meant to introduce and explain an evolutionary
principle whereby the greater beauty will through all eternity
usurp the lesser beauty—this is the 'eternal law'. But the implicit
teleology plucks our attention away from the evolutionary
principle. We have, I suggest, only the most perfunctory interest
in the question 'Where is it going?'—it isn't going anywhere
except onward and upward. 'Where did it start?' is the engaging
question, and Oceanus has drawn our attention to it by supplying
an unsatisfactory answer. According to Oceanus' Book of
Genesis, in the beginning was an intestine broil, in the course of
which Chaos and Darkness created light. One may very well find
that Oceanus' phraseology scarcely has an air of meaning, much
less meaning itself. It is difficult too, to know what he means by
'Light'. Since it is something other than and better than Chaos
and Darkness, it is presumably a rational order in the universe. If
Oceanus does mean this he appears to be overlooking Saturn's
supposed part in creation, though he has earlier alluded to the
king of the gods having 'sifted well the atom-universe'. The
problems increase as Oceanus proceeds—Light may certainly
bring order to Chaos, but how does it 'engender' upon it?
Oceanus' use of the sexual term suggests something which is
more creative, and perhaps more mystical, than mechanical.

In fact the whole passage may be a highly sententious way of
saying that Oceanus doesn't know how things began. But he
insists that he does: 'One avenue was shaded from thine eyes/
Through which I wandered to eternal truth.' His audience may
not know what he means, but he does—he has been granted a
knowledge which his words cannot express. This is a matter of
necessity, of course, because Oceanus knows something that
Keats doesn't know, 'eternal truth'. Hence Oceanus must have
recourse to a form of mystical symbolism that Keats does know.

His Book of Genesis is also his Book of Revelation—literally and symbolically the beginning and end of the Bible. For although Oceanus cannot describe his central conception, that of a being on which the whole contingent sequence depends, he has defined it by implication as that which Saturn is not: '... thou wast not the first of powers/ So art thou not the last; it cannot be:/ Thou art not the beginning nor the end.' St John describes his vision thus:

> And he that sat upon the throne said, Behold I make all things new. And he said to me, Write; for these words are true and faithful.
> And he said unto me, It is done. I am Alpha and Omega, the beginning and the end.
>
> (*Revelation* 21:5 - 6)

Let us now look again at the lines which follow Oceanus' allusion to Alpha and Omega:

> 'From Chaos and parental Darkness came
> Light, the first fruits of that intestine broil,
> That sullen ferment, which for wondrous ends
> Was ripening in itself. The ripe hour came,
> And with it Light, and Light, engendering
> Upon its own producer, forthwith touch'd
> The whole enormous matter into Life.'

Vague as this is ('broil', 'ferment', 'ripening' et cetera) it reads like an historical account of the beginning of things, and consequently one is first reminded of *Genesis* 1:3 - 4: 'And God said, Let there be light, and there was light. And God saw the light, that it was good; and God divided the light from the darkness.' But Oceanus is not merely speaking historically, he is conscious that the ripening took place for 'wondrous ends'. His cosmogony is less an explanation to be understood than a mystery to be meditated upon. We may remember again here that the image of light had apparently a special importance for Keats—in *Endymion* he alludes to the infant god of love as 'Dear unseen light in darkness'; in the sonnet *To Homer* he proclaims hopefully 'Ay, on the shores of darkness there is light', and in his letters he describes

himself as 'straining at particles of light in a great darkness' (2:80).
Such allusions indicate that he intended 'Light' in Oceanus' lines
to mean something more than a rational order in the universe,
more even than some anterior physical law by which the mass of
atoms were 'sifted' into that mathematical continuum. This in
turn suggests that we need to look further than *Genesis* for a
source:

> And the light shineth in darkness; and the darkness
> comprehended it not ...
> ... That was the true Light which lighteth every man that
> cometh into the world.
>
> *(John* 1:5;9)

> This then is the message which we have heard of him, and
> declare unto you, that God is light, and in him is no darkness at
> all.
>
> (1st *Epistle of John* 1:5)

Let us put these resemblances into perspective. If a
trustworthy comparative exegesis of Keats' and St John's words
were available, it would no doubt show considerable differences
between the two. St John is speaking in his own voice, affirming a
faith; Keats attributes his words to one of his characters for
dramatic and narrative purposes, and he is himself, perhaps,
merely exploring or re-examining another 'metaphysical
hypothesis'. One must not be tempted to think that Keats'
private thoughts were taking any particular direction. All that
one might reasonably say in this regard is that one of the tenets of
the doctrine of negative capability is that the mind should be a
thoroughfare for all thoughts. Our major interest, however, is
the literary effect of the Biblical memories, and that effect is to
add complexity and dimension to the dual symbolism of the
personae we see interacting in the poem. And of course it adds a
soberly ironic suggestion of what we have actually seen happen in
the poem called *Hyperion*—the fall of Apollo.

What we have also seen in the poem is an impressive
development of Keats' symbolism. Now more fully aware of the
complexity of his own responses to experience, he has greater
control of the artistic manifestation of it. Thus he has given his

fallen Titans a dual symbolic function by humanising them, so that they represent the failure of a certain kind of religious belief, and at the same time the most painful paradox in human nature—the sense of divine aspiration coupled with the knowledge of limitation and death. Inevitably the symbolic implications of the presentation of agonised gods become increasingly antithetical. But they are not yet, I believe, oxymoronic. It is in *The Fall of Hyperion* that the impossible union is achieved, in the image of the perpetual dying of one who cannot die, and in Saturn's strange cry of 'Death' as he perceives the inexhaustible life of things.

6

The Fall of Hyperion

For some time now many critics have accepted F.R. Leavis's judgement that the second version of *Hyperion* (which from now on I shall refer to as *The Fall*) is a greater achievement than the first. Leavis's main point was that Keats in the revision had humanised his myth by avoiding Miltonic rhetoric and pretentious diction, and by introducing himself into his narrative in order to graft the story on to his mature personality.[1] Later critics, more polemically minded, have approved the second version because they find there tragic vision and tough-minded humanism.[2] I believe both these points of view to be wrong, the first because it takes the attempt for the accomplishment; the second because it is solipsistic in its exegesis, and irrelevant in its application. If it is still possible to concur with the estimate of *The Fall* as the greater poem, it is because of two passages of richly symbolic verse, each of which constitutes an achievement not paralleled anywhere in *Hyperion*. In this chapter I propose first to show that Keats' use of direct address and exposition is disastrous rather than effective, and subsequently to demonstrate that the poem's principal quality is the richness of its symbolic structure. The view of the poem as a secular humanist statement I shall refute implicitly throughout the chapter.

When Keats characterised his publisher as a 'consequitive man' (*Letters* 2:218) he strongly implied that he himself was not—as his letters abundantly show. The lack of consistency and logic in the letters is of no importance—they are letters after all—and the delight we take in them springs from their vitality and fertility. They show an enormously energetic and fruitful intelligence, producing an abundance of stimulating individual thoughts, but with no overall shape, *ordonnance*, or consistency that we might strictly call 'thought'. One might reasonably say that this defect matters even less in poetry, for notoriously the poetic mind works by suggestion and symbol rather than by reasoned argument. However, when a writer proposes to use declarative exposition for a highly serious purpose, as Keats does in the first canto of *The Fall*, then one is inclined to suppose that if confusion and contradiction pass beyond a certain point, they will be destructive. Unfortunately, in *The Fall*, they are.

Let us examine the induction to the poem, which plainly has a very serious purpose:

> Fanatics have their dreams, wherewith they weave
> A paradise for a sect; the savage too
> From forth the loftiest fashion of his sleep
> Guesses at Heaven; pity these have not
> Trac'd upon vellum or wild indian leaf
> The shadows of melodious utterance.
> But bare of laurel they live, dream and die;
> For Poesy alone can tell her dreams,
> With the fine spell of words alone can save
> Imagination from the sable charm
> And dumb enchantment. Who alive can say
> 'Thou art no Poet; mayst not tell thy dreams'?
> Since every man whose soul is not a clod
> Hath visions, and would speak, if he had lov'd
> And been well nurtured in his mother tongue.
> Whether the dream now purposed to rehearse
> Be Poet's or Fanatics will be known
> When this warm scribe my hand is in the grave.
>   (1:1–18)

It appears to be a major purpose of these lines to distinguish between two kinds of dreams, the poet's and the fanatic's. The poet's dream is assumed to be superior, and though it is not explicitly stated why this is so, there is an implication that the fanatic's dream, in addition to being fanatical, will be circumscribed and exclusive—he weaves '*A* paradise for *a* sect'. It may also be implied that such a dream will be unsophisticated, since there is an implicit coupling of the fanatic's dream with the sleeping savage's 'guess at Heaven'. One might infer from this that the poet's dream will be sophisticated, humane, and universal; thus it will be more valid in itself as a religious view of

life. It looks as if we might sum the matter up as E.E. Bostetter
has done: 'The dream of the fanatic is false, unworthy of
preservation; the dream of the poet, true.'? Unfortunately the
next three and a half lines cast all in doubt:

> Pity these have not
> Trac'd upon vellum or wild indian leaf
> The shadows of melodious utterance.
> But bare of laurel they live, dream and die.

One would like to be sure, first of all, of the antecedent of 'these'.
Being plural it cannot relate to 'savage' alone, but does it relate to
both 'Fanatics' and 'savage?' If so, why does Keats, having
implicitly distinguished between them, now lump them together?
On the whole it seems better to ignore 'savage', and concentrate
on the distinction between fanatic and poet which the whole
paragraph seems to be making. The confusion is disturbing,
though, and is symptomatic of a more important confusion. The
discrimination between the fanatic's dream and the poet's dream,
implicitly a matter of intrinsic worth, may now be seen merely as a
matter of survival. Bare of laurel, the fanatic will 'live, dream, and
die'—and his dream will die with him; and this, says Keats, is a
pity.

One's first impression is that Keats is expressing regret merely
that the dreams of fanatics were not written down, implying that,
like the poet's dreams, they would have a value for posterity. But
a look at the imagery quickly corrects this—the fanatic's dreams
should not merely have been recorded, they should have been
rendered as poetry, 'The shadows of melodious utterance'. To
have a humanly valuable dream of paradise one must be a poet.
Clearly a large claim of this nature needs justification:

> For Poesy alone can tell her dreams,
> With the fine spell of words alone can save
> Imagination from the sable charm
> And dumb enchantment.

'Poesy' as used here obviously means something different from
what it appears to mean in 'I stood tip-toe' and *Sleep and Poetry*.
It now appears to be, or to include, a watchful and judicious

power which guards against imagination's errors and indulgences. Imagination too, we may note, has a different place in Keats' view of the nature of poetry—it is not to be trusted alone. But once more a closer look at the lines restores the confusion. What precisely is 'the fine *spell* of words'? And why does Keats allow the associations of 'spell', 'charm', and 'enchantment' to interact so disastrously?

Worse is to follow. If the poet's dream is to be preferred to the fanatic's, it would be encouraging for the dreamer to know that he is not merely a fanatic—and in the first four lines of the poem certain criteria for judgement were implied. However:

> Who alive can say
> 'Thou art no Poet; mayst not tell thy dreams'?
> Since everyman whose soul is not a clod
> Hath visions, and would speak, if he had lov'd
> And been well nurtured in his mother tongue.

Does Keats mean that every man who has a religious impulse (and apparently all men do) would, given a real command of language, become a poet? Again, is he returning to the view that the essential difference between the fanatic and the poet is that the latter's dreams are recorded memorably? If so, has he now abandoned the notion that 'Poesy' (which surely implies something more than being well nurtured in one's mother tongue) is a safeguard against wild speculations and imaginative excess? Are all men's visions valuable, or only poets'? Finally, what is the status of the new poem?

> Whether the dream now purpos'd to rehearse
> Be Poet's or Fanatic's will be known
> When this warm scribe my hand is in the grave.

Here, perhaps, is the cause of all the confusion—a frankly acknowledged misgiving about his project, his capacities, and his achievements. As Bostetter says, 'Inasmuch as the dream in its unfolding contains a judgement of all his past activity, becomes therefore a culminative, decisive poetic experience, Keats is staking his poetic future upon the poem.'[4] Posterity alone will be able to discriminate, and what posterity *has* discerned is the final muddle of the whole poem—the clash between this opening paragraph, and Moneta's admonition, in what has turned out to be the central scene of the fragment, against dreams of any kind.

The priestess' admonition, however, forms part of a confusion equal to that of the induction to the poem. In the first place we cannot be sure what her role in the poem was going to be. D.G. James, referring to her by the name she has in *Hyperion*, pertinently asks: '... were Mnemosyne and Apollo to appear in the story which Mnemosyne will show in vision to Keats?' We have no way of knowing what Keats intended to do about Apollo—though it is suggestive that he has himself displaced the god as the symbolic receiver of 'knowledge enormous'. James suggests however, that Moneta would indeed have been a protagonist as well as a chorus. In lines 1:386 – 88 she appears, though rather ambiguously, to be part of the picture she is revealing: 'The frozen God still bending to the Earth,/ And the sad Goddess weeping at his feet./ Moneta silent.' In lines 1:226 – 7 her allusion to herself as being left 'supreme/ Sole priestess of this desolation' suggests that she was to figure in the narrative. 'Now this,' says James, 'is clearly a clumsy arrangement, and ... is bound to make Keats' progress ... very difficult.'[5]

The goddess' change of name also adds to our difficulty. As Mnemosyne she is undoubtedly the mother of the muses, as Moneta less obviously so. The matter is aggravated by her change of place, and apparently, allegiance. In this respect Keats is not only muddled in himself, but the cause that muddle is in other men. Commenting on lines 1:161 – 9 in which Moneta condemns visionaries and explains that humanitarians have no need to come to the temple, Jack Stillinger says:

> The lines make a clear-cut distinction between non-poet humanitarians and poet-dreamers, and assert that the latter are 'less' than the former. Genuine humanitarians do not come to the temple (clearly the temple of poetry); among poet-dreamers, those who are aware of human misery make it up the steps (achieve fame as poets), and those who are unaware die on the pavement (fail as poets). And Moneta condemns the whole 'tribe' of poets.[6]

This last is an extraordinarily odd thing for Moneta to do, being 'supreme/ Sole priestess' of what is 'clearly the temple of poetry'. Stillinger is evidently assuming that Keats intended to erase lines 1:186 – 210, in which it is made clear that Moneta is condemning the 'dreamer tribe', whom she explicitly distinguishes from poets. But whether we include the lines or not, Stillinger's identification of the temple is doubtful. One needs to remember that Moneta is no longer Mnemosyne (though Keats himself forgets from time to time) and the god she serves is Saturn, not Apollo. These things being so, it is far from clear that the temple Keats finds himself in is the temple of poetry. The fact that Moneta seems to measure Keats not against non-dreaming poets, but against good people who are not poets at all indicates that the temple represents something much greater than poetry itself, that Keats has been brought to it in order that he might recognise the place of poetry in a universal scheme of things, and that as a poet himself he must be content to be a servant among other servants of this greater whole. This is perhaps the real sense in which *The Fall* is anti-Romantic—the poet may be a humanist, physician to all men, but he is no longer a hero. As Kenneth Muir has said: 'By the time he conceived Moneta he had come to think not only that the very condition of writing great poetry is that the poet should feel the miseries of the world as his own, but that ordinary good men and women are more valuable than "romantic" poets.'[7]

Moneta's symbolic function becomes much clearer later on in the poem, when she parts the veils and reveals herself to Keats, and the symbolic nature of the temple can be deduced, as I hope to show, from its relationship to the poem's symbolic action. But Moneta's lesson to Keats, as she teaches it directly, never becomes clear. It is in fact impossible to make continuous sense of what the priestess says—she contradicts herself at every turn. (This remains largely true even if one omits the disputed lines 1:186–210.)[8] Take, for instance, the matter of who may be admitted into the temple. Moneta seems to regard practical, philanthropic people as eligible, but they don't bother to come, they have no need of such grace as may be dispensed within the shrine. The ineligible are the dreamers, to which tribe she supposes Keats to belong. But the bar against them has no real function, for they 'find a haven in the world'; presumably they would no more seek out the temple than would the philanthropists who do not need to. But, it seems, they may stray into it, in which case they shrivel to death on the pavement where Keats' 'rotted half' (1:153). On the other hand Keats did not 'stray' into the temple, he seems to have been brought to it by a species of divine favour, and he only half died on the 'immortal steps'. Furthermore we are told that 'such things' as Keats are 'admitted oft' and 'suffered in these Temples' (the plural here provokes curiosity, and perhaps more confusion) so that happiness may 'be somewhat shared' (1:177 – 80).

In view of the fact that Keats is going to take the miseries of the world into his poetic sensibility, one might pause here to ask exactly what Moneta means by 'happiness'. But more importantly one has to try to understand the function of the temple itself, and to decide who precisely are the intended beneficiaries of its favour. We can only make sense of the matter if we suppose a distinction to be implied between a redeemable sort of poet-dreamer, and the incorrigible sort who risks blundering upon his death. But Moneta herself never explicitly makes such a distinction—on the contrary, she denies that there can be such a thing as a poet-dreamer: 'The poet and the dreamer are distinct,/ Diverse, sheer opposite, antipodes' (1:199 – 200). These lines are part of the disputed passage of course, and some critics will hold that Keats intended to erase them. I see no good reason for ignoring them, however, since they do not seem to me to be more muddled and inconsistent than the rest of Moneta's speech.

Let us look again at the oddity we noticed in the 'happiness' that Moneta says may be 'somewhat shared'. The eligible ones, the humanitarian, practical people, take on the sufferings of others, the miseries of the world are their miseries. Yet they seek 'a happy-noted voice' and wonder in a human face (1:164–65), and it is their happiness that reformed visionaries are to be allowed to share. Dreamers are those who find a haven in the world, they turn their eyes away from human suffering and refuse to share it—yet these are the ones who experience perpetual misery—'the dreamer venoms all his days,/ Bearing more woes than all his sins deserve' (1:175–6). Again, one might make sense of this by reading into it a religious paradox, that one finds happiness in accepting pain vicariously, and, by way of corollary, that a life of dedicated selfishness becomes a torment. But a sense of such paradox is not there in the poetry, as it is in Clymene's speech in *Hyperion*. All we have in confusion.

Moneta does, however, as I have already noted, make a firm distinction between the poet and the dreamer. Unfortunately this is a distinction which leads to deeper confusions:

> 'The Poet and the dreamer are distinct,
> Diverse, sheer opposite, antipodes.
> The one pours out a balm upon the world,
> The other vexes it.'
>
> (1:199-202)

Mario D'Avanzo has pointed out the oddity of these lines within the poem's structure:

> The distinction made between the dreamer and the poet reveals a meaningful sea-change in Keats' thought. The awestruck mortal of 'the dreamer tribe' in *The Fall of Hyperion* learns that 'the poet and the dreamer are distinct' (1:199), that the dreamer 'venoms all his days' (175); for only the true poet brings philosophical depths to his poems, which the baseless fabric of dreams cannot alone provide. The poet must identify himself with the problems of humanity, and serve as a 'humanist, physician to all men' (190). Yet it should be noted that *The Fall of Hyperion* is cast in the form of a dream, apparently suggesting that Keats still believes in its power to reveal truth.[9]

Another basic confusion concerns the unspecified nature of the balm the poet offers. The poet clearly belongs to the humanitarian group, to whom 'the miseries of the world are misery' (1:148-49). But what is the nature of the balm which he must apply to humanity's wounds? Is it, as many critics seem to suppose, the bare truth revealed by tragic vision? Is the poet to take the horrors of existence, record them vividly, and pass them back to his suffering audience? Is he to be not merely a man speaking to men, but a stoic preaching to stoics? Wouldn't mankind, in an indifferent universe, be better served by dreamers? Ought not Khayyam's book of verse to be as analgesic as his flask of wine? It is not unlikely that from time to time Keats suspected that this might indeed be so; in which case poetry was worth only what it would fetch, and one might labour for mortal good more effectively as a ship's surgeon. Such black moments no doubt

contributed to to the confusion here, reflecting once more the
απορια of the Ben Nevis sonnet.

I believe, however, that Moneta is suggesting a truly healing
balm here, not the quack remedy of despair. For one of the
confusions we noted earlier springs from the fact that she
conceives of the humanitarian heroes achieving a happiness that
forever eludes the dreamer. She also knows that by living in the
everyday world one can find wonder in the human face, and music
in a happy-noted voice. She also suggests, however, that
happiness and misery are separable: 'Every sole man hath days of
joy and pain ... The pain alone; the joy alone; distinct.' This, I
think, is inconsistent with the view of life that Keats was
developing at this time, which was, I reaffirm, an acknowledgement of the duality of things. Full perception reveals reality as
neither idyllic nor tragic, but incorrigibly ambiguous,—and this, I
believe, is the intended lesson in all that Moneta says. It is, as we
shall see, the lesson of her face—a more 'wondrous lesson' than
Apollo could read in Mnemosyne's—and it is presumably one to
be ratified and elaborated, as Clymene's speech in *Hyperion*
perhaps hinted, in the memories of titanic war through which
Moneta is to conduct Keats.

Whether or not Keats could have made the legend render this
cannot now be known—it is suggestive though that the second
attempt fails sooner than the first.

Perhaps the only safe conclusion we can draw from the
expository passages in *The Fall* is that Keats was attempting a
new philosophic orientation, and the muddle with which it is introduced is due at least partly to the painfulness of the effort.
Keats did not wish to see the world as he now had to see it; he far
preferred a world in which good and evil could be separated, the
one cultivated, the other as far as possible ignored. We may
remember that Lamia's most attractive but dubious virtue was
her ability to 'unperplex bliss from its neighbour pain'. To give up
his dreams, to abstain from selective experience and fantasy
living, and to renounce the spuriously godlike form of imagination was, for Keats, an extremely difficult exercise.

Let us now turn to those aspects of the poem in which its
strength really lies, its imagery and symbolic structure. The latter
appears at first sight to be a great deal more complicated than it
really is: the main body of the poem was to be a sequence of

visions experienced in a dream within a dream. Some readers will no doubt be tempted to postulate various abstruse purposes here, and find allegories of psychological encapsulation, or advanced and privileged states of consciousness. I doubt if such lines of enquiry would prove very valuable; we will do better, I think, to take Moneta's memories and the inner dream as useful mechanisms, obviating the need for difficult transitions, and thus allowing Keats to present a sequence of symbolic scenes and actions. The outer dream, beginning at 'Methought I stood' (1:19), which was to contain all the inner elements, and thus the body of the poem, we may usefully take as a 'disciplined dream', that is, an ideal vision guided by the intellect, whose particular purpose is religious inquiry.

There is good reason to suppose that this religious inquiry had a specifically Christian dimension, as several critics have noted. Stuart Sperry says: 'By this time Milton's grand conception of the Fall and Redemption of man had come to assume a profound relevance to Keats' own awareness of both the poet's plight and dignity, the key for ordering his tragic sense of life and human destiny into a meaningful allegory of the poetic soul.[10] John Jones comments, rather unsympathetically: '. . . the undertaking is befogged in a very private, near religious atmosphere, as if Keats had thought up the doctrine of the Incarnation all on his own, and then, to provide a home for his idea, had decided to invent the New Testament.'[11] But it is Jackson Bate who offers the most stimulating comment:

> Now, for the first time in any of his longer poems, the imagery and tone begin to move directly towards the religious and the sacramental. A strong magnetic attraction towards the Biblical (both Hebraic and Christian) is countered by a strenuous effort to universalise the religious quest that approaches the 'Burden of the Mystery' with awe, humility, and fruitful (if tortured) puzzlement. In the fifty lines or so that follow [Keats's awakening in the temple] we find a coalescence of mediaeval Christendom, Judaism, (with echoes of Jacob's ladder, and the horned altar of Jehovah), and Greek and Roman antiquity.[12]

My only quibble with this is that the strong attraction to Biblical imagery is not happening for quite the first time in Keats' longer poems, as I hope I have shown. But Bate's comment is most valuable in that it points out that the elements of Christian culture that we find in *The Fall* form a whole by coalescing with other elements, largely those drawn from Greek and Roman antiquity. Certainly Keats' enquiry involves a re-examination of a creed he had already rejected, but his bewilderment is too fundamental at this period to be cured either by sectarian ideals in the strict sense, or by purely literary theorising about the role of the poet. Thus, all the elements which are fused in the imagery of the poetry, Christian, Jewish, Greek, Roman, even, as Bate subsequently points out (*loc. cit.*), Egyptian and Druidic, are all necessary to create the sense of universal import in what is going on in the poem. As Douglas Bush says: '. . . the first phases of the vision might apply as well to the spiritual evolution of the race as to that of the poet. And throughout there is a sense of the mystery, only in part apprehended, of human existence.'[13]

Paradoxically, though not surprisingly, these universal concerns spring from an extremely personal difficulty. Keats wants to know, first of all, the nature of an authentic poet, and his responsibility to the world at large. That question can be answered, it seems, only by asking and hoping to answer a much larger question: what is the nature of mankind (the poet's audience), and its place in the universe? This question leads on, almost inevitably, to the question we heard Saturn and Apollo asking in *Hyperion*, 'Who had power?' 'Where is power?' But the beginning of the quest is individual and moral. Not surprisingly then, we begin in a garden:

> Methought I stood where trees of every clime,
> Palm, myrtle, oak, and sycamore, and beech,
> With Plantane, and spice-blossoms, made a screen;
> In neighbourhood of fountains, by the noise
> Soft-showering in mine ears; and by the touch
> Of scent, not far from roses. Turning round,
> I saw an arbour with a drooping roof
> Of trellis vines, and bells, and larger blooms,
> Like floral censers swinging light in air;
> Before its wreathed doorway, on a mound
> Of moss, was spread a feast of summer fruits,

Which, nearer seen, seem'd refuse of a meal
By Angel tasted, or our Mother Eve;
For empty shells were scattered on the grass,
And grape stalks but half bare, and remnants more,
Sweet-smelling, whose pure kinds I could not know.
Still was more plenty than the fabled horn
Thrice emptied could pour forth at banqueting
For Proserpine return'd to her own fields,
Where the white heifers low. And appetite
More yearning than on earth I ever felt
Growing within, I ate deliciously.

$$(1:19-40)$$

Immediately we recognise the special excellence of Keats' symbolic description at its best—that peculiar resonance when two memories are stirred at once, either harmoniously or with purposeful discord. There is a suggestion of pagan plenty here, the grape stalks 'but half bare' bring to mind a lolling Bacchus; the words 'banqueting' and 'horn' suggest the cornucopia of the old gods. But we are reminded of another source of bounty by the mention of 'Angel' and 'our Mother Eve'. The garden itself is familiar; the 'trees of every clime' which 'make a screen,' the 'spice-blossoms' and the fountains with a 'noise soft-showering'—all these derive from *Paradise Lost*: '. . . a circling row/ Of goodliest trees, loaden with fairest fruit' (4:146 – 7); 'Out of the fertile ground he caused to grow/ All trees of noblest kind for sight, smell, taste' (4:216 – 17); '. . . Now gentle gales/ Fanning their odoriferous wings, dispense/ Native perfumes, and whisper whence they stole/ Those balmy spoils' (4:156 – 59); '. . . through veins/ Of porous earth with kindly thirst updrawn/ Rose a fresh fountain, and with many a rill/ Watered the garden' (4:227 – 30). A more important memory is from Book 5; Keats' empty shells and grape stalks remind us, as does his food 'by Angel tasted', of the meal Eve prepared for Raphael:

For drink the grape
She crushes, inoffensive must, and meaths
From many a berry, and from sweetest kernel pressed
She tempers dulcet creams.

$$(5:344-7)$$

The reverberations touched off by Keats' passage are not due merely to two cultural sources—it is two moral possibilities we apprehend at once. Whose hospitality has provided this feast—that of mankind's first parents, or that of Bacchus? Who crushed the grapes, innocent Eve, or Proserpine? What is the nature of the act which the whole scene invites the poet to perform? The uncertainty here is not confusion, it symbolises moral perplexity. As Jackson Bate has said: '... this is something of an Eden, but an Eden strangely used ... A "feast of summer fruits" is spread as if in welcome. It is only on closer scrutiny that this feast is seen to be the refuse left by other visitors from an innocent remote past.'[14] But it is not entirely certain that this is a legacy from an innocent past, or that it is, as Bate suggests a little later, a sacramental meal. Why has it been so untidily left? Why has Keats been, as it seems, presented with it? What, in short, will the poet do if he eats and drinks?

Keats decides to do what the scene invites him to do, not knowing the significance of his action. There is a strong hint, though, of what that significance may be. Milton's Eve, in her dream of temptation, has the fruit at her lips:

> So saying he drew nigh, and to me held
> Even to my mouth, of that same fruit held part
> Which he had plucked; the pleasant savoury smell
> So quickened appetite that I methought
> Could not but taste.
>
> (5:82 – 6)

Keats is similarly overcome: 'And appetite/ More yearning than on earth I ever felt/ Growing within, I ate deliciously' (1:38 – 40). Having eaten he becomes thirsty, and drinks from 'a cool vessel of transparent juice' (1:42). As he does so he pledges 'all the Mortals of the world' (1:44). He is not, I think, merely wishing good health to all and sundry, he is recognising himself as momentarily representing 'all the Mortals of the world' in ritually re-enacting the sin of Adam. (That this in fact is what he has done is borne out, I suggest, by the fact that Moneta, in allowing him to enter her visionary memory, enables him to 'see as a God sees'—1:304.) Having drunk, he falls into a swoon, and awakes to find himself in the shattered remains of a temple sacred to a god whose identity he does not know.

I suggest that this awakening has a fairly simple symbolic function. Keats has, in re-enacting Adam's fault, acknowledged the fallen condition of man. I am not attributing this conception to Keats in the strictest theological sense—it has a wide application which sceptics may use quite happily. Man aspires beyond his capacities, and hungers beyond his means, and is confused, perverse and frightened. At the same time he is able to conceive of an ideal creature living in a perfect world. This disparity between the supposed potential and the perceived actual may dramatically be envisioned as a disastrous falling away from a former state. But it is the gap between the conceivable and the known that constitutes man's sense of 'fallenness', and this sense all men share. Keats awakes then, a confessedly fallen being, amid the ruins of a great religion. The parallel between Keats the protagonist in his own poem, and Keats the nineteenth-century liberal man is obvious. the temple is not, *pace* Stillinger, 'clearly the temple of poetry'; it represents the moral and social culture that Keats was born into—a culture based on a corrupt and apparently moribund Anglicanism. But there remains in the temple a sole priestess.

Not surprisingly then, an examination of the ruins sets off characteristically Keatsian resonances:

> I look'd around upon the carved sides
> Of an old sanctuary with roof august,
> Builded so high, it seem'd that filmed clouds
> Might spread beneath, as o'er the stars of heaven;
> So old the place was, I remembered none
> The like upon the earth: what I had seen
> Of grey Cathedrals, buttress'd walls, rent towers,
> The superannuations of sunk realms,
> Or Nature's Rocks toil'd hard in waves and winds,
> Seem'd but the faulture of decrepit things
> To that eternal domed monument.
> Upon the marble at my feet there lay
> Store of strange vessels, and large draperies,
> Which needs had been of dyed asbestos wove,
> Or in that place the moth could not corrupt,

So white the linen; so, in some, distinct
Ran imageries from a sombre loom.
All in a mingled heap confus'd there lay
Robes, golden tongs, censer and chafing dish,
Girdles, and chains, and holy jewelries—
    Turning from these with awe, once more I rais'd
My eyes to fathom the space every way;
The embossed roof, the silent massy range
Of columns north and south, ending in mist
Of nothing; then to Eastward, where black gates
Were shut against the sunrise evermore.

                                        (1:61 – 86)

Keats acknowledges the part played in building up this picture by
Fingal's cave, Crossraguel Abbey, and Winchester Cathedral, but
there is more than architecture to suggest Christian associations.
There is also what George Herbert called 'glorious household
stuff'.[15] The altar cloths, tongs, chafing dishes, censers and so on
are all as Christian as they are Greek. The Biblical echo now seems
inevitable: 'that place the moth could not corrupt' is a direct
allusion to *Matthew* 6:20. One can have no doubt that the
mythological doubling here is fully conscious. That being so, we
may also expect a certain hostility and resentment to show
themselves. Anti-clericalism has already provided the image of
'poison gender'd in close monkish cell/ To thin the scarlet
conclave of old men' (1:49 – 50). Perhaps also the black gates 'shut
against the sunrise evermore' constitute a symbolic thrust against
the puritanism and obscurantism of the church, or they may, as
Stuart Sperry suggests, represent the more punitive aspects of
Christian doctrine: 'The shut gates symbolise the impossibility of
a return to innocence or to the garden, they bring to mind the
great eastern gate of Paradise which closes behind the human
pair.'[16] What is surprising though, is that there are so few such
thrusts; the general tone of the description of the fabric and
furnishings of the shrine is detached, curious, and awe-struck. As
Douglas Bush has noted, we see here: '"the pious frauds of
Religion" ... contemplated with imaginative sympathy.'[17]

    This certainly reflects a new detachment in Keats' outlook.
One must remember that the revision of *Hyperion* was begun at
Shanklin, and continued at Winchester during September and

October 1819. Keats moved to Winchester for the sake of a library, but once there his letters proclaim his delight in the cathedral. He appears to have made daily visits to its precincts, and of the many allusions to it in letters to various correspondents, the most interesting is surely this, to Fanny Brawne:

> At Winchester I shall get your Letters more readily; and it being a cathedral City I shall have the pleasure always a great one to me when near a Cathedral, of reading them during the service up and down the Aisle.
>
> (2:137)

The following lines may be alluding to this practice:

> Towards the altar sober-pac'd I went,
> Repressing haste, as too unholy there;
> And, coming nearer, saw beside the shrine
> One minist'ring; and there arose a flame.
> When in mid-May the sickening East Wind
> Shifts sudden to the South, the small warm rain
> Melts out the frozen incense from all flowers,
> And fills the air with so much pleasant health
> That even the dying man forgets his shroud;
> Even so that lofty sacrificial fire,
> Sending forth maian incense, spread around
> Forgetfulness of everything but bliss.
>
> (1:93 – 104)

I don't know how much incense, if any, was burned at Winchester Cathedral at this time—but Keats had come across a small Catholic community in the town: 'We have a Collegiate School, a roman catholic School; a chapel ditto and a Nunnery!' (*Letters* 2:148). There is also a sprinkling of ecclesiastical Latinisms in his letters at this time (for example '*Incipit Epistola Caledoniensa*'—2:196); he may well have smelled incense being burned. But what is most interesting here is the tone of sympathy and respect as Keats moves 'sober-pac'd/ Repressing haste as too unholy there'. Also deserving notice is the delight he takes in ritual and its associated sensuous pleasure, for under the guise of rejoicing in the odours emanating from the flames he smuggles in a hint of Christianity's most seductive offer:

> When in mid-May the sickening East Wind
> Shifts sudden to the South, the small warm rain
> Melts out the frozen incense from all flowers,
> And fills the air with so much pleasant health
> That even the dying man forgets his shroud.

There is a vernal resurrection here, a sense of irrepressible and fragrant life released from winter; and this subtle odour is cunningly linked with the incense burnt on the altar. But most powerful of all is the implied prolepsis in the last lines—the dying man is already free from his coming shroud. Keats had not yet suffered his first haemorrhage, but his lingering sore throat must have given him fears that he might soon himself be a dying man. But we are all dying, and the gloom and fear of death increasingly 'shroud' our later years. It is precisely this 'shroud' that the doctrine of resurrection enables believers to forget, in the sense that they are no longer oppressed by it. There can be little doubt of Keats' increasingly urgent wish to believe such a doctrine, and the evidence is that from time to time he believed something like it. 'I have scarce a doubt of immortality of some nature or other' (2:4) he tells George and Georgiana Keats. But a few months later he writes despairingly to Fanny Brawne: 'I long to believe in immortality' (2:293). A confident and steady faith was beyond him, and 'things' as he had complained to Reynolds 'cannot to the will/ Be settled' (*Epistle* 76 – 7). Keats must now encounter the 'one minist'ring' at the altar.

   Moneta is certainly something greater than the mother of the muses. Kenneth Muir's more universal conception of her figurative role is probably right: 'Apparently Keats intended her to be the priestess of Truth, who had outlived the various manifestations of truth in different ages of the world.'[18] That being so her effect on Keats is appropriately paradoxical. He is both repelled and attracted by her, as people commonly are by the prospect of truth—'But for her eyes I should have fled away./ They held me back with a benignant light' (1:264 – 65); 'As near as an immortal's sphered words/ Could to a mother's soften were these last:/ But yet I had a terror of her robes,/ And chiefly of the veils ...' (1:249 – 52). But as I implied earlier, Moneta, as Keats first sees her, probably had an objective correlative in some ministrant at the altar of Winchester Cathedral; thus his ambivalence towards her may reflect his response to Christianity, with a bloodstained reality at the heart of its liturgical and mystical beauty. For Moneta is indeed a rather dubious saviour figure. Her very credentials are imperfect, for when we met her in *Hyperion* under the name of Mnemosyne (Keats twice calls her this in *The Fall*) she was a renegade Titan fostering the dynastic foe Apollo.

Now, like a scurvy politician, she seems to have changed sides again. Her manner of speech is not reassuring. Christ was often angry and forthright in denunciation, but never contemptuous as Moneta is. She refers to dreamers as a 'tribe', and speaks to Keats of 'such things as thou art', and asks 'What bliss, even in hope, is there for thee?' (1:169). The ordeal she imposes on the poet he feels as a form of 'tyranny' and 'fierce threat' (1:119 – 20). It is also, one may think, a cheat. Much ink has been vainly spilled in interpreting the change in Keats once he has reached the top of the steps, but there is no evidence in the poem that there has been any change whatsoever. Moneta indicates that all that the poet has won is a postponement of his fate. Keas has not wrung from this saviour what the dying thief achieved; he has merely 'dated on' his doom (1:144 –45) by passing a painful test. It is not his success that has gained this respite, but merely his ability to succeed, which was his before he mounted the steps: 'That thou hadst power to do so/ Is thine own safety' (1:143 – 44).

One cannot quite rule out the possibility that Moneta is the serpent rather than the saviour, just as the faith which Keats may now be re-examining may be the evil thing he has long thought it to be. For although Moneta is a figure within the inner dream, she knows about the garden where Keats ate his stupefying meal, and one may suppose that as 'supreme/ Sole priestess' of the temple, she arranges the admission of 'such things' as Keats. The meal then, may have been hers, and the offer, or temptation, may have been hers. But what was the food she offered—the eucharist or the apple? For although, as we have seen, Keats' eating and drinking was a ritualistic 'Fall' it may have been a necessary one, a *felix culpa* whereby he could gain the moral knowledge he longs for, and as a poet must have, 'the lore of good and ill'. Not surprisingly then, the reward of Keats' symbolic sin is knowledge, which he is to acquire by entering into Moneta's mind. What Keats was going to do with the sequence of Moneta's memories we cannot know. What we undoubtedly have, superbly rendered by the controlled ambiguity of the symbols and action of the poem, is the bewilderment of a bereaved and frightened man looking for help to what seems to him the remnants of a discredited tradition.

The symbolic ambiguity of the goddess is perhaps best epitomised in Keats' description of her face. This is one of the two passages in *The Fall* which I earlier cited as possibly justifying, in spite of all the expository muddle, the opinion that the poem is a greater achievement than *Hyperion*:

> This saw that Goddess, and with sacred hand
> Parted the veils. Then I saw a wan face,
> Not pin'd by human sorrows, but bright blanch'd
> By an immortal sickness which kills not;
> It works a constant change, which happy death
> Can put no end to; deathwards progressing
> To no death was that visage; it had pass'd
> The lily and the snow; and beyond these
> I must not think now, though I saw that face—
> But for her eyes I should have fled away.
> They held me back, with a benignant light,
> Soft-mitigated with divinest lids
> Half-closed, and visionless entire they seem'd
> Of all external things—they saw me not,
> But in blank splendour beam'd like the mild moon,
> Who comforts those she sees not, who knows not
> What eyes are upward cast.
>
> (1:255 – 71)

Claude Finney is probably right in suggesting that the human prototype for this picture was the face of Tom Keats.[19] The constant change towards a death which, to a compassionate nurse, seems to delay too cruelly, must have been the cause of Keats' most painful hours in the weeks of caring for his dying brother. But Moneta's face undoubtedly also has a kerygmatic prototype, and there is a wide consensus among critics on the identity of this. Joan Grundy has commented: 'Keats' Moneta is daringly conceived, perhaps more daringly than he realised, for she invites comparison with the King of Sorrows.'[20] Middleton Murry considers the passage: 'a great poet's vision of God—but of a godhead immanent in the changing enduring reality of the world.'[21] According to D.G. James, the chief character of the face is: 'the union of great suffering with luminous and profound peace. It is both frightening and comforting, exhausted and inexhaustible, agonised and calm, defeated and triumphant.' She does not represent, according to James, a 'high impersonal order', the worship which Keats as protagonist in the poem extends to her is: 'warmed with a love which is saturated by our values . . . We can hardly read the lines which portray the countenance of Mnemosyne without seeing the face of the agonised Christ.'[22]

Stuart Sperry, although agreeing in general terms with James's reading, enters a particular caveat: 'The conception of Moneta's suffering as an "immortal sickness" involves a paradox not ordinarily associated with the finality of Christ's passion. Her suffering is a living death, a misery that never ends, but must endure through countless ages.'[23] This is a shrewd point, but it can be answered. In the first place Sperry seems to conflate Christ's suffering and his redemptive act. I am not sure that this is justifiable, and I suspect that knowledgeable Christians might ascribe finality only to the redemption, leaving it a matter of speculation whether or not Christ continues to suffer. It is a nice point, about which one feels quite sure there must be a good deal of theological dispute from time to time. But much more pertinently, I suggest Sperry's understanding of James's phrase 'the face of the agonised Christ' is rather too literal. When I spoke earlier of a prototype other than Tom Keats for Moneta's face, I was careful to use the term 'kerygmatic'. By this I was alluding to the image of Christ crucified proclaimed not merely by apostles and churchmen, but by artists through the centuries. Leaving out of account highly disputable objects such as the vernicle and the Turin shroud, the only pictures we have of the suffering Christ are imaginative creations.

Let us consider this for a moment in the light of Sperry's description of Moneta's suffering as a 'paradox not ordinarily associated with the finality of Christ's passion'. In what does the paradox consist? Are we to imagine Moneta's face actually becoming ever more stricken with age, without the prospect of release in death? Did Keats have in mind for her a fate similar to Hesiod's Tithonous, growing always loathsomely older, yet remaining immortal?[24] Perhaps we might do well here to remember Saturn's decrepitude. In *Hyperion* we are simply presented with it, and accept it because it is so finely rendered. In *The Fall* however, Keats justifies it with magnificent economy when Moneta explains to the poet: '... this old Image here,/ Whose carved features wrinkled as he fell,/ Is Saturn's' (1:224 – 26). If we remember that Moneta shows her face to Keats because he cannot see the face of the god, we may draw inferences that ratify James's perception of the matter quite dramatically. When Moneta parts the veils, she does for the poet what Christ's death achieved for the religious consciousness of a large section of mankind: 'The veil of the temple was rent in the midst' (*Luke* 23:45).

According, once more, to D.G. James, 'Christianity has said that our imaginations can endure the huge reality of evil and pain only when we see it freely endured by God himself.'[25] Keats, knowing that he must, if he is to be a true poet, endure the 'huge reality', has asked to see Saturn as St Philip asked to see God; Moneta shows her own face, as Christ revealed his divinity to Philip: 'He that hath seen me hath seen the Father' (*John* 14:9). Also, Moneta is representing a god whose features 'wrinkled as he fell'—that is, while he suffered. But the marks of his suffering have been carved into his image. They are a permanent aspect of a devotee's consciousness of him. So with Christ, the marks of his passion are permanent in the consciousness of believers. The Christian can scarcely conceive of Christ in glory, but he can imagine that which some men did see, and that which he believes matters to him above all things. Christ's face too 'wrinkled as he fell'—his suffering is part of his descent from divinity to mortality. Like Saturn's sculptor, the Christian has carved into his image of an eternal God the suffering of a God caught in the aspect of limitation.

I put forward this interpretation not as a means of refuting Sperry, but as a means of reconciling his view with that of James. Chiefly though, I put it forward as a means of understanding the full power of the paradoxes in Keats' description. Moneta's face is a living face presented as an image, a clue to the nature of a god. It thus presents a god caught in mortal form. It suffering is divine suffering, but felt as mortals feel it; its mutable aspect is that of a god who, though immortal, has suffered the pangs of mortality, and who, in the consciousness of believers, will always do so. Bearing all this in mind, we can see that the paradox of change and stability that pervades the description is precisely the paradox of pictorial art—the look, gesture or position that suggests continuance, and the appearance that bespeaks process, are forever held still. Moneta's face, in Keats' lines, is like a great painting of a dying person, constantly changing as new aspects are discovered, yet always the same; the subject is always 'deathwards progressing/ To no death'. The face of the agonised Christ has been seen in the mirror of art.

The greatest image in the passage is not a paradox, though it is an antithesis. Moneta's countenance, 'had pass'd/ the lily and the snow'. The simple juxtaposition here perhaps deserves a place besides Wordsworth's sublime 'violet by a mossy stone'. Wordsworth's image emphasises community and contrast together—both objects are things of nature, but one is alive and mortal, the other dead and unchanging. The community in Keats' objects is at first glance greater than in Wordsworth's image; 'lily' and 'snow' both suggest beauty, purity, and transience. The effect is to emphasise the difference; the lily is alive and organic, suggesting growth, generation and return; snow is insentient, cold, inimical to the frail life of the bloom, yet itself providing the moisture that must nourish the corm, and itself vulnerable to the sun that will bring on the flower.

As an image of the interpenetration of life and death, of the manner in which these opposites are brought together in their complementary and mutually intensifying beauty, Keats' juxtaposition is superb. Also, we must remember that Moneta's face has 'pass'd/ The lily and the snow'. The inseparable doubleness of things is part of her consciousness; the experience which sickened Keats at Teignmouth, and wrinkled Saturn's features as he fell, has been accepted by her as a revelation of an eternal order in which the lily and the snow are reconciled. Yet the greatest paradox of the whole passage lies in the fact that it may indeed be read in a sense quite opposite to the one I have suggested. Though I am inclined to disagree with Sperry's reading, I acknowledge that what we see in Moneta may be 'the vision of the fallen Adam unrelieved by any promise of redemption'.[26] Both possibilities are always present, and this, perhaps, is the source of the deepest poignancy of the whole passage. For this is the ultimate doubleness of things, and constitutes the 'wondrous lesson' of Moneta's face.

I now wish to pass on to an aspect of *The Fall* that seems to me to have received too little attention—overshadowed no doubt by the dominant business of Moneta. When he revised his myth, Keats developed Saturn in an interesting, though not entirely successful way. The god's speeches seem to have been tinkered with in an attempt to make them less Miltonic and more Shakespearean—and this doesn't quite come off. Saturn's repeated 'moan' (1:412–38 *passim*) is almost ludicrous, and never approaches the pathos of Lear's repetitions of 'howl' and 'never'. But Keats does seem to have intended to strengthen Saturn's resemblance to Lear, and he seems at one point to give us a hint where to look to identify our memory:

> So he feebly ceas'd,
> With such a poor and sickly sounding pause,
> Methought I heard some old man of the earth
> Bewailing earthly loss
>
> (1:438–41)

Saturn's words alert us to his resemblance to the father of Goneril and Regan: 'Moan, Cybele, moan; for thy pernicious babes/ Have changed a god into a shaking palsy' (1:425–26). This also has the effect of strengthening our misgivings about the Olympians as the dynasty with whom we ought to sympathise.

But the most remarkable development in Keats' conception of Saturn consists in a passage of eight lines, entirely new in tone and substance, inserted into what was his first speech in *Hyperion* (1:95–134) and is his only speech in *The Fall* (1:412–38):

> '. . .for lo! the rebel spheres
> Spin round, the stars their antient courses keep,
> Clouds still with shadowy moisture haunt the earth,
> Still suck their fill of light from sun and moon,
> Still buds the tree, and still the sea-shores murmur,

> There is no death in all the universe
> No smell of Death.'
>
> (1:418–24)

These lines, as I have quoted them, isolated from their context, strike a note of marvellous philosophic optimism, and offer a religious vision of the highest and most reassuring kind. A Christian mystic might hear the voice of God promising that all shall be well, and all manner of things shall be well; Saturn seems to affirm that all things *are* well. Even the aspects of things that seem to mar the vision of eternal vitality in fact contribute to it—the clouds are full of sustaining moisture for the earth they cast in shadow, and they transmit to it the energy, the 'fill of light' they have sucked from sun and moon. Seasonal life and death is a tidal force, not merely repetitive, but inexhaustibly creative: 'Still buds the tree, and still the sea-shores murmur.' Change itself is the servant of permanence. Saturn seems to be proclaiming the same message that Coelus hints at in *Hyperion*, that of 'beauteous life/ Diffus'd unseen throughout eternal space'. Keats' fallen god does better than St Paul, who proclaimed that 'The last enemy that shall be destroyed is death' (1 *Corinthians* 15:26). In Saturn's vision 'There is no death in all the universe/ No smell of Death.' We might note not merely the optimistic substance of all this; there is in the tone of the passage a familiar note of reflective confidence. In particular the lines 'Clouds ... Still suck their fill of light from sun and moon,/ Still buds the tree, and still the seashores murmur' remind us, almost irresistibly, of Wordsworth's *Afterthought*, though it seems unlikely that Keats could have known the sonnet (published in 1820):

> For backward, Duddon, as I cast my eyes,
> I see what was, and is, and shall abide.
> Still glides the stream, and shall for ever glide.

In fact the only false note in Keats' passages as I have quoted it is the word 'rebel'.

When we replace the passage in its immediate context, the effect is strange to the point of perversity. Immediately before the first words of my extract is the half-line 'Moan, brethren moan', and at the end, after 'No smell of Death' Saturn cries out 'there shall be death'. The false note of 'rebel' soon becomes explicable; Saturn is wailing the fact that he and his fellow Titans are no longer responsible for the mechanical operations of the universe. He had begun his speech by literally bemoaning that 'we are swallowed up/ And buried from all godlike exercise/ Of influence benign on planets pale/ And peaceful sway above man's harvesting' (1:412–415). Thus deprived of powers, they could find comfort, and perhaps hope, if things were going amiss. Unfortunately things have gone on with unfaltering perfection; the new gods, it seems, are adequate to their task.

The vision of eternal harmony, unmarred by death, has thus become a nightmare vision for the vanquished gods. Hence Saturn's cry 'there shall be death' is an outburst of revanchist malice, rather like the Duchess of Malfi's curse to which Bosola replies 'Look you, the stars shine still.'[27] We begin to see depths of irony here. Beauty's triumph is the cause of all the pain and sorrow of the Titans, those 'families of grief' (1:461) who 'waste in pain' (1:462). But this is not the end of the damage done by beauty—there is to be another war, and the magnificent apocalypse envisaged by Saturn, with its 'hymns of festival', 'voices of soft proclaim and silver stir/ Of strings in hollow shells', and 'Beautiful things made new' is to be bought at the cost of 'other groans'. Even worse, perhaps, the hate and rage provoked by beauty's triumph has so distorted the vision of the defeated side that their king, viewing a universe of inexhaustible resource and harmony, can only cry 'Moan, brethren, moan', and vow to bring death into it.

There may be an even deeper irony. We do not know to what extent Oceanus' larger thesis in *Hyperion* was to be carried forward into *The Fall*. If it was to be assumed more or less intact into the second version, then the victorious gods remain as vulnerable as their victims—they too are limited. Apollo can no more interfere with the operations of the dawn than Hyperion could—he is not the first of powers nor the last. The continuing harmony of the universe which causes Saturn so much anguish is not evidence of the Olympians' superiority, it represents an immutable order anterior and superior to Titans and Olympians alike, to which both sets of gods are or have been privileged servants. And Oceanus' comfort to his fellows is seen once more to be valid. Peace and content can be restored to the Titans by their acknowledgement that they, like their conquerors are secondary powers. The nightmare vision will then become what it appeared to be, a vision of peace, order, and eternal vitality. To achieve this, of course, the Titans must 'die into life', acknowledging their status as dependent beings. Having done so, they may then experience Clymene's supereme paradox 'of joy and grief at once'.

Let us not assume from this that Keats was approaching some form of religious decision. He seems to postulate, implicitly, in Oceanus' larger thesis, and symbolically in Saturn's vision, an order of things to which the gods are servants. But he is careful not to identify this order of things. It may not be God, and it may not love us. On the other hand, he establishes clearly enough the unsatisfactory nature of the 'shap'd and palpable gods', and anthropomorphic theism is in some ways hard to distinguish from certain brash forms of humanism. One thinks naturally, of course, of Tamburlaine. We know how contemptuous Keats was of the 'Godwin-methodists', the 'perfectibility men'. In depicting the downfall of the Titans, and implying thereby the vulnerability of the Olympians, the poem may be saying that mankind must abandon its more hubristic aspirations, and recognise its dependency on that unidentifiable but 'beauteous life/ Diffus'd unseen throughout eternal space'. And this perhaps is Oceanus' vision, and such comfort as there may be in it is the balm which the true poet pours out upon the world.

7

Nightingale and Melancholy

Keats' love narratives were concerned principally with subjective judgement and the special difficulty the mind experiences, when stimulated by so powerful an emotion as sexual desire, of distinguishing between object and image. *Hyperion* and *The Fall* were meant to be even more subjective, for they were supposed to be, in narrative guise, examinations of the sensibility of a great poet, conducted, almost certainly, in the hope of finding that Keats' own sensibility corresponded sufficiently to the Apollonian ideal to justify the hazardous career for which he had abandoned Apollo's other demesne, medicine. In this sense even the early version of *Hyperion* was to have been Keats' *Prelude* rather than his *Paradise Lost*; and in both versions we may detect an aspect of the truly egotistical sublime. In both versions, however, we also see Keats being lured out of his private concern into an examination of the great common concerns of humankind—the pathetic dualism of the aspirations and limitations of human nature, and the universal hunger for the perception of some principle whereby the great human and natural paradoxes might be resolved.

The four greatest odes, which I am now going to consider, represent a return to private and subjective matters; but now, although there remains a substantial concern with the problem of perception, the most painful difficulty is what to make of reality rather than how to recognise it. The need to grasp some 'lore of good and ill' has been made bitterly sharp by personal grief, frustration, and fear. Consequently the symbolism by which these themes are expressed becomes astonishingly complex and oxymoronic. The imagery and diction of the odes is pervasively antithetical, and the richness of the poetry so engendered is perhaps the finest product of Keats' own negative capability. For the odes express an aporetic rather than a tragic vision of life, and they constitute something which may be unique in the greatest literature—the achievement of a highly ordered, controlled and sophisticated art springing from radical bewilderment.

For purposes of discussion I have chosen to group the odes in pairs. I take *Nightingale* and *Melancholy* together because although they differ greatly from each other in total effect, they have certain important aspects in common. Both are impassioned, reflecting personal anguish; both insist on the supreme value of unclouded consciousness. The *Grecian Urn* and *Autumn* are meditative rather than impassioned; both operate by means of symbolic picture-making, yet depend for their most important effects on modulation of tone; both form ironic commentaries on certain cherished doctrines of contemporary humanism. The element which all four odes have in common is implicit debate.

That the *Ode to a Nightingale* is a form of meditative disputation is by no means a new perception, and the poem has been most aptly described by Jackson Bate as a 'form of lyric debate that moves actively towards drama'.[1] I believe, however, that the ode has not yet been fully examined from this point of view, partly because the very concept of debate is apt to misdirect a reader's attention. One is tempted to suppose a single issue to be argued, a 'motion' in the Oxford Union sense. The proposer and the opposer become a pair of abstract adversaries; thus Allen Tate described the central problem of the ode as the 'antinomy of the ideal and the real'.[2] The consequences of this conception, which is now widely accepted, are distressing.

Take, for example, Jack Stillinger's view of the structure of the poem. As I mentioned earlier, he offers us a 'blackboard diagram', consisting of a horizontal line 'separating the actual world (below) and the ideal (above)', and the progress of the poem's supposed thought is represented by a broken line starting somewhere below the solid line at a point A, and proceeding to a point B somewhere above it. From point B the broken line returns at a rather obtuse angle to point A1, about the same depth below the solid line as point A, but much further to the right. Stillinger assures us that the poet could not have gone directly from A to A1. From this point on Stillinger becomes, I believe, oversimplistic. 'The two realms,' he tells us, 'have many common labels: earth and heaven, mortality and immortality, time and eternity, materiality and spirituality, the known and the unknown, the finite and the infinite, realism and romance, and so on.'[3] Stillinger seems to propose that since all the first terms in these pairs undoubtedly belong to the actual, all the second terms must be consignable to the unreal, hence they must all be of the same nature and status, and of equal value. Scientists and mathematicians may not, I think, agree that 'the unknown' belongs to the same realm as 'romance', and astronomers might be chary of setting finite limits to the actual.

One suspects that Stillinger's sorting of conceptions into ideal and real is much too tidy. A more important objection to his scheme concerns that very horizontal line itself. To suppose that such a line can be drawn is to ignore that central problem of human subjectivity that so painfully engaged Keats' attention in his love narratives, particularly *Lamia*. It ignores too the question of the status of the products of human subjectivity—the things which Keats calls 'semi-real', and Karl Popper assigns to his 'World Three'.[4] Also, it ignores, of course, centuries of epistemological striving. In the *Ode to a Nightingale* Keats' conception of the two worlds, and the relations between them, is much more complicated and much less assured than Stillinger's, and there is one point in the ode where the poet speculates that a line such as the 'blackboard diagram' postulates does not in fact exist, that materiality and spirituality may be neither separable nor discontinuous. As Bate has said, the poem is: 'no simple dialogue of the divided heart with itself between two choices.'[5]

Another danger in the notion of debate is the assumption that, a motion having been argued, a result must be declared. Richard Harter Fogle has said: 'In the *Nightingale* Keats is ... affirming the value of the ideal, and this is the primary fact.'[6] Cleanth Brooks and Robert Penn Warren on the other hand see the knowledge of mortality overshadowing the whole ode: 'The word "buried" conveys, in this context, (lines 77 – 8) a view of death very different from that conjured up by "embalmed darkness' in the fifth stanza.'[7] This itch to find a decision in the poem is perhaps connected with an itch to place the poet in a school of thought—'we have learned,' says Stillinger, '[to see] Keats primarily as a humanist.'[8]

My own view is that what is achieved in great poetry is much more interesting than decision-making; consequently I shall deny

myself the satisfaction of philosophic labelling. In reading the
Ode to a Nightingale I shall try neither to extrapolate a statement,
nor to recruit Keats into an ideological camp. Nor is it my
intention to trace a line of argument, for as Bate has said, this ode,
together with the *Ode on a Grecian Urn*, is the 'most striking
single precedent ... for the modern poetic development of
symbolic debate' (my italics).[9] David Perkins has identified the
singular vitality of Keats' symbols: 'With Shelley, for example,
symbolism provides a way of translating the abstract into the
concrete. His attitudes are already formed ... But with Keats a
poem is more likely to be a dynamic process of cognition carried
on by means of a symbol.'[10]

Although I cite this as a most valuable comment, I have two
reservations. First, Perkins seems to suggest that there is a single,
dominant symbol in such a poem as the *Nightingale*. I believe that
there are several symbols implicit in the poem, and that these interact with each other, as well as with the controlling one. Secondly, I
believe that there is also a dynamic process going on somewhat below the level of cognition, and I hope to identify such activity in the
course of this discussion. My object is to illustrate, by showing
the complexity of the interrelationships of the symbols and of the
imagery and diction Keats uses, the truth of Bate's further
comment: '... the Odes are analogous to experience as a whole.
We therefore continue to return to them as we could not if they
betrayed experience by oversimplifying it.'[11]

How far the *Ode to a Nightingale* is from such simplification we
can gauge from the fact that it is full of opposites and alternatives,
and it raises an extraordinary number of questions to which only
tentative answers may be possible. There is no single, formally
stated question to be discussed, as Tate, Stillinger and others
seem to imply, but a number of interrelated ones. 'Is human
consciousness immortal?' seems to be the dominating question,
but there is a moment in the poem where the prospect of
annihilation seems so restful that the matter of immortality
becomes secondary to the question whether or not life is worth
enduring.

Other questions in their turn become primary. Is
consciousness itself so valuable that either its extinction by death,
or its reduction by drugs, wine, or mere comforting fancy, must
be resisted to the very end? Is the traditional hope of immortality,

argued by Socrates and affirmed by the Bible, a matter of revelation, or merely another offering of wistful daydreams? All these questions, shifting and interchanging as they do, contribute to the fullness of the poem's meaning. But what makes the ode great is the fact that the problems are all debated subterraneously, in conflicting implications of the imagery, the nuances of diction and phrasing, and even in the rhythm of punctuation.

One does not expect a logical sequence in a debate so conducted; nevertheless the poem has an inner shape, a construction based on two pairs of opposed symbols, their relationship to each other, and to the controlling symbol of the bird's voice. First, and very obviously, we have two different worlds, represented by the substance of stanzas two, three, and five. Secondly, we have two kinds of burial, one represented by by lines 11 - 14, the other by lines 59, 60, 62. The first six stanzas of the ode are an intense, painful meditation on these opposites, tending steadily, in spite of momentary springs of vitality and joy, toward despair. But when despair itself seems to have been reached in the last lines of stanza six, the mood is obliterated by the astounding declarations of the first two lines of stanza seven. Nor does this confidence fade immediately; it is maintained through the next five lines, collapsing only in the last three lines of the stanza. But it would be wrong to suppose that the rest of the poem consists only in a return to the terms and feeling of the earlier debate. The uncertainty expressed in the final stanza is, because of what happens in stanza seven, of a very different quality from the wistful scepticism of the rest of the ode. Let us now try to follow the whole of this disputation as closely as we can.

The first major subject is introduced obliquely, and to understand the allusion fully we need to note that the statements in the first two lines of the poem are distinguished from each other. The painful numbness of the senses does not extend to Keats' heart (the fact that Keats is here using 'heart' figuratively does not, in this context, vitiate its allusive function). When we remember the physical details of Socrates' death, 'hemlock' becomes very specific in its implications. Keats is imagining his own early death to be a very immediate prospect indeed ('... when [the numbness] reached the heart Socrates would be gone').[12] We should remember how Socrates spent his last hours before accepting the executioner's cup, and it is a reasonable speculation that as he lay under the blanket, waiting for advancing coldness, his mind was once more engaged in an urgent rehearsal of the arguments for the immortality of the soul. But Keats may have flinched from quite such immediate apprehension of death, hence, perhaps, he provides a substitute for hemlock. The sense of ebbing consciousness becomes narcotically Lethean, not Stygian.

At this point Keats introduces another theme, associated with the theme of death. He shrinks from the hemlock which he suspects nature will soon force upon him, but he appears to choose opiate eagerly, emptying the alternative cup 'to the drains'. Hemlock would finally extinguish consciousness, laudanum would merely suspend it, or reduce it to dream consciousness—a welcome reduction in the face of hearbreak, pain and fear. The rest of the stanza implies, however, that Keats shrinks from the alternative too. The phrases 'happy lot', 'too happy in thine happiness', 'light-winged Dryad', 'melodious plot', 'beechen green', and 'Singest of summer in full-throated ease' strike such surprising notes of joy that they constitute a rebellion against the mortifying numbness offered by either chalice, and the heartache is transmuted by having its source in happiness. There is a curious shuttling of emotional states here; Keats' heart aches, line six implies, because the supreme happiness must end, but the fact of the inescapable end reveals and glorifies the happiness. Keats is surprised by joy not because he has found it at the heart of pain, but because he has found mortality to be a catalyst of happiness.

A third subject implicitly introduced in the last four lines of this stanza concerns the nature of the nightingale itself, and this problem may be associated with the doubt about whether the reader is to suppose himself experiencing the poem in darkness or daylight. In stanza four Keats speaks of moon and stars, in stanza six of midnight, and in stanza seven of 'this passing night', but the first stanza speaks of 'beechen green and shadows numberless'. The possible explanation that darkness falls during the progress of the poem is scarcely satisfactory, for there are no transitional images, no dusk or lingering sunset.[13] The matter may, of course, be merely a solecism, but it may be functional. Just possibly Keats is suggesting that amid the surrounding darkness the bird brings an idealising brilliance of its own to its immediate neighbourhood. Also just possibly Keats had this purpose in mind when he rejected an earlier version's 'small winged Dryad' for the final 'light-winged Dryad', suggesting the symbolic nature of the nightingale not merely by the classical allusion, but also by a deft and unassertive pun. Again if the bird is such a creature as this suggests, what is its song, and what is the summer which it celebrates 'with full-throated ease?'

One of the many remarkable features of stanza two is the oddity of its conclusion. The first eight lines constitute a paean not merely to wine, but to music, dance, laughter and joyous exuberance. We glimpse a festival that is the finale of an ideal summer, the summer, perhaps, of which the bird sings:

> O, for a draught of vintage! that hath been
>   Cool'd a long age in the deep-delved earth,
> Tasting of Flora and the country green,
>   Dance, and Provençal song, and sunburnt mirth!
> O for a beaker full of the warm South,
>   Full of the true, the blushful Hippocrene,
> With beaded bubbles winking at the brim,
>   And purple-stained mouth;

There is a sense in which this is an ideal world, but it is not a dream world; its pulse beats too powerfully for that. One can scarcely imagine therefore, a more inappropriate preliminary to the wish that completes the sentence:

> That I might drink, and leave the world unseen,
>   And with thee fade away into the forest dim:

Not merely the wish itself is inappropriate—who would turn away from the world Keats is describing?—but the means for leaving the world, as they have just been specified, are equally inappropriate. The long-cooled vintage tastes of summer warmth and peasant energy, and the 'blushful Hippocrene' inspires more intense consciousness. Nothing here suggests ebbing vitality, drugged sensibility, Lethean despair. A further oddity resides in the phrase 'leave the world unseen'. It is ambiguous, but the apparently primary meaning, that Keats wishes to slip away unnoticed, has little point. The apparently secondary meaning, that he wishes to leave the world without looking at it, is more dramatically effective. For Keats has already looked at the world and seen its marvellous gusto: 'Dance, and Provençal song, and sunburnt mirth,' and he has looked with eyes capable of the sharpest focus: 'With beaded bubbles winking at the brim,/ And purple stained mouth.' Yet, mysteriously it first seems, the reader does not protest against this inappropriateness—in fact most readers are unaware of it. I suggest we accept the paradox easily because we already know that a debate is under way about whether or not the gift of life is worth accepting. At the end of stanza two, Keats' momentary position is that the gift is not worth having, consciousness not to be endured, even though he knows the glories of life. The grape harvest is real, but it is only half, or less than half, of a real world.[14] The world which Keats wishes to leave unseen will follow in stanza three.

There is, however, another and perhaps more important debate initiated in stanza two: what is the nature of death? Many people are rightly suspicious of the business of digging up deeply fundamental universal images and expatiating on their tentacular ramifications, but one may safely recognise wine as an archetype. It is, moreover, an obviously religious archetype, dating back beyond the first miracle and the eucharist to the priesthood of Melchizedek. But I suggest that for a poet the greatest symbolic power of wine lies not in its Biblical associations, but in the nature of its own life-cycle:

> Cool'd a long age in the deep-delved earth,
> Tasting of Flora and the country green,
> Dance, and Provençal song, and sunburnt mirth!

It is scarcely necessary to explicate the suggestions of burial, resurrection and glorified life, or the suggestive paradox of warmth deriving from age-long coolness, vitality from deep stillness. It is necessary though, to remember that such suggestions operate not in the context of faith, but of debate. Meanwhile, the shape of the poem is being established. This is the first of our two kinds of burial.

The second stanza's vision of sunburnt joy, which I have called half, or less than half, of a real world, receives its complement in stanza three. The nightingale has never known 'The weariness, the fever, and the fret/ *Here*,' (the comma insists on a rhythmic emphasis). But when we examine the dying world that Keats locates 'Here' we cannot shake off the living festival world of stanza two, for the memory of its vitality intensifies the deadness of stanza three. There life was celebrated, 'Here' it is 'undergone'. Even the expression of pain is presented passively: 'men sit and hear each other groan.' The only transitive verb is attributed to a physiological condition, not an agent: 'palsy shakes a few, sad, last gray hairs,' and verbs active in form nonetheless denote something merely happening to their subjects: 'youth grows pale ... and dies,' 'Beauty cannot keep her lustrous eyes,/ Or new Love pine at them.' The last verb carries only the slightest trace of wilful effort. What gives this stanza its particularly tragic tone is not the physical dying, but the spiritual deadness it renders, the lack of transitiveness in what is merely happening. The argument between stanza two and stanza three is not only between a world without snags and a world full of them, it is an argument between active and passive, response and deadness, energy and despair. This argument is conducted not merely in diction and imagery, but rhythmically. In stanza two note the trochaic fling with which the pulsating iambics begin:

> Tasting of Flora and the country green,
> Dance, and Provençal song, and sunburnt mirth!

In stanza three the verse moves through weighted, long-vowelled spondees to an expiring breath:

> Where palsy shakes a few, sad, last gray hairs,
> Where youth grows pale, and spectre-thin, and dies.

The milieu that Keats calls 'here' may indeed be more than half a world, but it is not a whole world. In the common reality which is 'Here' for all of us, palsied despair may indeed be more widespread than sunburnt mirth, but when we have tough-mindedly acknowledged this fact, we still know that from time to time men and women abandon themselves to dance and song. Keats, I believe, held such a balanced view, in spite of his own desperate misery, and struggled to maintain such a genuinely realistic balance throughout the ode. For this reason, for this invincible grasping for fulness of living, F.R. Leavis distinguishes him from his decadent imitators.[15] Even at the end of stanza three we see this grasping for life beginning again. The mere presence of beauty, youth and love is in itself a positive force against what is present in the earlier part of the stanza. More powerful is the manner in which 'lustrous eyes' more than counterbalances 'leaden-eyed despairs', and more powerful still is the energy generated within the double-meaning of 'lustrous'.

The life of sunburnt mirth is too virile too be kept down, and has erupted into the deathly half-world of 'Here'. When we notice this, we realise that we are dealing with one world, the world we live in, where the extreme positives and negatives that have been expressed in these stanzas interpenetrate each other, and blend with much that is drab and neutral. Keats has disentangled and intensified these extremes in order to question more dramatically whether the life he dreads to lose is worth the keeping. But together the elements of stanzas two and three, whose common characteristic is reality, constitute one world, and it is our world. It is also the first of the two opposed worlds I spoke of earlier. The other is an imitation world, and Keats is about to construct it.

The expressions used to convey the wish to escape at the end of stanza two and the beginning of stanza four are worth comparing:

> That I might drink, and leave the world unseen,
> And with thee fade away into the forest dim:
>
> Away! away! for I will fly to thee.

In the first case we have a stretched diminuendo that suggests an effete pleasure in the sensation of failing consciousness. In the second we have abrupt energy (the vital strength we felt returning in the last lines of stanza three has broken through here), and an appearance of decisiveness. The energy, however, is quickly dissipated by the effect of certain intriguing false notes and ambiguities. The associations of 'Bacchus and his pards' are substantially different from those of the imagery of stanza two. Keats' mental savouring of the stored vitality of the wine and the vividness of its sparkle implies a measured, discriminating enjoyment. 'Bacchus' suggests gluttonous swilling and snoring oblivion. When Keats declines Bacchus' chariot he is rejecting an option he has not really proposed. Perhaps what he has proposed, an epicurean consolation in wine, now, for the moment, appears to him in another light, without the sophisticated gloss of connoisseurship. This is very much the manner in which symbolic debate may proceed, by presenting the same notion in two sets of images with very different associative powers.

The second false note is 'Poesy'. In the first place it is never easy to be sure exactly what Keats means by it, though in the last stanza of the ode he seems to equate it with 'fancy'. In the second place, many readers will feel that the word is sentimentally precious, the last traces of Keatsian mawkishness (cf. 'his erstwhile timid lips grew bold,/ And poesied with hers in dewy rhyme'—*Isabella*, 69 – 70). Yet the use of this doubtful word here may be a tactic rather than a lapse, for it is connected with two very fruitful ambiguities. In what sense are the wings of Poesy 'viewless'? The immediate suggestion is that they are wings of the mind or spirit, and therefore invisible. But as we carry on, during, say, a third or fourth reading of the poem, we may suspect that Poesy's wings offer no view, for 'here there is no light', and 'I cannot see what flowers are at my feet'.[16] There is rather more confusion with 'dull brain'. Poesy, it seems, would like to take to its viewless wings, but the brain is clumsy or protesting, and fancy is encumbered by it.

Poetry engages the intelligence as well as the sensibility, but perhaps Poesy is better off without the narrowly ratiocinative faculty. Or perhaps the dullness of the brain 'perplexes and retards'; a keen brain would speed the fancy on its delighted way. But one has to tease such a meaning out of the lines; the overriding impression is that intelligence ('dull' in the sense of 'boring, mundane'), is an obstacle to Poesy. 'Poesy' then may be a well-chosen word, signalling that Keats is proposing to surrender the faculty that tirelessly reaches for substance and wholeness.

One's suspicions about 'Poesy' are soon confirmed, for the Queen-moon only very momentarily suggests Greek myth or Elizabethan convention. Her 'starry Fays' make her more like Titania than Cynthia, and her function is to be decorative and comforting ('Tender is the night'). In a vital respect she is ineffective: 'here there is no light.' Like Poesy, however, the Queen-moon's faery triviality is, I suggest, Keats' tactic. He is describing a means of dealing with his agonised bewilderment that must fail, and to propose an ineffective solution in order to reveal it as such as a traditional debating ploy. Keats, therefore, will now attempt the pastiche world that fancy can manufacture, though, being a great poet and making his faery place for a valid strategic purpose, he will do better than ships of pearl and seas of amber.

In spite of the statement 'I cannot see . . ./ But guess', all the richness of stanza five is presented confidently. Precisely because 'here there is no light' Keats can be sure of his richness. David Perkins has described these lines as: 'a vivid assertion of the power of the imagination to see more than the sensory eye can see.' This is misleading, for the imagination here is merely remembering what the sensory eye *has* seen. Walter Evert's view makes better sense: 'One is struck . . . by the fact that what is seen in the imaginative vision includes nothing that the real world does not supply.'[17] This is, in fact, a constructed world, conceived in a mind that, while remembering reality, has deliberately tried to limit its consciousness. It is meant to be an expurgated world, from which all disagreeables have been evaporated, the sort of world we think the world ought to be, an Eden which some power called 'the seasonable month' perpetually 'endows'. Inevitably it is soft-focussed, there are no 'globed peonies', no 'sweet peas on tip-toe for a flight'.

The world created by wishing fancy cannot be looked at so sharply. Hence the sweets which Keats assures us are there are presented as little more than a catalogue: 'flower', 'boughs', 'grass', 'thicket', 'fruit-tree', 'hawthorn', 'eglantine'. Yet we sense that this stanza does indeed offer richness, a wealth that is, at least in part, made possible by the darkness and generalised vision. Other senses are wonderfully alert. 'Incense' and 'embalmed' bring exotic fragrance; 'eglantine' and 'musk' offer native scents. 'Dewy wine' brings a reminder of the taste of 'Flora and the country green'. Sharpest of all though, is the sense of hearing: we listen to a continuously rustling music, created by 'breezes blown/ Through verdurous glooms and winding mossy ways' (the motif actually begins in these lines), that modulates virtually unnoticed into the buzzing of insects. It would be tiresome to

explicate the onomatopoiea; I shall simply reproduce the stanza
and allow the reader to detect for himself the pervasive delicate
sibilance carried in language that might be entirely justified by its
connotative function:

> I cannot see what flowers are at my feet,
>   Nor what soft incense hangs upon the boughs,
> But, in embalmed darkness, guess each sweet
>   Wherewith the seasonable month endows
> The grass, the thicket, and the fruit-tree wild;
>   White hawthorn, and the pastoral eglantine;
>   Fast fading violets cover'd up in leaves;
>   And mid-May's eldest child,
>   The coming musk-rose, full of dewy wine,
>   The murmurous haunt of flies on summer eves.

I am going to suggest an interpretation of this sensory
compensation. In a poet as sharply intelligent as Keats, the
attempt to limit consciousness cannot succeed, even partially, for
very long. The imagery here, as Douglas Bush has noted: 'admits,
almost unwittingly, the fact of process, of transiency, of death
along with life.'[18] The attempt to make a world out of fragments
of fancy therefore quickly founders, and the dull brain, which
deals with reality, soon reassumes command. Indeed, intelligence
was always at fancy's elbow, offering vital hints. 'Embalmed
darkness' carries suggestions of fragrance, healing ('balm in
Gilead'), and oriental exoticism, but it may also suggest not
merely, as Perkins says, 'a scented, hushed burial', but grimmer
and more absolute images: mummification and burial chambers.[19]
'Seasonable month' proposes a timely bounty, but it also reminds
us that the seasonal cycle includes winter. Once we have picked
up these clues, we recognise that all the 'sweets' the stanza offers
bloom and fade in their turn, and 'embalmed's' reminder of burial
is renewed in 'Fast-fading violets cover'd up in leaves'.

  In other words, we now become aware of a stiffening ambiguity
throughout the stanza; the world of fancy is shot through with
reality, and therefore with time, death, and, paradoxically, life
again. Once the consciousness has been jogged into readmitting
death into its cognition, the outcome is renewed life. The burial
of the violets is ambiguous—they will bloom next year and die

next year. But there is nothing ambiguous in the assertion of life in the last three lines of the stanza. After the death of the violets we have the birth of the rose, 'mid-May's child', offering a form of that Provençal energy, 'dewy wine'. Finally there is the busy music of vitality, the warmth of mellow sunshine and life in the occupation of the flies on summer eves. The escape offered by fancy has failed; Keats knows that only a world that includes death can offer plenitude of life.

In stanza six the debate which has so far been conducted beneath the threshold of direct argument now breaks surface, and its main issues become clear. In spite of his claim 'Already with thee', Keats has not attained the world of the nightingale, the 'melodious plot/ Of beechen green', but he does seem to achieve what we might call communion with the bird, in an intimate, confessional moment. I suggest the notion of communion because I do not believe that Keats is merely conducting a conversation with an aspect of himself. The nightingale does not represent his poetic genius, or his conception of imagination or beauty; the expression 'Darkling I listen' (with its near-pun on 'Darling') indicates a true apostrophe. What then is Keats apostrophising? Perhaps it is an abstract principle, having such reality as principles have. The most attractive temptation is to say that the bird represents art, but there is a difficulty in this conception which I will deal with in the appropriate place. Whatever the objects of the apostrophe is, it is something to which Keats will attribute permanence. We should note too that Keats is obviously also addressing the physical bird itself; 'Darkling' suggests a tenderness towards the mere creature. That Keats can thus address himself to the ideal and the actual at once is significant, and will become more important in stanza seven.

Although the debate is now, for the moment, to be conducted in plain speech rather than impressionistically, it remains subtle and suggestive. There appears to be a simple statement: 'For a long time I have been attracted to the prospect of death.' But the contrary case is put in the reservations, of which 'half in love' is only the most obvious. Note also that Keats' expression 'for many a time' refers to numerous individual occasions, not a longstanding, settled state of mind. Also, he has been attracted only to a particular kind of death, 'easeful Death', entered into by a comfortable passage: 'Take into the air my quiet breath,' and the apostrophes to death never become actual, they remain 'mused rhymes'. At the moment though, Keats seems to be, in Shakespeare's phrase, 'absolute for death'. 'Now more than ever seems it rich to die'—but note how that dramatic absoluteness is undermined by 'seems'. The sentiment itself is an odd one—in what sense can it ever be rich to die? The romantic notion is that it may be rich to die in a moment of supreme happiness (See Naples and die!). Although Keats half suggests the notion, and partially supports it ('with no pain'), in fact he will have none of it, and his dismissal of it is managed by a beautiful rhythmic and structural allusion. Let us listen again to lines 5 and 6 of this stanza:

> Now more than ever seems it rich to die,
> To cease upon the midnight with no pain.

Hamlet is much taken with the same hope for bringing heartache to an end, but he goes on to reject the idea after conjuring with synonyms and their implications:

> 'Tis a consummation
> Devoutly to be wish'd. To die, to sleep;
> To sleep! perchance to dream: ay there's the rub.

Keats' debate, like Hamlet's, hinges on the play of synonyms, and the suggestiveness of a rhetorical pause: 'to die/ To cease.' Hamlet's attraction to death was counterbalanced by the fear that there might be life after death; Keats, while reminding us of Hamlet's argument, uses his device to make the opposite point—'To cease upon the midnight.'

It can hardly be rich to die when, as Walter Evert says: 'the brutal fact is that escape from the world of mutability entails as a necessary correlative the loss of that same world's beauty.'[20] Keats' recognition of this brutal fact perhaps now sends the debate underground again. Keats' position at this moment in the poem is that consciousness is extinguished by death, but the contrary case is offered by the conflicting implications of the diction. If Keats dies, he will cease, but the bird will continue to pour its *soul* abroad. In the next line Keats seems merely to be restating this 'rub' in plain terms: 'Still wouldst thou sing, and I have ears in vain;' but in the parallel complementary statement that follows, the submerged dialectic is activated again. If the word 'requiem' had carried no qualifying adjunct, its figurative nature would have been negligible, but 'high requiem' certainly renders the notion of a solemn funeral mass. The final word of the stanza not only denies the implication of this image, but conveys the burden of despair that the denial brings with it. Douglas Bush has identified not merely the evocative power of such implicit antitheses, but their function in the drama of the poem: 'The fact of death, real death, opens all the stops for what now becomes the dominant theme, the contrast between the mortality of man and the immortality of art.'[21]

I cannot, however, fully agree with Bush when he goes on to say of the succeeding stanza:

> The most wonderful thing about this stanza ... is that the climactic affirmation is also a tissue of implicit irony. For the conscious rejoicing in the immortal life and power of art turns—as it were unconsciously and inevitably—into recognition of the perpetuity of pain and sorrow through all generations of mankind.[22]

I believe the total effect of the stanza to be even more complex than Bush has indicated. The implicit irony is there, certainly, and the recognition of the inevitability of human suffering; but these are, I believe, tempered by the fact that Keats is not simply rejoicing in the immortality of art. He derives from the bird's song hints of something more important, as I hope, at length, to make clear.

The statement made in the first line of stanza seven should not surprise anyone, because the symbolic nature of the nightingale has been so strongly hinted from the beginning of the poem. The radiance suggested by 'light-winged Dryad', and 'beechen green', the marvellous happiness of the bird, its freedom from all knowledge of suffering, its unwearied song of summer, the ecstasy of its overflowing soul, all indicate that it represents some supremely good abstraction or principle, possibly, indeed, a spiritual being, but certainly something timeless. Nevertheless we are astonished, not by what is said, but rather by the incredibly swift change of mood from the end of stanza six: 'Thou wast not born for death, immortal Bird!' There is a rush of energy and bursting confidence in the line that we are utterly unprepared for. At this moment Keats' faith is so complete and secure that he can now deny his worst fears about death while expressing them with macabre vividness: 'No hungry generations tread thee down.'

Let us reflect for a moment on the image of death which is denied and presented in this exclamation. Keats was evidently influenced by certain lines from Wordworth's *Excursion*, but he has made the image so much more specifically gruesome that we need to look at his words very carefully.[23] We are not trodden down after death by living generations trampling over our resting places; the suggestion is that we are pressed down by succeeding dead generations buried in the same grave (the headstones of old churchyards give ample evidence). This interpretation raises two problems. First, why are the generations hungry? There is nothing in the poem to suggest social injustice, famine, and generations of starvelings. The most satisfactory explanation of the effect the word has on us is that it is a transferred epithet—it is the grave that is hungry for succeeding generations. All the energy of begetting and living implied in 'generations' ('The young/ In one another's arms, birds in the trees/—Those dying generations') provides unending food for the endless appetite of death. Secondly, there is the problem posed by the expression 'tread thee down'. I have already rejected the image of the living walking over our burial plots; in Keats' vision of the grave the dead are trampled by the dead. Now this is the nadir of pessimism, and yet the line retains that triumphant sense of happy and invulnerable faith that informs the previous line. This seems to need more than the 'No' at the beginning of the line to account for it fully, more even than the carry over of visionary enthusiasm from 'immortal Bird!'

Near the beginning of this chapter, in describing the symbolic shape of the ode, I claimed that we could find two images of burial with conflicting implications. The first of these was the burial of the wine, 'Cool'd a long age in the deep-delved earth'. In the succeeding lines there is an implicit, but vivid, resurrection image; when the wine is brought out of its cellar it has new rich life. There seems to be no parallel to this in the line we are now examining, yet the two images are implicitly connected. Before the wine can be buried, the grape must be trodden down in the winepress. I am suggesting we might make a rather long and tenuous connection here, but I think it may not unreasonably be made. By far the most powerful suggestion of the line we are discussing is of death piled on death, but the vineyard associations of 'tread ... down' are strong enough, perhaps, to remind us of the poem's earlier symbol of burial with all its implications of vitality and renewal. It is not impossible that such a connection contributes something to the strange retention of joy in a line expressing so grimly final a picture of death. Keats' moment of joy cannot be accounted for merely by his conviction of the nightingale's immortality (symbolising the immortality of art); somehow his vision seems to raise a more human hope.

In the worst of his despair ('I have ears in vain/ To thy high requiem become a sod') Keats is again surprised by joy, and perhaps relieved by hope. Both joy and hope are momentary, the ecstatic vision becomes itself a subject for debate, and its status decays to a thing of 'magic' and 'faery'. But not yet. The nightingale's song, as a symbol, modulates in a more complicated way than many readers have been inclined to suppose—the visionary moment does not fade smoothly into fancy, as Perkins, for example, suggests: 'But throughout the seventh stanza the nightingale, even as a symbol, continues to move farther away from the human world. It is first heard by "emperor and clown", figures presumably out of the historical past, then by Ruth in a world of biblical legend, and finally it is heard in "faery lands".' This is an odd comment. Perkins seems to assume that the story of Ruth is a legend, though we have no means of knowing whether it is fact or fiction. There is nothing inherently unlikely in the narrative, and Ruth's situation was probably not uncommon. The Jewish laws and customs concerning property inheritance involved in the story have a factual, commonplace atmosphere about them.

More to the point immediately though, is the firm reality of Ruth as the poem presents her: a heartbroken woman longing for, yet resisting comfort. As Claude Finney has said, this tercet 'which distills the essence of the story of Ruth from the Hebrew Bible, is the poetry of human emotions'.[24] Perkins is perhaps a little too anxious to trace a smooth decline from fact to faery—there is no such smoothness. The world in which the voice is heard remains fully human until it plunges into faery. There is then, I believe, a dramatically sharp change from the humanity of

Ruth amid the busy working world of hired hands on a prosperous farm to the emptiness and sterility of faery lands.

One can only speculate why Keats' choice of 'emperor and clown' as hearers of the nightingale's song seems so remarkably right. The conjunction of the two, combined with the stretch of time between their 'ancient days' and Keats' 'passing night' indicates the universality of the voice, and the summer of which it sings perpetually. But one seems to hear fainter resonances, and perhaps Keats has chosen his personae from Rome's eastern empire. Perhaps he has in mind the fabled work of Grecian goldsmiths, the 'Miracle, bird or golden handiwork . . . Planted on the starlit golden bough'—the jewelled mechanical nightingales with their artificial songs which reputedly kept a drowsy emperor awake, and perhaps his drowsy jester; and which, because such toys seemed to be a form of art and to be comparatively immortal, drew the curious soul of W.B. Yeats to Byzantium. If Keats does have such products in mind, he is making better use of the image than Yeats does, for he is casting a quizzical eye on his symbol. Is the voice a mere human artifact, or does it have a greater provenance? I suggest that at this point Keats' confidence rallies as he examines another possible source of hope than immortal art.

It is certainly not a fabricated voice that sings in the succeeding lines. In relation to Ruth we most clearly perceive that Keats thinks of the song as a message not originating within his own subjective being, nor yet within the realm of human art, for the nightingale's voice appears to meet a good deal of resistance here—it is obliged to 'find a path' through Ruth's 'sad heart'. But why is Ruth mentioned? This question puzzled H.W. Garrod: 'Whence Keats fetched, in this stanza, the thought of Ruth . . . it is idle to conjecture . . . I have the fancy, for what it is worth, that the image of Ruth amid the corn came to Keats, by some obscure process of association from Wordsworth's *Solitary Reaper*.'[25] Conjecture is in fact unnecessary; Keats fetched the thought of Ruth from the Old Testament. Ruth in the scriptural scene Keats so vividly pictures is not solitary, nor is she cutting and binding. She is in a field with busy labourers and she is gleaning. Perhaps what Garrod is really trying to ask when he inquires 'Whence Keats fetched the thought of Ruth' is what purpose the image is meant to fulfill. We can answer this, at least provisionally, when we answer other questions. Why is she homesick and why is the corn alien? Does the nightingale's song indeed find a path to her consciousness? We know that Keats read the Bible regularly, and that he was particularly impressed with this episode. The *Book of Ruth* is now less well-known than it used to be; I shall therefore recall the most significant features of the story.

Orpah and Ruth were the Moabite wives of the Hebrews Mahlon and Chilion, sons of Elimelech and Naomi of Bethlehem-judah, but at that time living in Moab. After the early deaths of Mahlon and Chilion, and that of Elimelech, Naomi released her daughters-in-law, so that they might seek fresh husbands. Orpah left, but Ruth, with a matchless declaration of love, determined to remain with Naomi. The two widows returned to Bethlehem-judah at the beginning of harvest, and Ruth took the opportunity to glean in the fields of Boaz, a wealthy kinsman of Naomi. The ruse succeeded, Boaz took kindly to the Moabitess, redeemed for the family the patrimonial lands Naomi had been obliged to sell, married Ruth, and begat a line that was finally royal.

Keats' mention of Ruth places her at the point in the narrative where she is newly arrived in Bethlehem-judah, at the beginning of harvest. Her homesickness and tears are Keats' attributions, but understandably so. In the biblical phraseology the Almighty had dealt very bitterly with both Naomi and Ruth, and the latter, though she has totally adopted Naomi's racial and spiritual heritage, is now among a foreign people worshipping a strange god. She also has much to be thankful for. She is wonderfully well-received; Boaz invites her to take her meals with him, instructs his field-hands not merely to allow her to glean, but to 'let fall some of the handfuls of purpose for her'. Of course she is presumably confident about how things must turn out; in purely human terms her salvation is at hand. But her greatest blessing is unknown to her; the end of the story is a genealogy: 'Boaz begat Obed, and Obed begat Jesse, and Jesse begat David.' Christ therefore will be of her flesh. Yet she is in exile and doubtless sick for home, not yet consolable by the family love that now surrounds her, the resources of wealth that must now work on her behalf, and the natural riches and joy of harvest. Keats imagines her, in Eliot's phrase, 'fearing the warm reality, the offered good'. Grief and homesickness may be proof for a long time against such gifts. Even the harvest may seem foreign in a strange land, even corn in the fields near Bethlehem, the house of bread.

At this point in the poem I believe it is the whole of this 'offered good' that constitutes the nightingale's song, and is obliged to 'find a path' through Ruth's heart. Ruth, I suggest, is in the poem because, although her circumstances as the Bible describes them are widely different from Keats', the emotional and psychological difficulty Keats attributes to her is very much his own. The Almighty had dealt very bitterly with the young poet; death had knocked on his door regularly since childhood and now seemed to be calling for Keats himself. But he has just had a visionary movement, an ecstasy which he speculates was not generated within himself, nor was merely a response to a creature's song. It may be that something has been offered, as something was offered to Ruth. But the thing offered is associated with a religious tradition that Keats despises. He could not imagine ever being at home in this tradition; this harvest, for him, must always be 'alien corn'. But the fact that he considers, even so obliquely and momentarily, the prospect offered by a tradition of incarnational idealism erases Stillinger's line between two worlds.

The greatest significance is that the image of Ruth, with all the implications I have indicated, should occur at this point in the poem. The first four lines of the stanza may be read as a momentary conception of the nightingale's song as a symbol of the immortality of art, but 'Perhaps' it is something more humanly satisfying. Here we have a major obstacle to perceiving the bird throughout the poem as a symbol of the immortality of art, for the assumption behind all the speculations of the ode is that such a symbol must be inadequate. The immortality of a symbol or an abstraction offers only spurious satisfaction; what Keats hungers for is the immortality of consciousness itself, and 'Perhaps' this is what the bird offers. The visionary climax of stanza seven is not the first two lines, but the fifth, sixth, and seventh, where the offered hope almost finds a path through Keats' sceptical defences. If breached at all, these defences are rapidly mended. The visionary moment is quickly reduced to a matter of charm, magic, and faery. Yet there is little that is charming in these magic charms; the landscape viewed by faery fancy is a prospect of ominous shores and dangerous tides. If the moment when the nightingale's voice promised more abundant life was a moment of illusion, imagination and art can offer nothing better, nor even as good. Compared with the 'alien corn' their world is romantically barren, so Keats travels swiftly back to what must appear to be waking reality—'Here,' where there is no light, and where the fading song of the nightingale is punctuated by a mournful bell: 'Forlorn ... Forlorn ... toll ... sole.'

Although stanza eight expresses the withdrawal of the vision, it is not an anticlimax, for something has been gained. The bird's anthem becomes plaintive with distance, but the bird is not a failed illusion, it continues to exist and sing, though more and more remotely: 'Past the near meadows, over the still stream/ Up the hillside ... in the next valley glades.' As Katherine Wilson has said: 'The experience of the nightingale's song was a reality—a reality experienced for too short a time. That an experience comes to an end does not mean it never was. Keats does not repudiate it.'[26] Nothing has been settled in the course of the lyrical argument, but something has been added to the range of the debate—the nightingale experience itself. Was it indeed a spiritual reality making itself known to Keats, or was it the subjective product of painful longings? Is the nightingale's world, the rich summer of its song, a real world or faery land? Or (the parallel and opposite question) is 'Here, where men sit and hear each other groan' a lesser reality from which we may awake? The debate is inconclusive, but the questions which Keats asks at the end of the poem could not have been asked at the beginning. Perhaps Harold Bloom has made the most perceptive comment on the last lines of the poem: 'Once back in experience, the honest answer is only in the continued question ... "Do I wake or sleep" '[27]

The *Ode on Melancholy* has long been thought to typify a characteristic Romantic posture. E.C. Pettet has summed up the agreed placing:

> ... the Hamlet mood, and all the various shades of unhappy sentiment, are fundamental constituents of the Romantic temper. Most of the major poets of this period produced at least one important poem that can be grouped with the *Ode on Melancholy*, and this ode was written by one who, on his own

confession, had luxuriated in a 'love of gloom' and who felt it necessary to warn his sister against dieting the mind with grief.²⁸

Pettet's final relative clause ought to sound a cautionary note against this too easy and convenient classification of the poem. The warning to Fanny Keats indicates that the poet saw real danger in this particular romantic sentiment; however much he had luxuriated in his own love of gloom he was anxious that his young sister should not contract the habit. The fact is that the poem is too complex in its structure to justify this kind of critical assumption, for it is an argument, strenuously conducted, which is gradually transformed into a contemplative monologue. Unfortunately it is also a seriously flawed poem, for in the transition from dialectic to meditation Keats seems to lose his sense of direction. The resulting ambiguity is not of the fruitful kind.

The ode is the one short poem of Keats' that is undoubtedly a dramatic lyric (we can, if we like, make all the odes dramatic lyrics by pretending that we hear someone other than the poet speaking). But in the first two stanzas of *Melancholy* someone who may or may not be the poet is heard talking urgently to someone who is not the reader. Even if half-Keats is talking to half-Keats, the sense of dramatic interplay is there—we overhear the speech of one party in an implicit dialogue, and from this side of the colloquy we can deduce the sentiments of the unheard partner. In the third stanza, however, either the poet has abandoned his persona and is speaking in his own voice, or the persona has forgotten his interlocutor, for the dramatic urgency—the sense of sentiments being answered and a different attitude promulgated—has faded out, and a contemplative monologue has taken its place.

The debate then, in the first part of the poem, is between two voices, one heard, one unheard. Keats suggests what the 'other' voice has already said, and/or would say if allowed to speak, by means of disciplined counterproductivity. This is particularly clear in the opening lines, and reminds us of Donne's 'For God's sake hold your tongue and let me love!' Empson's famous comment on the first lines of *Melancholy* that 'somebody, or some force in the poet's mind, must have wanted to go to Lethe very much if it took four negatives ... to stop them' can scarcely be bettered, except that we might note also the urgency of the speech rhythm, the sense almost of a fist beating a table: 'No, no, go *not* to Lethe ...'[29] The voice is loud, tinged with alarm, as the voice of Donne's persona is loud with exasperation. In the rest of the stanza, the voice becomes quieter, but the device of counterproductive emphasis goes on—there are five more prohibitions in five lines, all rendered ambiguous by their force.

There is however a less theatrical but more important ambiguity in the stanza. The powerful negatives do not counterbalance the prevailing sense of self-pitying gloom that emerges on a first reading of the poem; on the contrary, they strengthen it. The sense we have after repeated readings of the poem that it is more complex than the 'indulgence' that F.R. Leavis considered it to be, springs from at least two other sources.[30] Of these the most easily identifiable is the force of 'wakeful anguish'. Let us look at the phrase in its context. After all the negatives forbidding narcotic escape, the speaker explains that 'shade to shade will come too drowsily,/ And drown the wakeful anguish of the soul'. We have in the first of these lines a pun that draws attention to itself and asks to be explained, and in the second line an explication of the pun and its significance. The first 'shade' seems to mean the darkness of approaching unconsciousness ('too drowsily' suggests the narcotic lethargy that precedes sleep); the second 'shade' seems to mean the remaining consciousness, the phantasmal spirit that in ancient mythology inhabits Hades after death, and this meaning is subsequently made explicit and less classical by the plain term 'soul'.

The argument, in so far as one can paraphrase it, seems to be a circular one: 'Do not, by any of the means specified here, obliterate your consciousness, because if you do, your consciousness will be obliterated.' The unheard voice in the dialogue might well protest here that was exactly what he wanted to do; but such a rejoinder is pre-empted by 'wakeful anguish'. Its very unexpectedness gives 'wakeful' at least as much force as 'anguish'. The implication is that wakefulness itself has a value that must not be surrendered. The words battle against each other, and while the reader may have doubts about the outcome, Keats plainly intends that 'anguish' submits to 'wakeful'.

The other source of complexity in the stanza is less startling, but ultimately more effective and pervasive. The images of the stanza are predominantly drawn from what one might think of as the dark side of folk-lore, and the punctuation of these by classical allusions has little balancing effect. 'Lethe', 'wolfe's-bane', 'poisonous wine', 'nightshade', 'beetle', 'Proserpine', 'yew-berries', and 'downy owl' all point in one direction only, and suggest a state of mind where despair is dramatically savoured. Even Psyche is presented as 'mournful', and her symbol is not the delightful butterfly, but the ominous moth with the death's-head markings on its wings.

'Rosary', however, is significantly different from the other images, and is also more important, since it has greater extension within the stanza; after being named once specifically it is alluded to twice more in a subsequent line, and in such a way that the reader's attention is directed to its real meaning rather than the popular misconception of it. The poet recognises that a rosary is not in itself a symbol of melancholy, and not an 'approximate equivalent of the beetle or the downy owl'.[31] The meaning of Keats' lines is that one can make it so by concentrating on one aspect of it, thus making it 'of yew-berries', but the symbol itself commands a far wider range of awareness and response. Keats means by 'rosary' what the informed Catholic means by it.

To most people the term signifies a string of beads, a pretty bauble containing things which Chaucer called 'gaudies'. The poet here seems at first glance to ratify this notion by suggesting that for the melancholy man a suitably dismal bauble might be made of yew-berries (because of the prevailing counter-productivity, we tend not to notice that he is actually saying that his interlocutor should not do this). A rosary is not a set of beads, however, the beads merely represent the rosary. That the real meaning of the term is implied in Keats' use of it becomes clear a little later, providing we can make the necessary connection:

> Make not your rosary of yew-berries,
>   Nor let the beetle nor the death-moth be
>   Your mournful Psyche, nor the downy owl
> A partner in your sorrow's mysteries.

'Yew-berries', 'beetle', 'death-moth', and 'downy owl' are so powerfully and morbidly earthy that they put more distance than three lines of verse between 'rosary' and 'sorrow's mysteries'. However, once we have overcome the gloomy force of the paraded *memento mori*, the balancing force of the rosary as a set of prayers is inescapable. The prayers actually recited in this devotion, 'Our Father', 'Hail Mary', and 'Glory be' are meant to accompany and in part to express a meditation on the fifteen mysteries of the Christian faith. These mysteries are grouped in three sets of five, the Joyful Mysteries, concerned with the nativity; the Sorrowful Mysteries, concerned with Christ's passion and death; and the Glorious Mysteries, concerned with the resurrection and subsequent events. A recitation of the full rosary is an arduous affair, involving fifteen 'Our Fathers', fifteen 'Glory be's', and one hundred and fifty 'Hail Marys'. While a devout Catholic may say the rosary privately, alone, its public recitation is usually an antiphonal affair: the leader of the prayers, usually a priest, says the first halves of the 'Our Father', 'Hail Mary', and 'Glory be', the congregation completing them from 'Give us this day', 'Holy Mary, Mother of God', and 'As it was in the beginning' respectively.

If Keats expected many of his readers to have this much knowledge of the Catholic tradition of prayer, it was rather unreasonable of him; but the evidence is strong in the poem that he knew this much himself.[32] Not merely is the phrase 'sorrow's mysteries' a literal reference to the Sorrowful Mysteries of the rosary, the warning not to take the downy owl as partner surely alludes to the tradition of antiphonal recitation.

It has been necessary to digress into the most popular form of Catholic prayer (other than the mass itself) because the force of Keats' allusions seems to have been missed by commentators and editors, and it is possible that it has been missed by the majority of readers. Keats himself, with his intervening relish of beetles, death-moths and downy owls has made it difficult even for an informed reader to make the vital connection. We must add to this, of course, the fact that the allusion is so unexpected; Keats' hatred of the Church of England was so strongly expressed that the liberal-minded Anglo-Saxon reader will assume that he hated the Catholic church even more. Nevertheless the allusion is there, and we must now examine the work the rosary symbol does in this stanza, and possibly in the first few lines of the next.

The contemplation of Christ's suffering and death, with the

grief, fear, bitter disappointment and sense of defeat that it brought to his mother and friends, is at the centre of the rosary, as suffering is at the centre of human experience. But on either side of it are more positive things, and the cycle is completed with 'Glorious' promises. Keats, at the time of writing was almost certainly not confident of a glorious destiny for man, but he was honest enough to acknowledge in this way that grief, though apparently central and predominant in life is not all-pervasive. The prime function of the rosary image here is to place the melancholy mood in context—grief, pain, and fear there may be in experience, but there is also joy and renewal. To make a rosary of yew-berries and to pray only the sorrowful mysteries, antiphonally, with a downy owl for partner, is to pretend that this is not so; it is to parade one's melancholy as a posture of romantic stoicism. Keats does not recommend this, on the contrary he repeatedly warns against such dramatising self-indulgence.

What the Catholic rosary image works against in the poem is not the physical poison of wolf's-bane or nightshade, but an intellectual poison which takes the form of the exclusive, undiversified, and continuous recitation of the yew-berries' rosary. One must remember that these Christian images and the traces which, as I am about to suggest, they may have left on other images, are almost certainly being used dramatically, and we must not take them as evidence of a particular direction in Keats' thought. What is important is their balancing function within the poem.

The rosary symbol does more than render a sense of perspective, it exerts an influence on the imagery around it. By reminding us of the passion and death of Christ, the allusion alerts us to possible implications in earlier lines: 'Nor suffer thy pale forehead to be kiss'd/ By nightshade, ruby grape of Proserpine.' In Burton's *Anatomy of Melancholy* Keats would have come across the treatment of 'head melancholy' by washing the forehead with a potion containing juice crushed out of hellebore.[33] Just as self-intensifying melancholy would substitute a death-moth for Psyche's butterfly, so here she substitutes a more treacherous poison; nightshade, whose fruit looks wholesome, the 'ruby grape of Proserpine'. Similarly a kiss looks like an expression of love, but was the means of an appalling betrayal. To surrender to the poisonous luxury of despair is to play Judas to one's own mind. Consciousness, or wakefulness, must be held on to, however anguished—'Life must be undergone' (*Letters* 1:293). The soul must not, however drowsy, submit to the ultimate 'shade'.

The second stanza begins with a remarkable number of positive implications. The melancholy 'fit'—the word surely indicates a passing mood—falls from Heaven, and the 'weeping cloud' is necessary for the hill to be green, and the flowers to be fostered. Cleanth Brooks, commenting on an aspect of Keats' poetry that he finds akin to the Metaphysicals, 'thinking through images', has said of these lines:

> Keats' 'April shroud' in the *Ode on Melancholy* is as characteristic of Keats as Donne's more famous shroud is characteristic of Donne. First of all it is an *April* shroud, and the associations of joy and fruitfulness clash sharply with the more sombre associations of grave clothes. But the phrase is not merely a showy but incidental flourish of rhetoric. The 'weeping cloud' covers the 'green hill' with an April shroud, and the descent of the cloud is used to describe the falling of the 'melancholy fit'. But such a description argues that melancholy is fruitful as well as sad. It catches up the reference to 'droop-headed flowers ...'.[34]

Brooks is surely right, for there is a spring-like freshness in the images which somehow gets through the ostensible gloom. There is also an implication that the melancholy mood is part of a cycle, as necessary to the development of man as rain to the natural world. There may also be resonances from the rosary image in 'green hill' and 'April shroud'.

We now arrive at the major problem of the ode, its central ambiguity (it comes almost exactly in the middle):

> Then glut thy sorrow on a morning rose,
>   Or on the rainbow of the salt-sand wave.
>   Or on the wealth of globed peonies.

What does Keats mean by 'glut thy sorrow'? How we interpret this phrase will determine our understanding of the rest of the poem. If we take it as meaning 'Nourish to excess your feeling of misery' (the ostensible meaning), then the rest of the poem is indeed an emotional indulgence. The poet is saying: 'Make yourself even more miserable by reminding yourself that the beauty of the rose and the peony last only for a season, the rainbow of the sea-spray an instant, the mature beauty of a woman a mere few years. The posturing infatuation of the lover is still briefer. Surrender then to unhappiness, and try to wring from it a perversely luxurious pleasure.'

The difficulty with this reading is that it conflicts with all the prohibitions of stanza one, and the spring-like freshness of the imagery of the first four lines of stanza two. Keats' interlocutor has been told not to commit suicide, not to drug himself into oblivion, and not to make a litany of morbid suggestions. He has been encouraged implicitly to a balanced consciousness of reality, to see sorrow as necessary to refreshment and renewal. It seems most unlikely that he should now be given quite contrary instructions, particularly as the word 'But' at the beginning of stanza two implies that what follows will be a more positive prescription. How then may we read 'glut thy sorrow' so that the rest of the poem will follow the changed direction implied by 'But'? It is perhaps possible to understand the words as forming an unusually compressed phrase, which might be expanded thus: 'Satiate your sorrowing consciousness with images of beauty.' This might still be an indulgence—an escape into the cult of the exquisite and the religion of beauty.

But what strikes the reader about the images which follow is not merely their beauty but, once more, a sense of natural freshness: 'the morning rose', 'the wealth of globed peonies', 'the rainbow of the salt sand-wave.' Such beauty is simple, concrete, and is offered by nature as part of her rich ordinariness. Note again the positive tone struck by 'wealth', 'globed' and 'rainbow'. The escape, if one is being recommended, is not to aestheticism or indulged emotions, but to reality, which has such pearls among its rubbish.

The last three lines of the stanza, however, present a serious difficulty:

> Or if thy mistress some rich anger shows,
>   Emprison her soft hand, and let her rave,
>   And feed deep, deep upon her peerless eyes.

There is nothing fresh or healthy about the boorish silliness Keats seems to be recommending here. It is possible, of course, that he is not recommending it; there is something in the tone of 'let her rave' that is half flippant, and the exaggerated vowel emphasis of 'feed deep, deep ... peerless' may equally suggest either a determined aesthetic intensity or a mockery of it. But if irony was intended, it scarcely comes off; the abiding impression is of a relapse into the cult of beauty. Robert Gittings attempts to solve the problem by resurrecting from a manuscript version (the draft known as K) a capital 'M' for Mistress. Assuming, as I cannot, that Keats' capitalisation was always logical and purposeful, Gittings suggests that 'Mistress' is a personification of Melancholy, and thus we can interpret the rest of the poem as an invitation to become the thrall of such a mistress.[35]

Leaving aside one's doubts about Keats' punctuation, there are difficulties in the figure itself. While one can allow personified Melancholy to have a soft hand and peerless eyes, one cannot imagine in what way she can be angry—even richly so—or for what reason. Anger is an emotion which might have a personification of its own. One must not endow a state of mind with an existence independent of the mind, and thus with the power of will and motivation. One is more impressed with Ian Jack's point that the lines in the ode recall the sentiments concerning Jane Cox which Keats expressed in a letter to the George Keatses: '... she has fine eyes ... When she comes into a room she makes an impression the same as the Beauty of a Leopardess ... I always find myself more at ease with such a woman; the picture before me always gives me a life and animation ... I forget myself entirely because I live in her.'[36] Unlike the abstraction Melancholy, a real woman is quite capable of the kind of anger that enhances her eyes, and many young men may find her beauty a sovereign remedy for the blue devils, even if only temporarily. But few, one hopes, will bully her in the way Keats seems to recommend.

Perhaps the principal difficulty, the source of the reader's confusion, is syntactical. The final 'or' in the series of three which begin lines six, seven and eight of the stanza may in fact not be part of the series. If 'mistress' is introduced, according to the traditional reading of the lines, as another object of beauty on which one may glut one's sorrow, then the image is in certain ways inappropriate. It is not merely that 'mistress' is human, while 'rose', 'rainbow', 'wave', and 'peonies' are not (though modern readers will be quick to detect an attitude implied by thus adding a woman to a list of objects); the major point is the nature of the transience of the beauty of the objects. The roses and the peonies will bloom again, the waves will roll to shore again tomorrow and there will be a spectrum in their clouds of spray. They are transient, but cyclical. The beauty of a woman is transient, but not cyclical; as she fades, she fades for ever.

One must consider, then, that the third 'or' may be introducing an alternative to the whole concept of glutting one's sorrow on beautiful objects. Instead of trying to improve one's mood by simple Hartleian therapy, one may make a cult either of Melancholy itself, as Gittings suggests, or of pleasure, as Ian Jack's citation implies, or of both. If this is so, and the lines about letting one's mistress (or Mistress) rave are not ironic, then the poem has changed direction again, and Keats has returned to his vomit. However we take them, the lines fail, and constitute a major flaw in the poem, for their ambiguity is distracting, not dramatic.

In stanza three we find the most explicit expression of that sense of time passing that is not a stoic posture but a necessary part of true fullness of living. There is something fundamentally healthy in the dialectic of the first four lines of the stanza, something clear-eyed that insists on seeing things as they are:

> She dwells with Beauty—Beauty that must die;
> And Joy, whose hand is ever at his lips
> Bidding adieu; and aching Pleasure nigh
> Turning to poison while the bee-mouth sips.

There emerges from the clash of opposites an implicitly equal valuation of positive and negative. Beauty dies, but first lives; Joy bids adieu, but has first been welcomed; Pleasure's ache accompanies its intensity. Stuart Sperry has pointed out a peculiar doubleness in the symbolic figure of Joy eternally bidding farewell: 'Yet one realises that the gesture is forever suspended, forever withheld, forever in the process of being made.'[37]

Nevertheless the lines appear to clash with those in stanza two recommending recourse to natural beauty as a cure for melancholy. That being so they may well be a way of ratifying a lapse into exquisite self-pity, as many critics seem to suppose. Quoting a passage from Burton to the effect that one must accept and make use of the advantages of melancholy, Robert Gittings says: 'Keats indeed took this philosophy to a much finer conclusion in the last stanza of the ode, to a creed of luxurious acceptance which might stand as the Romantic poet's solution for the dilemmas of life: "His soul shall taste the sadness of her might/ And be among her cloudy trophies hung." '38

This is clearly meant as high praise, yet in its effect, particularly in the use of the word 'luxurious', it is more deadly to Keats' reputation than Leavis' most magisterial strictures. If one can luxuriate in one's unhappiness, is one really unhappy? What kind of poet luxuriates in his sense of 'the giant agony of the world'? What kind of solution is it to any of the 'dilemmas of life' to become the thrall of any particular state of mind? What justification is there for assuming that Keats is recommending this creed to his supposed interlocutor? Can we really suppose that whoever is referred to by the second person pronouns in stanzas one and two is being asked to share the besotted state of 'him' in stanza three? Again, in what sense is this self-dramatising surrender a finer thing than Burton's more sober advice that one should make use of the advantages of melancholy? Finally, before we assume that Keats is offering this prescription to himself or anyone else, should we not bear in mind the advice he really did offer to his sister? 'Do not suffer Your Mind to dwell on unpleasant reflections—that sort of thing has been the destruction of my health ... Do not diet your mind with grief, it destroys the constitution.' (*Letters* 2:329 - 30).

It is possible that in these lines Keats meant to sound a cautionary note against the cult of pleasure, and perhaps the lines about feeding deep upon a woman's eyes really were meant as part of an ironic transition that failed. The notion may be that although the way to deal with the melancholy fit is to refresh one's sensibility with beautiful objects, it is a deadly mistake to replace the cult of sorrow with the cult of beauty. The fate of the sorrowing romantic and the epicure will be similar: the melancholy man will deaden his consciousness with drugs, or more insidiously with a self-dramatising relish of morbidity; the epicure, finding beauty and pleasure always slipping from his grasp, and the wine of life turning to poison (Proserpine's 'ruby grape') while the delicate palate is savouring, will become the thrall of melancholy. Keats is not referring to the common human joy in the beauty that can be experienced from time to time in everyday living, he is referring to the obsessive pursuit of enjoyment, the 'strenuous tongue' forcing all things to disgorge their last increment of sensation. The sybarite loses his soul as humiliatingly as the melancholy man—it will be a trophy in misery's holy place, a gossamer flag in a mystic chapel.

8

Grecian Urn and Autumn

The final riddle of Keats' urn has received so much explanatory comment that it has directed attention away from a more important, though soluble, difficulty at the beginning of the poem: 'Thou still unravish'd bride of quietness,/ Thou foster-child of silence and slow time.' Bernard Blackstone has spoken of his own struggle 'to understand how the urn can be at one and the same time a *bride* of quietness and a *foster-child* of silence and slow time, a difficulty ...in comparison with which the celebrated truth-beauty equation seemed clarity itself. These were points that the commentators disdained to raise, much less answer.' What I hope to do now is to be a little more precise about the urn's symbolic status, and to show that the poem's main concern is wiser and more humane than an examination of aesthetic functions and values. It is in this connection that the first two lines of the poem are so important.

In approaching an understanding of them, it is helpful to note that there are two appositions. 'Quietness' we may reasonably suppose to be in apposition to 'silence', and close enough in its implications to be virtually synonymous. Both 'silence' and 'quietness' are implicitly distinguished from 'time'; they represent, then, something other than time. The second apposition is 'bride' and 'foster-child'. These terms are clearly not synonymous—we must take them then as alternative symbols or, better perhaps, as paired symbols, both being necessary to express fully a complex significance. However we take them, they seem to make the sense of the lines more than a little confused. The urn is the bride of timelessness, but is also the child of such a union. To add to the confusion, the bride is unravished, and the child is a foster-child. These two difficulties, however, may be thought to cancel each other out. If the bride is unravished, then no union has taken place, the child is merely in the care of surrogate parents. It is this assumption, based perhaps on a too literal reading of 'foster-child' that has misled Jackson Bate and others to suppose an 'actual parentage' for the urn, and subsequently to imagine the urn after the death of its 'father' as fostered by the silence and slow time of a museum or gallery. I find it difficult to suppose that Keats was saying, or trying to say, no more than this.

Let us look at the imagery again, without supposing an antecedent 'actual parentage'. The urn is clearly the product of the union of a temporal thing (the potter who turned the clay, or the craftsman who sculpted the marble) with a timeless, immaterial thing (inspiration, imaginative vision, ideal form). But it is also a material thing (clay or marble) shaped by an ideal conception (the form in the artist's mind). It is thus both a child of the union of time and timelessness and, at the same time, a partner in such a union. Thus the term 'foster-child' need not suggest an orphan put in the care of substitute parents—Keats is using the term, I think, as the most appropriate term available to describe the product of a non-biological union—the union of shaping hands and mental image. Similarly the material that is shaped is not ravished or possessed by the mental image—there is no sexual correlative available to describe what has happened. True enough some critics see the urn as a womb, or as a whole female body, but nobody finds a phallic image.[1] The clay or marble was informed by the inspiring vision, not penetrated.

If this interpretation of Keats' terms is acceptable, then perhaps we have arrived at a slightly more precise understanding of the urn as a symbol of art. However, I believe that these opening lines indicate a larger symbolic function. Earl Wasserman has commented that: 'such tender reverance for what normally is an undesirable condition—to say nothing of the startling force of the word "unravish'd" applied to "bride"—calls for some inquiry.' Wasserman goes on to describe the notion of an 'Unravish'd bride' as, borrowing Kenneth Burke's term, a 'mystic oxymoron'.[2] Now there is an extraordinarily similar kind of 'mystic oxymoron' deeply rooted in western consciousness, expressing another form of the union of time and eternity, also producing a 'foster-child' (*The Times* of London recently noted March 19 as 'the feast of St Joseph, foster-father of Christ'.)

Keats is not, I would emphasise seeing the urn as another type of Madonna and Child—what he does perceive in the urn, I suggest, is a non-believer's equivalent. (I have used the term 'non-believer' discriminatingly here; I do not wish to synonymise tacitly non-belief and disbelief.) Gilded, richly jewelled pictures of Mary and the infant Jesus are now the most popularly recognised ikons of the Christian churches (though ikons can represent any aspect of the Christian religion), and many of them are wonderfully beautiful works of art. But let us consider their religious function. They are not in themselves objects of devotion (or are not supposed to be); they are representations which enable the worshipper to concentrate his attention on what he takes to be the reality behind the image. That reality is God, his relationship with his creatures, and his promise of an eternal destiny for man. An ikon may ratify an already held faith, or perhaps may on rare occasion promote a new-found faith, but its principal function is to focus the meditations of those who already believe.

What, then, of the bewildered man, whose faith has been weakened or lost, who at best can now believe only fitfully and vaguely? What can be helpful to, and clarify the perceptions of, a man who, agnostic in the strictest sense of the word, is dismayed by knowing that he cannot know? The urn is certainly a symbol of art in so far as the mystic oxymoron of its origin is common to all the arts, and by virtue of its function as an object lesson on what art can do. But it also has a power to stimulate and focus meditation which is not common to all forms of art, nor confined to any of them. It is because of this function that it is an agnostic's ikon, as the intense debate within the poem demonstrates. That debate is concerned with man and his hungers, his relation to the gods, his longing for permanence. The urn's power to stimulate not an act of faith, but meditative bewilderment about these matters, is perhaps given poignant modification by its funerary function—it may, in addition to what I have already suggested, be unravished in the sense that it has not yet been impregnated with the ashes of the dead.

Let us now examine how the poem expresses this meditative bewilderment. The organisation of the ode is in one sense very simple—the poet slowly turns the urn in his hands and comments on the scenes depicted on its sides. Ian Jack has made an exhaustive study of the likely sources of these scenes. The Townley Vase, which Keats could have seen in the British

Museum, shows naked male and female figures, but nothing suggesting 'mad pursuit'; the Sosibios Vase in the Louvre, of which Keats is said to have made a tracing (presumably from a sketch) has a religious procession, a youth with pipes, and is leaf-fringed, but has no heifer; the Borghese Vase, also in the Louvre, has a scene of Bacchic abandon, a bold lover, pipes and timbrels, maidens loth, but no religious procession; the Holland House urn does portray a sacrifice, though the victims are a pig, a sheep and a bull,—it has also a piper, trees, fruit and leaves; the Elgin Marbles provide a heifer which may indeed be lowing; Claude Lorrain's painting (*View of Delphi, with a Procession* has a little town, mountain-built with peaceful citadel; Poussin's *Autumn, or the Grapes of the Promised Land* also has a mountain citadel.[3]

Clearly the imagined pictures on Keats' urn are selected from these sources. They are not, however, merely 'a very generalised picture of the Greek scenes depicted'.[4] As Claude Finney has said, 'The imaginary Grecian urn which Keats described is untrue . . . to the pure conventions of Greek art. A Greek sculptor would no more think of mingling a Bacchic throng with a pious sacrifice than a Greek dramatist would think of mingling tragedy and comedy in a play.'[5] Keats' un-Grecian breach of unity of tone, however, may have a more important explanation than Finney suggests—that he was influenced by the example of Sosibios, whose vase does display a certain amount of heterogeneous matter. Keats, I believe, selected from his sources with a particular purpose in mind. We cannot be sure how many scenes we are to suppose are pictured on the urn,—there may be three or four, but there are certainly two principal ones, and I believe Keats chose these with deliberation, for they display two universal and apparently ineradicable human instincts; the pursuit of sexual pleasure, and the offering of sacrifice to the gods.

We should remember that Keats sometimes found it hard to reconcile these two instincts. He seems to have experienced from time to time a painful distaste for sexuality itself; one remembers, for example, his fury at Bailey's sudden marriage, and his stigmatising his friend's motive as 'that of a Ploughman who wants a wife' (*Letters* 2:67). More to the point for my present purpose is the incident on board the *Maria Crowther* reported by Joseph Severn:

In the ship when we were performing Quarantine—it was proposed that the Sailors should sing us some songs to kill the time—2 or 3 sung—coarsely and brutally enough—but I was astonished at the effect on Keats—he started up—and said —'O! god! I doubt the immortality of my Soul—this grossness takes away my belief—I fall into a brute even to hear it—why do I live if these are my fellow creatures?'[6]

One may cite also his dismay on contemplating the fact that the English word 'love' was used both for sexual attraction, 'goatish, whinnyish, lustful love', and 'the abstract adoration of the deity'. This, to Keats, was 'the old plague spot, the raw scrofula'. Such violent expressions may be the product of passing moods, but that such moods happened from time to time perhaps indicates a deeper problem. The fact that the urn shows to the poet, on one side, goatish lust, and on the other side worship of the gods, and bearing in mind that the two sides are in fact fully contiguous, indicates that the principal topic for debate in this poem is perhaps not the nature and function of art, but the nature and destiny of man, whose lust and piety are not separate parts of his nature, but are inherent in his wholeness.

If we now reconsider the organisation of the poem we see that it is wider in scope and more complex in detail than we first supposed. The poet is not merely commenting in turn on each of the scenes depicted as they appear to his gaze; they are, after all, imaginative constructs of his own careful and purposeful choosing. Stanzas one and four represent seemingly opposite aspects of human nature; stanzas two and three, coming spatially between them, represent also an argument between them; a dialogue between the appetites of soul and body, the hunger for eternity and the need for time. The agnosticism which the urn symbolises is implicit in the failure of the art object to suggest any form of reconciliation of these opposites, thus rendering it impossible to conceive of a divine destiny for creatures so diversely constituted. The first two lines of the poem indicate the urn's symbolic nature, the last stanza comments on the lamentable success of its function as an ikon of unknowing. The unifying principle of the poem is the dialectic conflict implicit in the language and phraseology throughout the ode. Bearing this organisation in mind, let us now examine details.

The scene in the first stanza is not described directly, but is revealed by a series of questions. It has been said that these are questions that any curious observer might ask.[7] Surely not *any* curious observer, one might demur, but a gifted and philosophically troubled one. As E.E. Bostetter has pointed out: 'the urn and the poet raise questions they do not pretend to answer.'[8] They are in fact aporetic questions, even in their simple significance. We cannot know who the figures are who are represented on the marble frieze, their names and backgrounds are forever out of reach. But behind the ten questions (seven in stanza one, three in stanza four) through which the two principal scenes are revealed to us, there may be an anterior question, and this too may be aporetic, in a far more important way: what kind of a piece of work is man, crawling between earth and heaven? If such a question is being asked, the explicit questions of the opening stanza bear a double load of ambiguity:

> What leaf-fring'd legend haunts about thy shape
>   Of deities or mortals, or of both,
>   In Tempe or the dales of Arcady?
>   What men or gods are these?

Let us look at the simple ambiguities first. Keats may be asking: 'Are the characters shown here all gods or all men? Or are some of them divine and some human?' But he may also be asking, in the phrase 'or of both', 'Are some of the characters both divine and human?' Earl Wasserman has said of the passage:

> Mortal and immortal move close to the knife edge, but Keats' question, although it brings them together in the same context, expresses a hesitation that prevents them from fusing. The same loose mingling appears in the line 'In Tempe or the dales of Arcady', Tempe being that earthly region which the gods, especially Apollo, were inclined to favour—an earthly heaven—and Arcady that region that man thought to approach most nearly a paradise—a heavenly earth. In each name both the divine and the mortal are present, but with inverted emphasis.[9]

Wasserman shrewdly illustrates the debate within the imagery—a 'loose mingling' only, but with hints of possible fusion. Keats' questions approach but do not explicitly reach the primal question: 'Is there indeed a spark of the divinity in man?'

Let us now look at the deeper ambiguity, which introduces not merely a fresh possibility of meaning, but a more sophisticated modulation of tone. What the questions may be asking is: 'Can there really be sparks of divinity in appetitive creatures such as these?' There is little tenderness in the picture Keats unveils, there is 'mad pursuit' and 'struggle to escape', and no suggestion of mutuality in 'wild ecstasy'. As Wasserman again shrewdly notes: 'Only our fecund talent for recognising the rapacity of love, and not anything in the explicit description, leads us to see the pursuit and struggle as a love game instead of a brutality.'[10] The tone therefore of the repeated 'What' in these lines may be ironic as well as quizzical. Could any such creatures become divine, as Keats' Apollo is evermore about to do in *Hyperion*? Could any god ensnare himself in such flesh, or propagate himself upon it? Is mankind's divine aspiration a leaf-fring'd legend merely?

The puritan irony that I suggest here is, I think, subdued—a possible tone that seems at times to creep into the poet's voice. What I have called the simple ambiguities remain the most important ones. Do the gods mingle with us, and perhaps inspire us? The question seems to be constantly asked in Greek mythology, and is usually answered affirmatively; and even if the gods and goddesses who come to us are predatory, spiteful and gluttonous, does not their mingling with us offer hopeful prospects? Stanzas two and three of the ode constitute an allusive debate on such intimations.

Two problems face us when we examine these stanzas. To some people they seem a digression. 'We have only to apply the simple test of omitting them both, or else the third alone, and we find that what remains will still be a poem, though admittedly less rich.'[11] This difficulty may be resolved if we consider that the ode's real debate is about the nature and destiny of humankind, and the poet's difficulties in reconciling man's apparently conflicting appetites. For Keats here begins to meditate on man's possible spiritual capacity. The contrast between the boisterous, sportive lust of stanza one and the serene idealism with which stanza two begins is both sharp and deliberate:

> Heard melodies are sweet, but those unheard
> Are sweeter; therefore, ye soft pipes, play on;
> Not to the sensual ear, but, more endear'd,
> Pipe to the spirit ditties of no tone.

The paradox of unheard music repays careful attention. The immediate temptation is to think of a peculiar intensity of pleasure in music—as Eliot expressed it: 'the music heard so deeply/ That it is not heard at all, but you are the music/ While the music lasts.' A more romantic, and consequently less satisfying notion is that since we must imagine the music being played on the urn, our aural fancy can provide a better music than has ever been performed. It can't, of course. The real significance of the lines is both more philosophical and more scientific.

The number scribed on a tuning fork ought to remind us that the physical basis of music is a pattern of precisely calculated vibrations, which, as numerical values, might be said to exist formally and independently without being actualised in time. We can notate music as lines and symbols on a score; a physicist might record it as a sequence of numbers. Now one of the consequences of popular theology is the development of the idea that after death the soul will know all things directly: beauty, truth, love, God himself, will be known by an act of simple apprehension, unmediated through sensory experience. Keats seems to express precisely this idea in a letter to the George Keatses written shortly after Tom's death:

> ... there you are with Birkbeck—here I am with brown—some-times I fancy an immense separation, and sometimes, as at present, a direct communication of spirit with you. That will be one of the grandeurs of immortality—there will be no space and consequently the only commerce between spirits will be by their intelligence of each other—when they will completely understand each other—while we in this world comp[r]ehend each other in different degrees.
>
> (2:5)

St Paul may have promoted the notion in Christian belief and culture: 'For now we see through a glass, darkly; but then, face to face' (1 *Corinthians* 13:12), and in so doing made it not so much a Platonic notion as a puritan form of idealism, for implicit within it is an attitude to the senses which, if it does not actually despise them, reduces them to the status of dispensable aids. Newell Ford has shown that in his early poems, and particularly *Endymion*, Keats had conceived of a bodily post-mortal state, where all sensory pleasures would be enjoyed 'in finer tone'.[12] But the *Ode on a Grecian Urn* seems to imply that heaven, if there is such a place, will not be like that. In the lines before us Keats is certainly inclined towards the kind of bodiless immortality he had described in his American letter: '. . . therefore, ye soft pipes, play on;/ Not to the sensual ear, but, more endear'd,/ Pipe to the spirit ditties of no tone.' The puritan emphasis shows itself not only in the tone of the word 'sensual', but in the pun in 'endear'd'—we must love and trust the spiritual ear more than the fleshly one.

There is supporting evidence for this view within the very texture of the lines themselves. Keats we know was greatly concerned with the manipulation of vowel sounds, and he seems to have considered the possibility of vowel patterns conforming to principles such as govern melody in music. Benjamin Bailey says, in his memoir of Keats at Oxford: 'One of his favourite topics of discourse was the principle of melody in verse, upon which he had his own notions, particularly in the management of open and close vowels.'[13] When we listen carefully to the first four lines of stanza two we become aware of a deliberate pattern of repetition and return of vowels: 'heard—unheard', 'sweet—sweeter', 'ear—endear'd', 'spirit—ditties', that might possibly correspond to a composer's management of tonic, dominant, and so on. But of course we can also see the pattern at a glance, on the page before us. 'Pipe to the spirit ditties of no tone' seems to say, then, that the pattern, which can be apprehended in an instant, is all; sense experience unfolding in time merely a crutch that can be dispensed with by the unbodied soul. We are locked into our senses though, we cannot imagine seeing 'face to face' in the way Paul means, or hearing 'ditties of no tone'. Hence the difficulty many people feel in conceiving such a kind of post-mortal existence—it is not merely a matter of doubting whether heaven exists, but of doubting that one would like it if it did. It is this last consideration that forms the substance of the debate in this stanza and the next, and gives it a strangely rich poignancy.

When we continue reading stanza two, the second problem that I alluded to earlier arises immediately. Are we now looking at a different scene from stanza one, or a detail of that scene brought into sharper focus? 'Ye soft pipes' appears to refer back to 'What pipes and timbrels?' and thus to imply that we are now scrutinising a detail, or possibly several details in turn. But if this is so, the details are in strange contrast to the suggestions of the whole picture. If we keep in view the whole scene while examining particular areas of it—in other words if we remember stanza one while looking closely at stanza two, we see the uniquely generative way in which Keats' images seem to argue with one another. Let us remember the accelerating pace of the last three lines of stanza one:

> What men or gods are these? What maidens loth?
> What mad pursuit? What struggle to escape?
> What pipes and timbrels? What wild ecstasy?

The climax re-enacted by sense and rhythm here is probably not supposedly represented on the urn—we are not asked to see copulating figures—but the 'wild ecstasy' is irresistibly suggested by the pictorial dynamism of the scene as Keats has described it. Although the figures are fixed on the urn, swift movement, struggle and satisfaction are all conjured into the observer's mind as he gazes at the imagined still scene. But let us now look at what we may suppose to be a detail of the picture:

> Bold Lover, never, never canst thou kiss,
> Though winning near the goal—yet do not grieve;
> She cannot fade, though thou hast not thy bliss,
> Forever wilt thou love, and she be fair!

All the dynamism is gone, along with all the lustful joy; nothing urges the mind to make the picture move. The beauty is formal, statuesque, and strangely wistful. So great is the change that one instinctively supposes that Keats has rotated the urn and is looking at a separate scene, but the link implied in 'soft pipes' makes this unlikely. On a closer inspection of the Bacchic scene, the sexual gusto has been etherealised, or realised anew 'in finer tone'. It is not a goatish spirit that apprehends unheard melodies.

We are now well launched into the debate about spirit and sense. The figures on the urn represent a paradigm of immortality—the bodiless immortality that was part of the popular beliefs of the Protestant tradition in which Keats had been reared. The discussion in stanzas two and three does not concern whether such immortality is indeed man's destiny; Keats, for the immediate purpose of his argument, assumes that it is. The real point at issue is whether the immortal state will really be a blessed one. Newell Ford assumes that Keats thinks it will be:

> The third stanza rings over and over the theme of unfading happiness ... If there were any doubt in the previous stanza of the desirability of a perennial spring time, or any fear that the lovers would be unhappy because they could not, like Endymion and Cynthia, embrace, there is assuredly neither doubt nor fear in this stanza ... A less empathic poet would have remembered the irony implicit in his theme: eternity belongs to lifeless representations, fixed and cold, rather than to living, breathing things.[14]

My own view is that Keats, marvellously empathic poet that he was, and perhaps indeed because he was more fully so than Ford realises, was keenly aware of the irony of his theme. It is because he could so powerfully project his own feelings into the inanimate figures on the urn that the 'theme of unfading happiness' is so deeply undermined with sadness. The mere perpetuation of individual consciousness is undoubtedly the most widespread and ineradicable of human longings, yet the everlasting disappointment of the lover on the urn, his longing ever sharp, his failure unending, may be regarded as more genuinely tragic than mere annihilation would be. To the despairing lover on the urn the situation is an eternal teasing—the rapid sequence of contraries in the relevant lines in stanza two—the juxtaposition of benefit and drawback is almost cruel and almost humourous:

> Bold Lover, never, never canst thou kiss
> Though winning near the goal—yet do not grieve;
> She cannot fade, though thou has not thy bliss,
> For ever wilt thou love, and she be fair.

But we do not need to carry even these immediate memories into our reading of stanza three to be dubious of that ringing

happiness that Ford proclaims. Perhaps a corollary to the theory
of the affirmative possibilities of 'not' is the negative power of
affirmation. Somewhere there is great sadness latent in the
picture on the urn if it takes six 'happys' in five lines to reassure
the poet and his readers. Also this sadness is not merely due to the
fact that 'more is being deprived the figures on the urn than is
bestowed',[15]—there is a debilitating sense of limitation which we
detect more fully if we note Keats' choice of verbs, both in stanzas
two and three:

> Fair youth, beneath the trees, thou canst not leave
> Thy song, nor ever can those trees be bare;
> Bold Lover, never, never canst thou kiss . . .

> She cannot fade . . .
> Ah, happy, happy boughs! that cannot shed
> Your leaves . . .

If the trees, the melodist, and the lovers are happy, it is a
straitened happiness, for the timeless state must by its nature
exclude not only physical joy, but a kind of beauty that is
wonderfully fitted to temporal creatures—the beauty of change
and sequence. In spite of the piper's 'unheard melodies' the
beauty of music cannot be known in a timeless instant, it is phase
beauty, depending on memory and expectation. Likewise an
eternal spring is no spring at all, following no winter, heralding no
summer, hoping for no harvest. Eternity, as art represents it, is a
prison.

   Although Keats has, in these stanzas, by means of controlled
ambiguity and the contrary suggestiveness of emphasis, exposed
the limitations of this idealist conception of immortality, we
must not suppose too readily that he dismisses the idea, or that it
did not remain in some ways attractive to him. To recover a truer
perspective on the argument that has gone on in these stanzas, let
us bring together once more the contending opposites:

> Heard melodies are sweet, but those unheard
> Are sweeter; therefore, ye soft pipes, play on;
> Not to the sensual ear, but, more endear'd
> Pipe to the spirit ditties of no tone . . .
> . . . All breathing human passion far above,

That leaves a heart high sorrowful and cloy'd,
A burning forehead, and a parching tongue.

The lines describing the unheard music are perfectly balanced, both in their rhythm and vowel music. Their sense unfolds simply and with assurance; there is a classical serenity in almost every aspect of the poetry that conceals the flaw in the state of being that is postulated—perhaps only the calculated disappointment in the false rhymes prepares us for the sad bathos of 'no tone'. The lines dealing with the snags of bodily life, however, contain stronger ironies. They begin deceptively, as if mocking the idealism of the rest of the stanzas—such idealism being 'far above' the thing it so painfully lacks—'breathing human passion'. But the very pulse of the lines, and the expression 'a heart high sorrowful' seem as if they are leading us to some intense romantic tragedy. We get instead the word 'cloy'd', a more disastrous bathos than the unheard music's 'no tone'.

Pleasure is not merely transient, it is a cheat, fulfilment is anticlimax, satiety a kind of surfeit. 'The enjoyment of the Spring', as Keats had written in the lines on *Fancy*, fades just as inevitably as the actual 'blossoming'; the ripeness of autumn ultimately 'cloys' the most beautiful eye will soon 'weary'; nor is there any 'voice, however soft', that 'one would hear too oft'.[16] Pleasure, even without snags, loses its gusto. But there is a snag for the finely tuned sensibility—the aftermath—'a burning forehead and a parching tongue.' The more scrupulously we weigh the implications of Keats' diction and symbols, the more delicately the balance trembles, but the scale never comes down.

So far we cannot be sure whether we have been looking at one scene, and subsequently scrutinising details, or two or three separate scenes. In stanza four there can be no doubt that the poet has turned the urn in his hands, for the new scene is so different in subject matter from that of stanza one that it seems to constitute, as Finney pointed out, a breach of classical unity. Douglas Bush sees stanza four as 'logically a digression', and F.W. Bateson considers it as a: 'relapse into Romanticism. The "green altar", the "mysterious priest" and the "little town" were alluring invitations to reverie.'[17] If, as I believe, Keats selected from his sources the scenes revealed in the first and fourth stanzas for the particular purpose of examining the nature of man in the light of his apparently incongruous instincts, then stanza four is neither a digression nor a relapse, and it is certainly not a reverie. The stanza is not merely vitally connected to the examination of human nature, it is organically united to the theme of idealism by virtue of its inquiry into that instinct which Keats seemed at times to consider antipodean to sexuality. The religious procession does not, as Ian Jack thinks, 'unforgettably *intrude*' [my italics] into the poem, it is Keats's preordained means for continuing, from another aspect, his meditation on his principal theme.[18] We would do well to remember Wasserman's judgement: 'Keats is far from being merely an associative poet whose only control over structure is the subjective pattern that his feelings spontaneously dictated to him. Quite to the contrary, Keats conceived of a poem as a perfectly ordered cosmos.'[19] Bearing this in mind let us review the questions by means of which the ritualistic scene is revealed to us:

> Who are these coming to the sacrifice?
>   To what green altar, O mysterious priest,
> Lead'st thou that heifer lowing at the skies,
>   And all her silken flanks with garlands drest?
> What little town . . .
> Is emptied of this folk, this pious morn?

In the second version of *Hyperion* the name 'Saturn' was not a full answer to the questions '. . . tell me where I am,/ Whose altar this; for whom this incense curls;/ What image this . . .?' Only the sight of Moneta's face could tell the poet what he really wanted to know, the nature of the deity he had encountered. Similarly, in the fourth stanza of the ode, names will not do; neither the group name of the people, nor the names of their town, priest, god or goddess would be adequate to Keats' perplexity. The real questions, I suggest, are: 'What is it in man that urges him to make sacrifices to the gods? Is there in fact a god, and does he accept these offerings? What sort of man devotes his life to serving such a people and their god, and to celebrating the sacred mysteries (there is surely a pun on 'mysterious')?' Apart from religious faith, answers to these deeper questions are no more available than they are to the questions in their simple forms. Like the questions in stanza one, they are doubly aporetic.

There are two images in this stanza which need particular attention. The heifer, it seems to me, is central in a double sense. She is the sacrificial victim whose death will, it is hoped, propitiate the god. As such she is the honoured cynosure of the whole occasion. It may be, however, that she is ironically representative of all the worshippers and the ceremony itself. She is animal life, with all its attractiveness ('silken flanks') given a meretricious dignity by being dressed in garlands. There is perhaps a double significance in her 'lowing at the skies'. This may be what the whole ceremony amounts to, animal beings dignifying themselves not merely with dress and ornament, but with the ritual itself. Perhaps the townsfolk and their priest are, like their victim, merely crying to an indifferent heaven.

The second image which needs attention is the 'little town'. The form of Keats' question: 'What little town, by river or sea-shore,/ Or mountain-built with peaceful citadel . . . ?' implies that the town is not represented on the urn (he does not ask 'What is *this* little town?' and he is ignorant of its whereabouts). However in the next lines the town seems to appear on the urn, as if the image had created itself there as Keats asked his question:

> And, little town, thy streets for evermore
> Will silent be; and not a soul to tell
> Why thou art desolate, can e'er return.

Keats sees the town's emptiness, and endows this condition with the permanence of all the other images on the urn. Why has he, almost as an afterthought, it seems, projected this image onto the established scene? Also, why does he describe the town as 'desolate'? It has been suggested that one reason is the urn's function as a 'sylvan historian': 'It is not simply because the figures are forever imprisoned on the urn that no one can ever return to the empty town, but because the actual inhabitants disappeared in the remote past—a past from which no one remains except as figures on an urn or in other works of art.'[20] This is stimulating, for undoubtedly one of the emotions Keats wishes to arouse is a sense of the apparently utter finality of death. Another suggestion, not inconsistent with this, is that the empty town symbolises the deadness of idealism: 'We have been carried into a world that is permanent, but permanently empty, just as the art on the urn is permanent but permanently lifeless.'[21]

Both these suggestions go a fair way to justify the force of 'desolate', but not far enough. They do not account for the use of the verb 'return', and this seems to me important. If the figures were able to tell why the town is desolate, that is, establish the nature and validity of the ceremony for which they have left the town, they would not have to return to it to do so; they are there, before our eyes, forming their procession. Perhaps the turn of phrase 'not a soul ... can e'er return' sets off echoes here; perhaps Keats was remembering Hamlet's description of death as: 'The undiscovered country from whose bourne/ No traveller returns.' If so the memory helps us to divine Keats' purpose, and thus perhaps to explain why 'desolate' and 'return' seem so right. The town represents ordinary commercial and social living, the ceremony spiritual yearnings and immortal longings. But no one who could supply a real answer to the deeper questions that have been asked in the stanza can ever return from the undiscovered country to the town of the living. It is this knowing that we cannot know that renders the town desolate.

The concluding stanza is an elegantly wistful comment on the urn's limitations both as a symbol of art and its relation to life, and, paradoxically, its lamentable success as an ikon for the non-believer. Like the great images of faith, it has wonderful beauty, but little warmth and human significance other than the warmth and significance the gazer projects onto it—the leaf-fring'd legend is merely legend, not myth. The figures in the 'brede' have no human genesis, they are a *breed* of 'marble men and maidens'. The urn has answered none of the questions Keats asked, it has merely been the occasion of them, and they are questions beyond the power of human thought to answer, just as eternity is a concept beyond imagination. There is an almost bitter disappointment in Keats' pun, 'Cold Pastoral.' The urn has no more power to warm or enlighten us than bucolic love tales; it is an episcopal letter to the faithful that answers none of their deep needs. Yet though the urn explains nothing, it offers a kind of comfort, being itself immortal:

> When old age shall this generation waste,
>   Thou shalt remain, in midst of other woe
>   Than ours ...

An equivocal and characteristically cold comfort, one may think. The urn's immunity emphasises our disease. It will still be there, from age to age of human sorrow, frailty and death. Nevertheless Keats seems to see it as in some way a friend to man, and to derive an apparently consoling message for the urn to convey:

> Beauty is truth, truth beauty,—that is all
> Ye know on earth, and all ye need to know.

If these lines in their entirety, and not merely the aphorism, are indeed spoken by the urn, there seems little comfort in the implicit rebuke that all the questions that the poet has been asking so urgently are unnecessary and irrelevant, and mankind must be satisfied with the knowledge that two abstract nouns are coterminous. Yet I suggest that this ending to the poem is not the failure some critics have thought it, nor yet the arcane triumph which others have so energetically praised.

Keats had doubts about the value of art. Poetry, he conceded, may be a mere 'Jack a lanthern to amuse whoever may chance to be struck with its brilliance' (*Letters* 1:242). The artist ought to be a friend to man—a physician to all men—but how can an artist labour for mortal good and ease the giant agony of the world? At times it seemed to Keats that a ship's surgeon might do better. It seems possible that the last lines of the poem expose the quasi-religious pretensions of art. 'The immortality of art, promised by the Grecian Urn, may be itself only the coldness of another kind of death.'[22] What can the urn do to make bearable the worst of our distresses, when its only answer to the riddle of life is another riddle? Some critics, following the Arnoldian heresy, believe that Keats and other Romantics regarded art as a surrogate for religion. Its seems probable that in the *Ode on a Grecian Urn* Keats is denying this very notion, or at least casting serious doubt upon it. For if the last two lines are the urn's deposit of faith, there seems little point in meeting at Nicea. If this is indeed the wisdom of art, 'the highest wisdom available to man', then the urn's function as the ikon of agnosticism has been almost perfectly fulfilled.

To the philosophically inclined or biographic critic, *To Autumn* is a strange poem. Written several months after the odes of

May—after, that is, the perplexity of the *Grecian Urn* and the
struggles with pain, grief and fear in *Nightingale* and *Melancholy*,
To Autumn seems inexplicably serene—'the most serene poem in
the English language,' according to Gittings.[23] This is the more
puzzling because in the three or four months' interim Keats'
personal situation had not improved. He had been worried by
news from George in America, was sufficiently impoverished to
begin trying to call in loans from his friends (including Haydon),
and to consider taking a job, possibly as a ship's surgeon.
Towards the end of the period he adds to his misery by exiling
himself from Fanny Brawne, to live with Brown in Winchester.
Why then this seeming tone of deep and secure happiness?

> Season of mists and mellow fruitfulness,
>   Close bosom-friend of the maturing sun;
> Conspiring with him how to load and bless
>   With fruit the vines that round the thatch-eaves run;
> To bend with apples the moss'd cottage-trees,
>   And fill all fruit with ripeness to the core;
> To swell the gourd, and plump the hazel shells
>   With a sweet kernel; to set budding more,
> And still more, later flowers for the bees,
> Until they think warm days will never cease,
>   For summer has o'erbrimm'd their clammy cells.

Nothing in the poet's life, or in what he had written or revised
during these months prepares us for this. Gittings believes that
the source of this marvellous calm was: 'the joyful peace which the
countryside always brought him, if the pressures of the world did
not intrude.'[24] There is much in this, but one suspects that by this
time, even under the most comforting influences of nature, Keats
was not able to exclude the pressures of the world from his
consciousness. No healing influence could alter the fact that the
orphan family was broken by death and departure—Tom was in
his grave, and George in Kentucky—and yet we have in these lines
not merely a description of autumn, but a celebration of it. Let us
look at the diction, imagery and structure to see not only their
poetic excellence, but their implications.

It should be noted straight away that there seems to be no
debate here—everything apparently points in the same direction.

The verbs, for instance, 'load', 'bend', 'swell', 'plump', 'o'erbrimm'd', all indicate not merely a tireless vitality, but an overwhelming benevolence. The same sense of nature's rich kindliness is hinted in the notion of sun and season 'conspiring' to 'bless' the trees with fruit. Whether or not God's in his heaven, all is undoubtedly right with the world. But 'bless' has no spiritual connotation here—this magnificent world, providentially arranged though it seems, is entirely material. Thus although it reminds us strongly of Marvell's *Garden* ('the nectarine and curious peach/ Into my hands themselves do reach'), it has in fact more in common with stanza three of *Nightingale*, representing the fulfilled promise, it seems, of the seasonable month that so abundantly endows: 'The grass, the thicket, and the fruit-tree wild;/ White hawthorn and the pastoral eglantine.' In other words, the world shown in stanza one of Autumn is not a prefigurative vision of a spiritual reality to come, nor a backward glance to 'that happy Garden state'. It is the real world with all the drawbacks of reality except time removed. If it were an ideal world it would not be so English, so locally placed by the potent details: 'thatch-eaves', and 'moss'd cottage-trees'. Nor would it contain the temporal hints of 'season', 'mellow fruitfulness', 'maturing sun', and 'later flowers'. The cottage trees are not the marble trees on the Grecian urn, they, are, one feels certain, Hampshire trees. The ideal world of the urn was not merely fixed and cold, it was also silent, offering only 'ditties of no tone'.

The world of Keats' autumn is alive with music. In this stanza we hear the first rustlings of the wind that is soon to lift Autumn's hair, its low murmurings suggested by the frequency of 'm', 'n', and 's' sounds throughout the stanza—a sound that blends easily with the noise of the bees. But when the humming of the bees rises above the wind, when in fact the onomatopoeia becomes obtrusive, 'For summer has o'erbrimm'd their clammy cells', we hear not only the humming of the insects, but a faintly indicated murmur of satiety that almost becomes sickly in 'clammy cells'. Keats at his greatest was a master of the controlled false note. The stanza has suggested not merely abundance, but overabundance:

> To bend with apples the moss'd cottage-trees,
>   And fill all fruit with ripeness to the core;

> To swell the gourd, and plump the hazel shells
> With a sweet kernel; to set budding more,
> And still more, later flowers ...

To this point the riches and sweetness are still entirely delightful, but in 'o'erbrimm'd their clammy cells' the palate curdles. The first hint of a possible snag has been made. As Douglas Bush has said: 'We canot escape the melancholy implications of exuberant ripeness.'[25]

If we listen to the whole rhythm of this stanza we may detect another hint. Accompanying the imagery and plain statement of overabundance, there is a rhythmic sense of surplus; the stanza seems to go on longer than we expected, as if 'warm days would never cease'. It actually does, of course, if we have grown used to the stanza pattern of *Nightingale*, *Grecian Urn*, and *Melancholy*, for there are eleven lines. But there is also something in the rhyme scheme, the significance of which Jackson Bate has pointed out: 'The effect of the couplet, placed thus [immediately before the last line] is to sustain the approaching close at a momentary crest before the stanza subsides in the final line.'[26] The effect in this stanza is minimal—there is the merest hint of 'too much'—but there is also (and this is the effect Keats was looking for) a trace of anti-climax. In this stanzaic shape we have the pattern of the whole poem. The superb achievement of nature, the joy of its wealth, the sense of inexhaustible resource is something we are encouraged imaginatively to sustain 'at a momentary crest' before subsiding into a perception of an aspect of reality which the poem refrains from specifying.

The second stanza is dominated by the personification of the season. Northrop Frye sees this figure as a corn goddess, though one finds it difficult to imagine a corn goddess gleaning, or stepping cautiously across a stream.[27] She would need to be a fruit goddess too, for she presides over the cider making. One suspects Frye may be oversimplifying. Ian Jack is more specific about the identity of the goddess, finding in the personification: 'a slight suggestion of the classical figure of Ceres.' On the other hand he sees Autumn in the threshing floor as possibly modelled on Psyche in Giulio Romano's painting, *Psyche asleep among the Grain*. This painting illustrates part of the story of Cupid and Psyche, where Psyche is punished by Venus with the task of sifting a mingled heap of 'wheat, barley, mill, poppy seed, peason, lintels and beanes'. The ants came and did the job for Psyche, but Jack, noting that in the picture Psyche's hair seems to be soft-lifted, suggests that perhaps a winnowing wind helped too.

Autumn keeping steady her laden head across a brook, Jack suggests, may owe something to Poussin's *Autumn, or the Grapes of the Promised Land*, but I suspect he is on better ground when he suggests the same artist's *The Summer of Ruth and Boaz*.[28] I am inclined to think that Keats' figure has more in common with Ruth than with either Ceres or Psyche, and the memory of his Old Testament reading perhaps influenced Keats as much as the mirror of art. Autumn sometimes looks like a gleaner, Ruth 'kept fast by the maidens of Boaz to glean unto the end of barley harvest' (*Ruth* 2:23); Autumn sits careless on a granary floor while the breeze from the threshing lifts her hair, Naomi told Ruth that Boaz 'winnoweth barley tonight in the threshing floor' (3:1 - 2); Autumn is found on a half-reaped furrow sound asleep, Ruth rests near Boaz, who 'went to lie down at the end of a heap of corn' (3:7). There is also the possibility, suggested by Gittings, that she bears some affinity with Iphigeneia of Cyprus, whom Burton describes: 'by a brookside, in a little thicket, fast asleep.'[29]

Although I think that the Old Testament probably provided the most important single source for the figure, one should note the ways in which Autumn differs from Ruth. Ruth was an impoverished widow in a foreign land, looking for employment in someone else's fields. Autumn is in charge of her world, she need importune no one, she is not among 'alien corn', it is her corn. Indeed she is in this respect more like Boaz than Ruth, she is the provider of this natural wealth. All her postures are superbly and economically pictured—sitting careless, her hair soft-lifted (her hair is seen in the glinting yellow of the flying chaff), asleep among the poppies and convolvulus. 'Autumn is ... a female overcome by the fragrance and soft exhaustion of her own labour. She is passive, an embodiment of the earthly paradise.'[30] Only when strenuously balancing across a brook is she anything less than assured and at ease. In the final image she is savouring her wealth: 'And by a cider press with patient look/ Thou watchest the last oozings, hours by hours.'

The figure of Autumn is so dominant, the beauty of her attitudes and her surroundings so delightful to the inward eye that we may need to read the stanza several times before we become fully aware of all the work that is being done by sound. True, we hear at once the onomatopoeia of 'soft-lifted by the winnowing wind', but the very obviousness of this may deafen us for a time to the stanza's prevailing undersong. The rustling wind from stanza one blows gently through the harvest field in carefully spaced sibilants:

> Who hath not seen thee oft amid thy store?
> Sometimes whoever seeks abroad may find
> Thee sitting careless on a granary floor,
> Thy hair soft-lifted by the winnowing wind.

Perhaps 'seen ... oft' in the first line is an aural preparation for 'soft-lifted'—this is Keats' vowel music at its most adroitly beautiful. We should note too that there is more here than the rustling 's' sounds, there are deftly manipulated nasal consonants: 'Sometimes', 'find', 'winnowing wind'—so that the rustling modulates into the hum of complacent sleepiness; and these sounds intensify, with the help of long 'o' sounds, and one superbly positioned 'u': 'Drows'd with the fume of poppies.' By the end of the stanza the sound has modulated again to the wakeful busy murmur of the harvest field—an effect Arnold was to make explicit in 'All the live murmur of a summer's day'—mingled with slow liquid tricklings in 'last oozings, hours by hours'. Here again, in the eleventh line, there is a faint sense of subsiding, as Bate puts it, a slightly less happy tone. Autumn waits by the cider press, patiently, while the utmost yield of the press is squeezed out. This, in a sense, is characteristic of the figure, in all her postures she symbolises the extraction of the utmost good from the earth. In this she is achieving that 'sustained' but nonetheless 'momentary crest'—the closure, nevertheless, must come. The oozings she watches for so many hours are the last oozings and, as Jackson Bate says: 'The pervading thought in what follows is the withdrawal of autumn, the coming death of the year, and of course the familiar archetypal relevance of the association to our feelings of sequence in our own lives.'[31]

So far there has been little symbolic debate in the poem, the images of serenity and fulfilment have been so powerful that the faint contra-indications have been almost overwhelmed. From now on, however, the disturbing implications of the imagery grow steadily more effective. The first two lines of the stanza are rich with hidden significance: 'Where are the songs of Spring? Ay, where are they?/ Think not of them, thou hast thy music too.' In spite of the prohibition addressed to the figure of Autumn, the effect of the second line is to cause the reader to think of the songs of Spring; something he might not have done had Keats not issued his rhetorical caveat. The reiteration of the question as supposed reassurance to Autumn ('Your rivals are dead') has precisely the opposite effect on the reader. The name Autumn occurs only in the title, not in the poem; the sudden naming of Spring reminds us that we are not contemplating an invulnerable state of things, but a passing season. The songs of Spring were of energy and hope; those of Autumn of rich fulfilment. Those of Spring have passed away; those of Autumn will pass away. From this point on: 'every item carries an elegiac note. The day is dying, and gnats and lambs and crickets and birds all seem to be aware of approaching darkness.'[32] The other significance in these lines is that Keats is specifically drawing the reader's attention to the onomatopoeia, hitherto pervasive, but subsidiary to the visual imagery. From now on it will be both pervasive and primary—'the music of time.'[33]

We hear at once a dramatic modulation in the sound. The tones of the bees and the winnowing wind may have been drowsy, but they were as happy in their ways as we may suppose the songs of spring to have been. But Autumn's later music is a solemn melody:

> While barred clouds bloom the soft-dying day,
>   And touch the stubble-plains in rosy hue,
>   Then in a wailful choir the small gnats mourn
>   Among the river shallows borne aloft
> Or sinking as the light wind lives or dies.

The same notes appear to have been struck as earlier, the vowels in 'bloom', 'hue', 'mourn', pick up the humming theme of 'fume', 'oozings', 'hours', but the effect is different in the way a minor key differs from a major—our usual expectations are slightly cheated. The difference is perhaps signalled in the downshift from 'soft-lifted' to 'soft-dying'. But now we have an explicit clash of opposites: 'bloom-dying', 'borne aloft—sinking', 'lives—dies'. 'Wailful choir' and 'mourn' ratify what has already been suggested. The change in the tenor of the poem has been effected quickly, though subtly, and it is a sombre change. The 'momentary crest' of life's richness has been sustained to the utmost, to the last gleanings and the last oozings, but now it must subside. There are two backward glances: 'hedge-crickets sing', but 'full-grown lambs' (reminding us by their growth that spring is gone) 'loud *bleat* from hilly bourn'. The final images look forward: 'The redbreast whistles from a garden-croft;/ And gathering swallows twitter in the skies.' There remains a certain vitality here, but it is the nervous energy of departure, or of stealing oneself to endure. The music is now thin, without timbre. Man: 'has his winter too, of pale misfeature,/ Or else he would forego his mortal nature.'

Although the serenity of the first two stanzas has been undermined in this sombre fashion, it remains in many ways the prevailing tone of the poem, the impression one takes away even after several readings. As Ian Jack has noted: 'the remarkable thing is that Keats does not allow melancholy to cloud the poem. There are no dead leaves in the ode, and there is no cold autumnal wind.'[34] This has led critics to find some kind of 'resolution' in the final lines. David Perkins, for example, finds 'acceptance':

> ... the repeated suggestions of gentleness or softness—'small gnats,' 'light wind,' 'lambs,' 'treble soft,' 'twitter'—suffuse the stanza with a tone of tenderness; and the objectivity of the last few lines suggests an acceptance which includes even the fact of death ... The symbol of Autumn ... permits, and the poem as a whole expresses, an emotional reconciliation to the human experience of process.[35]

Critics have been finding this kind of reconciliation in works of literature ever since Gertrude Stein accepted the universe. If not meaningless, it is highly equivocal, and akin to that relish of unhappiness that Gittings finds praiseworthy. The principal objection to the notion here is that nothing in the poetry justifies it—the 'suggestions of gentleness or softness' and the 'tone of tenderness' convey rather an impression of vulnerability in the face of oncoming bleakness. But there is no mock-stoic posturing, no tasting the sadness of Melancholy's might. Jackson Bate finds a less precious resolution, a suggestion of renewal in the very perception of process. He refers to Keats'

> inability to conceive fulfilment without a spring of promise still implicit within it . . . as the mind conceives the present, the past and future are incorporated in it, and the conception of the 'greeting spirit' thus matches, in fidelity to fact, both the unfolding promise and the laden past that are part of the very nature of the object it is attempting to greet and to rescue into consciousness.[36]

Bate is using Keats' notion that things 'semi-real' require a 'greeting of the spirit' to make them wholly real rather inappropriately here. The scenes presented in *To Autumn* are entirely real, though the 'disagreeables' of reality have been excluded rather than evaporated, from them. They certainly need no greeting of the spirit. Yet Bate's main point is a good one—the reminder of seasonal process in the allusion to the songs of spring, and in words such as 'maturing' and 'later' remind one of the return of spring as well as its passing. If there is an assurance to be gained from the sense of seasonal return, the implication is certainly there in the poem. Harold Bloom finds another kind of resolution, an obliquely religious one: 'Keats' swallows gather for a flight beyond winter.'[37] It requires, however, another 'greeting of the spirit' to see the lines in this way, and a spirit of a different temper might see the swallows simply as symbols of life departing.

My own view is that if we are really going to find a resolution in the poem—that is, something which we believe the poem finally says—we are going to have to be more specific. Only now, after we have examined the poem closely, noting as many as possible of its poetic tactics, can we properly perceive its organising shape and central symbol. The shape is precisely that which Bate perceives for its individual stanzas, a crest of well-being in a perfect environment, prolonged and enjoyed to the limit of possibility, and then subsiding inevitably into the flow of time. The central symbol is the personified figure of Autumn, not a goddess but a mortal—looking something like Ruth, but rich and complacent as the Moabite widow could never be. The sex we attribute to Keats' figure (and we have only the implications of the lifted hair to go on) perhaps misleads us; nevertheless one's imagination finds it hard to conceive of anything other than a female figure. But we might modify this bias if we add Eve as a possible prototype, along with Ceres, Ruth, Psyche, and Iphigeneia of Cyprus, for Eve represents mankind generically even more than Adam does. Autumn in her barns and fields may look something like Eve in her garden, ominously complacent, greedy for the last oozings of every fruit. The objection to seeing her thus is that the whole poem does not look back to Eden before the Fall, it has death in its implications throughout. Nevertheless, Autumn is like Eve in one important respect, for she represents mankind, not in a 'happy Garden state', but in an Eden-substitute, a postulated secular world to come. If we are to find a statement in the poem, it will consist in an implicit comment on this figure and her relation to her world.

The use of Keats' letters to prepare the reader to find a meaning in a particular poem is a risky business—the temptation is to distort the poem by extrapolating from it a message which conforms to a known prose statement. The risk may be lessened, however, if one uses the letters to provide an afterword to the poem and one's examination of it. The material basis of the poem, its objective correlative in the simplest sense of the term, is described in a letter to Reynolds, 21 September 1819:

> How beautiful the season is now—How fine the air. a temperate sharpness about it. Really, without joking, chaste weather—Dian skies—I never lik'd stubble fields so much as now—Aye better than the chilly green of the Spring. Somehow a stubble plain looks warm—in the same way that some pictures look warm—this struck me so much on my sunday's walk that I composed upon it. (2:167)

Autumn in the real world can be very pleasant, if not quite like autumn in the poem. But it can also be unpleasant: 'Autumn is encroaching: for the autumn fogs over a rich land is like the steam from cabbage water ... the damp exhalement from the glebe.' (*Letters* 2:156). Even without this reminder of the season's more rheumatic aspect, it is clear that the poem is a selective enhancement of the actual. There is, I think, a purpose in this—Keats is not creating a poetic otherworld, nor consoling himself momentarily by 'glutting' his imagination on the beauties of fulfilment. Still less is he, in the undermining of these comforting images, relapsing into the pleasures of pessimism. His purpose is certainly hardheaded, but more particular and sophisticated than any of the popular forms of evasion.

We know from Keats' intention to seek a living in journalism that he considered himself 'on the liberal side of the question' (*Letters* 2:176). No doubt he would also consider himself a liberal in a more general, philosophical sense of the term—and, in our own jargon, a liberal humanist. There was one aspect of contemporary liberal philosophy, however, which Keats scornfully and sometimes irritably dismissed. Although the Romantics are popularly supposed to have been anti-scientific ('Philosophy will clip an angel's wings'), Shelley hailed the advance of science as liberating mankind from the annoyances of nature, with its floods, famines, pestilences, etc. It seemed not impossible to believe that science would, in the not too distant future, make the natural world virtually perfect. To Keats this was nonsense:

> Let the fish philosophise the ice away from the Rivers in winter time and they shall be at continual play in the tepid delight of summer. Look at the Poles and at the sands of Africa, Whirlpools and volcanoes—Let men exterminate them and I will say that they may arrive at earthly Happiness—The point at which Man may arrive is as far as the paralel state in inanimate nature and no further—for instance suppose a rose to have sensation, it blooms on a beautiful morning it enjoys itself—but there comes a cold wind, a hot sun—it cannot escape it, it cannot destroy its annoyances—they are as native to the world as itself. (2:101)

Accompanying this primitive 'scientism' was a belief in the effectiveness of Hartleian psychology. By arranging the human environment so that each man was exposed to sensations which would necessarily form benevolent clusters of associations, the race could be brought to moral perfection. Keats found this the greater nonsense, and even his contempt for the Christian clergy scarcely exceeds his disdain for the 'perfectibility men', the 'Godwin-methodists':

> The whole appears to resolve into this—that Man is originally 'a poor forked creature' subject to the same mischances as the beasts of the forest, destined to hardships and disquietude of some kind or other. If he improves by degrees his bodily accomodations and comforts—at each stage, at each accent there are waiting for him a fresh set of annoyances—*he is mortal* [my italics] and there is still a heaven with its Stars above his head. The most interesting question that can come before us is, How far by the persevering endeavours of a seldom appearing Socrates Mankind may be made happy—I can imagine such happiness carried to an extreme—but what must it end in?—Death—and who could in such a case bear with death—the whole troubles of life which are now frittered away in a series of years, would then be accumulated for the last days of being who instead of hailing its approach, would leave this world as Eve left Paradise—but in truth I do not at all believe in this sort of perfectibility. (2:101)

The figure in stanza two of *To Autumn* is, I believe, mankind made perfectly happy by the efforts of succeeding Socrates and Hartleys, in a world made perfect by succeeding Newtons. But it remains a world of time and season—'there comes a cold wind' and the rose must die. The Godwinian world to come has been marvellously celebrated and totally undermined. Hedge-crickets sing, the robin whistles, the swallows gather, and Eve leaves Paradise.

To Autumn was Keats' last complete great poem. There is a narrow sense in which we may say that the view of life we may derive from it represents Keats' 'final position', for although the man died in Rome, February 1821, the poet's life ended in Winchester, September 1819. His last letters, and Severn's account of his final weeks in the house on the Spanish Steps, indicate an agonised inner drama of longing and despair, but this engages our wider human sympathies rather than our specifically literary interest. How then may we characterise the stage Keats' development had reached when swallows gathered in his skies?

The Godwinian world we experience in *To Autumn* is one

where all which can be amended in human life has been amended. But after the utmost practical humanistic amelioration has been achieved, the great paradox remains untouched and unexplained. The evil from which aestheticism turns its eyes and the good which despair must ignore remain indissolubly compounded. The world seen in the poem is the actual world at its conceivably possible best, and it remains a world which delights, torments and puzzles us. This is not tragic vision, it is the comprehensive vision which negative capability makes possible. Such a view of things may be ultimately religious, and in this regard it is interesting to compare Keats' state of awareness with that of John Updike, as represented by Jonathan Raban. Commenting specifically on a collection of Updike's critical essays, Raban says:

> It is a Christian vision in the broadest sense, with an acute theological grasp of the metaphysical implications of doubleness and paradox ... He is—to borrow two more of his favourite terms—attentive to creation.
> All the best pieces in the book come to grips with the contrary fabric of things with a kind of intelligent wonder.[38]

Except for the theological and metaphysical elements, one is astonished to see how applicable this is to all of Keats' greatest work. On the other hand one must remember that Matthew Arnold, who also aspired to see life steadily and whole, and was perhaps Keats' most intelligent and perceptive imitator, could only hear faith's melancholy, long, withdrawing roar.

It is perhaps safer to say that the comprehensive vision that is 'attentive to creation' and 'comes to grips with the contrary fabric of things' is not itself the product of a philosophic structure, it is rather the basis on which such a structure might be founded. In Keats' case, whether the philosophy would have been sceptical or theistic is irrelevant. Our interest as readers of literature is in the fullness of apprehension itself, and the greatness of the art it makes possible. I hope I have managed to trace the development both of the vision and the art, from aestheticism to maturity, and from luxurious association to oxymoronic symbolism.

Notes

Chapter 2: The Nature of Keats' Development.

1. *John Keats: A Reassessment*, ed. Kenneth Muir (Liverpool University Press, Liverpool, 1969), p. ix.
2. 'The hoodwinking of Madeline: scepticism in the Eve of St Agnes', *Studies in Philology*, LVIII (1961). Republished in *The Hoodwinking of Madeline and Other Essays on Keats' Poems* (University of Illinois Press, Chicago, 1971). All subsequent references to this essay will be to the latter publication.
3. *Twentieth Century Interpretations of Keats' Odes*, ed. Jack Stillinger (Prentice Hall, Englewood Cliffs, NJ, 1968), p. 2.
4. *The Letters of John Keats 1814—1821*, ed. Hyder Edward Rollins (Harvard University Press, Cambridge Ma, 1958), vol. 1, pp. 241 - 43. Henceforth quotations from this work will be noted by an intext reference citing only volume and page numbers, e.g. (1:241 - 3), or where necessary to avoid confusion, thus (*Letters* 2:241 - 3).
5. *Objective Knowledge*, (Clarendon Press, Oxford, 1972).
6. *See* for example, *Letters* 1: 293, 341, 404; and 2:20, 127, 266. *See* also 'Woman, when I behold thee, flippant, vain,' and 'Ah! who can e'er forget so fair a being?' in *The Poetical Works of John Keats*, 2nd edn, H.W. Garrod, (Clarendon Press, Oxford, 1958), pp. 26 - 7.
7. *See* for example, Aileen Ward, *John Keats: The making of a Poet* (Secker and Warburg, London, 1963), pp. 9 - 11, 15 - 16, 309 - 10.
8. Robert Gittings, *John Keats*, (Penguin, Harmondsworth, 1968), pp. 446 - 50.
9. *The Making of a Poet*, p. 171.
10. Mario L. D'Avanzo, *Keats' Metaphors for the Poetic Imagination* (Duke University Press, Durham NC, 1967), p. 142.
11. 'O Poesy For Thee I Hold My Pen,' in *Psychoanalysis and Culture, Essays in Honor of Géza Róheim*, eds George B. Wilbur and Warber Muensterberger (International Universities Press, New York, 1951), p. 441.
12. It is not the only example. *See*, for example, his cruel humour on the subject of Henry Wylie's sweetheart, 'Miss H', (*Letters* 2:68 - 9).
13. *The Romantic Comedy* (Oxford University Press, London, 1948), p. 121.
14. *Scrutiny*, Reprint in 20 volumes (Cambridge University Press, Cambridge, 1963), vol. 4, pp. 376 - 400.
15. *Keats and Embarrassment* (Clarendon Press, Oxford, 1974), p. 104.

16. *Journal of English and Germanic Philology*, LI (1952), p. 337n. *See* also Beyer's *Keats and the Daemon King* (New York, 1947), pp. 124 fn, 306 – 8.
17. *John Keats' Dream of Truth* (Chatto and Windus, London, 1969), p. 88.
18. Robert Ryan, *Keats: The Religious Sense* (Princeton University Press, Princeton NJ, 1976). Stuart Sperry, 'Keats' Skepticism and Voltaire,' *Keats-Shelley Journal*, XII (1963), pp. 75 – 93. Henceforth references to this Journal will be abbreviated to KSJ.

Chapter 3: The Love Narratives.

1. Jacob D. Wigod, 'The meaning of *Endymion*', PMLA 68 (1953), 779 – 90.
2. Peter Quennell, *Byron, A Self-Portrait, Letters and Diaries 1798 – 1824* (John Murray, London, 1950), vol. 2, p. 533.
3. George Sandys, *Ovid's Metamorphosis Englished, Mythologized, and Represented in Figures*, eds Karl K. Hulley and Stanley T. Vandersall, Introduction by Douglas Bush (University of Nebraska Press, Lincoln, Nebraska, 1970), p. 243.
4. *John Keats*, (Harvard University Press, Cambridge MA, 1963), p. 554.
5. Robert Burton, *The Anatomy of Melancholy* (11th edn, London 1813). The copy referred to belonged to Keats, and is now in the Keats Museum, Hampstead.
6. *John Keats: His Life and Writings*, (Weidenfield and Nicolson, London, 1966), p. 160.
7. 'On the Subject in Art (No. 1)', in *The Germ: Thoughts towards Nature in Poetry, Literature and Art* (Aylott and Jones, London, 1850), no. 1, p. 18. Reprint with an Introduction by W.M. Rossetti (AMS Press, New York, 1965).
8. 'The Critic as Artist', in *The Artist as Critic: Critical Writings of Oscar Wilde*, ed. Richard Ellman (W.H. Allen, London, 1970), p. 380.
9. See again his attitude to Jane Cox, (*Letters* 1:394 – 5).
10. 'The Significance of the Humour in "Lamia"' KSJ, 8 (1959), pp. 20 – 21.
11. *The Evolution of Keats' Poetry*, 2 vols, (Harvard University Press, Cambridge MA, 1936), p. 701.
12. *The Finer Tone: Keats' Major Poems* (Johns Hopkins University Press, Baltimore, 1953), p. 168.
13. *The Hoodwinking of Madeline*, pp. 84 – 5.
14. *John Keats: His Life and Writings*, p. 111.
15. 'The Bishop Orders his Tomb in St Praxeds', 73 – 5.
16. *Poetical Works*, pp. 238n and 252n.
17. *John Keats: The Complete Poems*, ed. John Barnard, (Penguin, Harmondsworth, 1973), p. 620.
18. *Poetical Works*, p. 256n.
19. *The Hoodwinking of Madeline*, p. 77.
20. Hesiod, 'Theogony', 188 – 200, trans. Dorothea Wender, in *Hesiod and Theognis* (Penguin, Harmondsworth, 1973), p. 29.
21. Hesiod, *The Homeric Hymns and Homerica*, trans. H. Evelyn White (Heinemann, London, 1954), p. 423.

22. 'Has Keats' "Eve of St Agnes" a Tragic Ending?', in *Twentieth Century Interpretations of 'The Eve of St Agnes'*, ed. Allan Danzig (Prentice Hall, Englewood Cliffs, NJ, 1971, p. 14.
23. *Evolution of Keats' Poetry*, p. 549.

Chapter 4: Endymion and Glaucus.

1. John Middleton Murry, *Studies in Keats* (Oxford University Press, London, 1930), pp. 46 – 7.
2. *Keats and his Poetry*, (Chicago University Press, Chicago and London, 1971), p. 60.
3. *Keats, Skepticism and the Religion of Beauty* (University of Georgia Press, Athens, Ga., 1979).
4. *Keats' Metaphors*, p. 141.
5. *John Keats' Dream of Truth*, p. 62.
6. Sandys' *Ovid*, p. 621.

Chapter 5: Hyperion.

1. *Keats and Shakespeare* (Oxford University Press, London, 1925), p. 85.
2. On at least nine occasions Keats ends his letters with 'God bless you', on one occasion he speaks of 'our Creator' (1:143), on another of 'the wonders of the great Power' (1:299), and on another he prays for the support of 'a High Power' (1:141).
3. *Aesthetic and Myth in the Poetry of Keats* (Princeton University Press, Princeton, NJ, 1965), pp. 30 – 31.
4. *Keats: The Religious Sense*, pp. 67, 103.
5. *John Keats: The Complete Poems*, p. 519.
6. *The Consecrated Urn*, p. 234.
7. 'John Keats, who was killed off by one critique,
   Just as he really promised something great
   If not intelligible without Greek,
   Contrived to speak about the gods of late
   Much as they might have been supposed to speak.'
                                    (*Don Juan*, Canto 9, stanza 60)
8. C.A. Brown, in *The Keats Circle*, ed. Hyder Edward Rollins (Harvard University Press, Cambridge Ma., 1965), p. 63; and Keats 'Read me a lesson muse,' *Poetical Works*, p. 495.
9. *Keats the Poet*, (Princeton University Press, Princeton NJ, 1973), p. 159.
10. *John Keats' Dream of Truth*, p. 90.
11. *The Romantic Comedy*, p. 126.
12. *Keats and the Mirror of Art* (Clarendon Press, Oxford, 1967), p. 165.
13. 'The Dry Salvages,' Section 3, in *Four Quartets* (Faber and Faber, London, 1944, p. 30).
14. *John Keats' Dream of Truth*, p. 82.

Chapter 6: The Fall of Hyperion.

1. *Scrutiny*, 4:397 – 400.
2. Stillinger, Ford and Sperry are notable examples.
3. *The Romantic Ventriloquists* (University of Washington Press, Seattle, 1963), p. 164.
4. *Ibid*, loc. cit.
5. *The Romantic Comedy*, pp. 144 – 5.
6. *The Hoodwinking of Madeline*, p. 61.
7. *John Keats, A Reassessment*, p. 115.
8. Brian Wicker, 'The Disputed Lines in "Hyperion"', *Essays in Criticism*, 7 (1957), pp. 28 – 41.
9. *Keats' Metaphors*, p. 66.
10. *Keats the Poet*, p. 316.
11. *John Keats' Dream of Truth*, p. 111.
12. *John Keats*, p. 591.
13. *John Keats, His Life and Writings*, p. 164.
14. *John Keats*, p. 594.
15. 'Affliction (1)', see lines 7 – 10.
16. *Keats the Poet* p. 321.
17. *John Keats, His Life and Writings*, p. 165.
18. *John Keats, A Reassessment*, p. 113.
19. Finney, *The Evolution of Keats' Poetry*, p. 468.
20. 'Keats and the Elizabethans', in *John Keats, A Reassessment*, p. 15.
21. *Keats and Shakespeare*, p. 183.
22. *The Romantic Comedy*, pp. 81, 149 – 50.
23. *Keats the Poet*, pp. 330 – 31.
24. Hesiod, *The Homeric Hymns*, trans. Evelyn-White, p. 423.
25. *The Romantic Comedy*, p. 150.
26. *Keats the Poet*, p. 332.
27. *Duchess*: I could curse the stars.
    Bosola: O, fearful.
    Duchess: And those three smiling seasons of the year
             Into a Russian Winter; nay the world
             To its first chaos.
    Bosola: Look you, the stars shine still.
    (John Webster, *The Duchess of Malfi*, 4:1:115 – 20)

Chapter 7: Nightingale and Melancholy

1. *John Keats*, p. 500.
2. 'A Reading of Keats,' in *On the Limits of Poetry* (Swallow Press, New York, 1948), p. 177.
3. 'Imagination and Reality in the Odes of Keats,' in *Twentieth Century Interpretations of Keats' Odes*, ed. Stillinger (Prentice Hall, Englewood Cliffs, NJ, 1968), pp. 2 – 3.

4. See *Objective Knowledge*, passim.
5. *John Keats*, p. 500.
6. 'Keats' "Ode to a Nightingale" ', in *Twentieth Century Interpretations*, p. 36.
7. 'The "Ode to a Nightingale" ', in *Twentieth Century Interpretations*, p. 46.
8. 'Imagination and Reality', in *Twentieth Century Interpretations*, p. 15.
9. *John Keats*, p. 500.
10. *The Quest for Permanence*, (Harvard University Press, Cambridge, Ma), p. 231.
11. *John Keats*, p. 500.
12. Plato, *The Last Days of Socrates*, trans. Hugh Tredennick (Penguin, London and Baltimore, 1957), p. 157.
13. Douglas Bush suggests: 'The poem had begun in an hour of sunlight; now, [stanza four] when the poet's imagination has carried him to join the bird in the forest, it is midnight, in a secluded fairy world of sense that is almost cut off from moon and starlight.'—*John Keats: His Life and Writings*, pp. 134 - 5. But Keats has already imaginatively seen the bird in stanza one—he does not see it in the 'secluded fairy world' of stanza four.
14. I believe it is a mistake to suppose, as many critics have done, that the scheme depicted here belongs to an unreal or visonary world. Bernard Blackstone, for instance, implies a lesser reality when he says, 'Provençal song and sunburnt mirth he [Keats] has only imagined!' (p. 326). This does not make them unreal. Though Keats never saw them, they do exist.
15. *Scrutiny*, 4:388.
16. John Barnard suggests that 'viewless' may imply 'that the flight of "Poesy" is so high as to make the world invisible', *John Keats: The Complete Poems*, p. 656.
17. *The Quest for Permanence*, p. 250; *Aesthetic and Myth*, p. 263.
18. *Life and Writings*, p. 135.
19. *Quest for Permanence*, p. 251.
20. *Aesthetic and Myth*, p. 265.
21. *Life and Writings*, p. 135.
22. *Ibid*, p. 136.
23. 'And countless generations of mankind/ Depart, and leave no vestige where they trod.' (4:761 - 2).
24. *Quest for Permanence*, pp. 254 - 5; *The Evolution of Keats' Poetry*, p. 630.
25. H.W. Garrod, *Keats*, p. 111.
26. *The Nightingale and the Hawk* (George Allen and Unwin, London, 1964), p. 138.
27. *The Visionary Company* (Doubleday, Garden City, New York, 1961), p. 403.
28. E.C. Pettet, *On the Poetry of Keats*, p. 298.
29. *Seven Types of Ambiguity* (Chatto and Windus, London, 1947), p. 205.
30. *Scrutiny* 4:391.
31. David Perkins, *Quest for Permanence*, p. 286.
32. There is also some evidence in the letters from Winchester. *See*, for example, *Letters* 2:148, 189. One might note also an occasional whimsical liturgical phrase such as *Incipit Poema Lyrica de Staffa tractans'* (2:199).

33. 'Irrigation of the head shaven, of the flowers of water-lillies, lettuce, violets, camomile, wild mallows, wether's head, &c must be used many mornings together. Montanus would have the head so washed once a week. Laelius a Fonte Eugubinus, for an Italian count troubled with head-melancholy, repeats any medicines which he tried, but two alone which did the cure; use of whey made of goat's milk, with the extract of Hellebore, and irrigations of the head . . . upon the suture of the crown.—*Anatomy of Melancholy*, Part 2, Sect. 5, Memb. 1, Subs. 5.

34. Cleanth Brooks, 'The Artistry of Keats: A Modern Tribute,' from *The Major English Romantic Poets: A Symposium in Reappraisal*, eds Clarence D. Thorpe, Carlos Baker, and Bennet Weaver (Southern Illinois University Press, Carbondale, 1957), p. 247.

35. Robert Gittings, *The Odes of Keats and their Earliest Known Manuscripts* (Kent State University Press, Ohio, 1970), p. 79.

36. Ian Jack, *The Mirror of Art*, p. 108, and *Letters* 1:395.

37. Sperry, *Keats the Poet*, p. 284.

38. Gittings, *John Keats: The Living Year, 21 September 1818 to 21 September 1819* (Heinemann, London, 1954), p. 143.

Chapter 8: Grecian Urn and Autumn

1. *See* Blackstone, *Consecrated Urn*, p. 331, and Charles I. Patterson, 'Passion and Permanence in Keats' "Ode on a Grecian Urn",' *Twentieth Century Interpretations*, pp. 50 – 51.

2. *The Finer Tone*, pp. 14 – 15.

3. *Keats and the Mirror of Art*, pp. 217 – 18.

4. Robert Gittings, *Keats' Odes*, p. 69.

5. *The Evolution of Keats' Poetry*, p. 642.

6. *The Keats Circle* 1:267 – 8. *See* also Severn's biographical notes, 2:134 – 5.

7. Jacob Wigod, 'Keats' Ideal,' *Twentieth Century Interpretations*, p. 59.

8. *The Romantic Ventriloquists*, p. 158.

9. *The Finer Tone*, p. 17.

10. *Ibid*, p. 21.

11. Bate, *John Keats,* p. 514.

12. *The Prefigurative Imagination of John Keats*, pp. 30 – 86. (Stanford University Press, Stanford CA and Oxford University Press, London, 1951), pp. 30 – 86.

13. *The Keats Circle*. 2:227.

14. *The Prefigurative Imagination*, pp. 138 – 9.

15. Bate, *John Keats*, p. 514.

16. *Ibid*, p. 513.

17. Douglas Bush, 'Keats and his Ideas', in *The Major English Romantic Poets*, p. 154; F.W. Bateson, 'Ode on a Grecian Urn', *Twentieth Century Interpretations*, p. 108.

18. *Keats and the Mirror of Art*, p. 220.

19. *The Finer Tone*, p. 82.

20. Bate, *John Keats*, p. 515.

21. Charles I. Patterson, 'Passion and Permanence,' *Twentieth Century Interpretations*, p. 48.
22. Gittings, *Keats' Odes*, p. 13.
23. *The Living Year*, p. 186.
24. *Ibid*, p. 188.
25. *Life and Writings*, p. 177.
26. *John Keats*, p. 581n.
27. 'The Drunken Boat: The Revolutionary Element in Romanticism', in *Romanticism Reconsidered: Selected Papers from the English Institute*, ed. Northrop Frye (Columbia University Press, New York and London, 1963) p. 21.
28. Ian Jack, *The Mirror of Art*, pp. 236 – 7.
29. *The Living Year*, p. 188.
30. Harold Bloom, *The Visionary Company*, p. 423.
31. Bate, *John Keats*, p. 583.
32 Bush, *Life and Writings*, p. 177.
33. Bloom, *The Visionary Company*, p. 423.
34. Ian Jack, *The Mirror of Art*, p. 234.
35. *The Quest for Permanence*, p. 294.
36. *John Keats*, pp. 584 –5.
37. *The Visionary Company*, p. 423.
38. 'Updike: Criticism by Stealth,' a review of John Updike's *Hugging the Shore* (Deutsch, London, 1984), in *The Sunday Times*, 15 January, 1984.

Selected Bibliography

The following is a list of books and articles which I have found either genuinely helpful or in some ways stimulating.

Allen, Glenn O, 'The Fall of Endymion: A Study in Keats' Intellectual Growth,' *Keats-Shelley Journal*, VI, (1957), pp. 37 - 57.

Bate, Walter Jackson, *John Keats*, Cambridge MA: Harvard University Press, 1963.

Blackstone, Bernard, *The Consecrated Urn: An Interpretation of Keats in Terms of Growth and Form*, London: Longmans Green, 1959.

Bloom, Harold, *The Visionary Company*, Garden City NY: Doubleday, 1961.

Bostetter, Edward E, *The Romantic Ventriloquists*, Seattle: University of Washington Press, 1963.

Bush, Douglas, *John Keats: His Life and Writings*, London: Weidenfeld and Nicolson; 1966.

Combellack, C.R.B, 'Keats' Grecian Urn as an Unravished Bride,' *KSJ*, XI, (1962), pp. 14 - 15.

Cook, Thomas, 'Keats' Sonnet "To Homer," ' *KSJ*, XI, (1962) pp. 8 - 12.

D'Avanzo, Mario L., *Keats' Metaphors for the Poetic Imagination*, Durham, NC: Duke University Press, 1967.

Dickstein, Morris, *Keats and his Poetry: A Study in Development*, Chicago and London: Chicago University Press, 1971.

Dunbar, Georgina S, 'The Significance of the Humor in "Lamia," ' *KSJ*, VIII, (1959), pp. 17 - 26.

Evert, Walter H, *Aesthetic and Myth in the Poetry of Keats*, Princeton NJ: Princeton University Press, 1965.

Finney, Claude Lee, *The Evolution of Keats' Poetry*, 2 vols., Cambridge MA: Harvard University Press, 1936.

Fogle, Richard Harter, *The Imagery of Keats and Shelley, a Comparative Study*, Chapel Hill NC: University of North Carolina Press, 1949.

Ford, Newell F, *The Prefigurative Imagination of John Keats: A Study of the Beauty-Truth Identification and its Implications*, Stanford Cal.:

Stanford University Press, and London: Oxford University Press, 1951.

Frye, Northrop, '*The Drunken Boat: The Revolutionary Element in Romanticism*,' in *Romanticism Reconsidered: Selected Papers from theEnglish Institute*, ed. Frye, New York and London: Columbia University Press, 1963.

Garrod, H.W. *Keats*, Oxford: Clarendon Press, 1939.

Gerard, Albert. 'Romance and Reality: Continuity and Growth in Keats' View of Art', *KSJ*, XI, (1962) pp. 17 – 29.

Gittings, Robert. *John Keats: The Living Year 21 September 1818 to 21 September 1819*, London: Heinemann, 1954.

——*The Odes of Keats and their Earliest Known Manuscripts*, Ohio: Kent State University Press, 1970.

——*John Keats*, Harmondsworth: Penguin, 1968.

Jack, Ian, *Keats and The Mirror of Art*, Oxford: Clarendon Press, 1967.

James, D.G., *The Romantic Comedy*, London: Oxford University Press, 1948.

Jeffrey, Lloyd N., 'Keats and the Bible,' *KSJ*, X, (1961), pp. 59 – 70.

Jones, John, *John Keats' Dream of Truth*, London: Chatto and Windus, 1969.

Leavis, F.R., 'Revaluation: Keats', *Scrutiny*, reprint in 20 vols, Cambridge: Cambridge University Press, 1963, pp. 376 – 400.

Matthews, G.M. (ed.), *Keats: The Critical Heritage*, London: Routledge and Kegan Paul, 1971.

Muir, Kenneth. (ed.), *John Keats: A Reassessment*, Liverpool: Liverpool University Press, 1969.

Murry, John Middleton, *Keats and Shakespeare*, London: Oxford University Press, 1925.

——*Studies in Keats*, London: Oxford University Press, 1930.

Perkins, David, *The Quest for Permanence: The Symbolism of Wordsworth, Shelley, and Keats*, Cambridge MA: Harvard University Press, 1965.

Pettet, E.C., *On the Poetry of Keats*, Cambridge: Cambridge University Press, 1957.

Ricks, Christopher, *Keats and Embarrassment*, Oxford: Clarendon Press, 1974.

Ridley, M.R., *Keats' Craftsmanship: A Study in Poetic Development*, New York: Russell and Russell, 1962.

Rollins, Hyder Edward (ed.), *The Keats Circle*, Cambridge MA: Harvard University Press, 1965.

Rosenberg, John D., 'Keats and Milton: The Paradox of Rejection,' *KSJ*, VI, (1957), pp. 87 – 95.

Ryan, Robert M., *Keats: The Religious Sense*, Princeton, NJ: Princeton University Press, 1976.

Saly, John, 'Keats' Answer to Dante: *The Fall of Hyperion*,' *KSJ*, XIV, (1965), pp. 65 – 78.

Sharp, Ronald A., *Keats, Skepticism, and the Religion of Beauty*, Athens, GA: University of Georgia Press, 1979.

Sperry, Stuart M., *Keats the Poet*, Princeton NJ: Princeton University Press, 1973.

——'Keats' Skepticism and Voltaire,' *KSJ*, XII, 1963, pp. 75 – 93.

Stillinger, Jack, *The Hoodwinking of Madeline and other Essays on Keats' Poems*, Chicago: University of Illinois Press, 1971.

——(ed.) *Twentieth Century Interpretations of Keats' Odes*, Englewood Cliffs, NJ: Prentice Hall, 1968.

Thorpe, Clarence D., *The Mind of John Keats*, New York: Oxford University Press (American Branch), 1926.

Van Ghent, Dorothy, 'Keats' Myth of the Hero,' *KSJ*, III, (1954), pp. 7 – 25.

Ward, Aileen, *John Keats: The Making of a Poet*, London: Secker and Warburg, 1963.

Wagner, Robert D., 'Keats' "Ode to Psyche" and the Second "Hyperion," ' *KSJ*, XIII, (1964), pp. 29 – 42.

Wasserman, Earl R., *The Finer Tone: Keats' Major Poems*, Baltimore MD: Johns Hopkins University Press, 1953.

Wicker, Brian. 'The Disputed Lines in *The Fall of Hyperion*,' *Essays in Criticism*, (1957), pp. 28 – 41.

Wigod, Jacob D., 'The Meaning of *Endymion*,' PMLA 68, (1953), pp. 779 – 90.

Acknowledgements

All quotations from Keats' poems are taken from *The Poetical Works of John Keats*, 2nd, edition by H.W. Garrod, (1958), and are reprinted by permission of Oxford University Press. All quotations from Keats' letters are taken from *The Letters of John Keats 1814 - 1821*, edited by Hyder Edward Rollins in 2 volumes, (1958), and are reprinted by permission of Harvard University Press. I am grateful to Professor George Sanderson of St Francis Xavier University, Nova Scotia, for permission to reprint the second half of Chapter Three, which first appeared as an article, 'Aphrodite and the Virgin: A Note on Keats' "Eve of St. Agnes,"' in *The Antigonish Review*, 47, (1981), pp. 99 - 108.

My thanks are also due to the Reverend R.B. MacDonald, Dean of Arts of St Francis Xavier University, and to my colleagues in the English Department who willingly shouldered extra burdens in order to make this project possible. I am also grateful to my wife for her constant encouragement, positive criticism, and practical help at all stages of this work; and to my son Philip for writing a computer program which greatly facilitated the preparation of the index.

Index

207